The Wars of the Roses Volume 1

The Triumph of York 1455-1461

David Grummitt

Helion & Company

Helion & Company Limited
Unit 8 Amherst Business Centre
Budbrooke Road
Warwick
CV34 5WE
England
Tel. 01926 499 619
Email: info@helion.co.uk
Website: www.helion.co.uk
Twitter: @helionbooks
Visit our blog https://helionbooks.wordpress.com/

Published by Helion & Company 2025
Designed and typeset by Mach 3 Solutions (www.mach3solutions.co.uk)
Cover designed by Paul Hewitt, Battlefield Design (www.battlefield-design.co.uk)

ISBN 978-1-804518-33-5

British Library Cataloguing-in-Publication Data.
A catalogue record for this book is available from the British Library.

For details of other military history titles published by Helion & Company Limited contact the above address or visit our website: http://www.helion.co.uk.

We always welcome receiving book proposals from prospective authors.

Contents

Chronology		iv
Abbreviations		vi
Acknowledgements		viii
Introduction		1
1	The Road to War	12
2	The First Battle of St Albans	22
3	The Battle of Blore Heath and Ludford Bridge	33
4	Calais and Ireland: The Forgotten War	52
5	The Battle of Northampton	69
6	The 'Battle' of Wakefield	82
7	The Battle of Mortimer's Cross	98
8	The Second Battle of St Albans	108
9	Ferrybridge and Towton	122
Epilogue		148
Colour Plate Commentaries		152
Appendix: The Nobility and the Wars of the Roses, 1459–61		155
Manuscript Sources		165
Index		167

Chronology

1399
Usurpation of Henry Bolingbroke and deposition of Richard II.

1415
Renewal of the Hundred Years War and Henry V's victory at the Battle of Agincourt.

1420
Treaty of Troyes: Charles VI of France recognises Henry V of England as heir to the French throne.

1422
Death of Henry V and Charles VI and accession of Henry's nine-month-old son, Henry VI, as King of England and France.

1449
French reconquest of Normandy after five years of truce.

1450
English defeat in Normandy and the murder of Henry VI's leading councillor, the Duke of Suffolk. This is followed by Jack Cade's Rebellion against the King's 'evil counsellors' and the return to England from Ireland of Richard, Duke of York.

1453
17 July: An English army led by the Earl of Shrewsbury is defeated at the Battle of Castillon, leading to the fall of Bordeaux and loss of Gascony. Henry VI suffers from a mental and physical collapse.

1454
27 March: Richard, Duke of York, is appointed Protector of the Realm for the first time. He remains in office until the King's recovery around Christmas.

1455
22 May: First Battle of St Albans leads to the death of the Duke of Somerset, the Earl of Northumberland and Lord Clifford at the hands of the Duke of York and his allies.
17 November: York is appointed as Protector for a second time. He is dismissed from the office in March the following year.

1458

25 March: 'The Loveday' at St Paul's Cathedral sees Henry VI and the moderate lords attempt to reconcile the rival factions led by the Duke of York and Queen Margaret of Anjou.

1459

23 September: A Lancastrian army, led by Lord Audley, is defeated by the Earl of Salisbury at the Battle of Blore Heath.

12/13 October: The retreat of the Yorkist lords at Ludford Bridge. York flees to Ireland and the earls of Warwick and Salisbury and York's eldest son, the Earl of March, to Calais.

20 November: The 'Parliament of Devils' meets at Coventry for the attainder of the Yorkist lords.

1460

16 March: Warwick arrives in Waterford, Ireland, for discussions with the Duke of York.

23 April: Lord Fauconberg defeats the Duke of Somerset at Newnham Bridge near Calais.

26 June: Warwick, Salisbury and March land at Sandwich and march to London.

10 July: The Yorkist victory at the Battle of Northampton results in Henry VI being taken prisoner by the earls of Warwick and March.

19 July: The Lancastrian defenders of the Tower of London, led by Lord Scales, surrender to the Earl of Salisbury and Sir John Wenlock.

13 September: The Duke of York returns to England, landing near Chester.

10 October: Richard, Duke of York, arrives at the Westminster Parliament and makes his formal claim to the throne. He is recognised as Henry VI's heir by the terms of the Act of Accord.

29 December: York, Salisbury and York's son, the Earl of Rutland, are captured by the Earl of Northumberland and Lord Clifford at Wakefield and subsequently murdered.

1461

3 February: The victory of Edward, Earl of March and the new Duke of York, over Lancastrian forces led by the earls of Pembroke and Wiltshire at the Battle of Mortimer's Cross.

17 February: The Earl of Warwick is defeated by Margaret of Anjou's army at the Second Battle of St Albans. The Lancastrians are subsequently refused entry into London.

4 March: The Earl of March is acclaimed King Edward IV in London.

28–29 March: The Yorkists emerge victorious from the battles at Ferrybridge, Sherburn-in-Elmet and Towton. The Lancastrian royal family and their surviving supporters flee to Scotland.

Abbreviations

BL	The British Library
BNF	Bibliothéque National de France
Calendar of Close Rolls	*Calendar of the Close Rolls, Henry VI – Henry VII*, 4 vols (London: HMSO, 1953-63)
Calendar of Patent Rolls	*Calendar of the Patent Rolls, Henry VI – Henry VI* (12 vols, London: HMSO, 1901-14)
Contemporary English Chronicles	*The Contemporary English Chronicles of the Wars of the Roses*, ed. D. Embree and M. T. Tavormina (Woodbridge: Boydell and Brewer, 2019)
Calendar of State Papers, Milan	*Calendar of State Papers and Manuscripts, in the Archives and Collections of Milan 1385– 1618*, ed. A. B. Hinds (London: HMSO 1912)
An English Chronicle	*An English Chronicle, 1377-1461: A New Edition*, ed. William Marx (Woodbridge: Boydell and Brewer, 2004)
Hall's Chronicle	*Hall's Chronicle*, ed. H. Ellis (London: J. Johnson, 1809)
The House of Commons, 1422-1461	*The History of Parliament: The House of Commons, 1422-1461*, ed. Linda Clark (7 vols, Cambridge: Cambridge University Press, 2020)
John Benet's Chronicle	*John Benet's Chronicle, 1399-1462: A New English Translation with New Introduction*, ed. Alison Hanham (Basingstoke, Macmillan, 2016)
Letters and Papers	*Letters and Papers Illustrative of the Wars of the English in France During the Reign of Henry the Sixth, King of England*, ed. J. Stevenson (2 vols in 3, London: Rolls Series, 1861-4)
Paston Letters and Papers, ed. Davis	*Paston Letters and Papers of the Fifteenth Century*, ed. Norman Davis, Colin Richmond and Richard Beadle (3 vols, Oxford: Early English Text Society, 1971-2004)
Polydore Vergil	*Three Books of Polydore Vergil's English History*, ed. Sir Henry Ellis, Camden Society old series 29 (London, 1844)
Parliament Rolls of Medieval England	*The Parliament Rolls of Medieval England 1275-1504*, ed. C. Given-Wilson et al (16 vols, Woodbridge: Boydell and Brewer, 2005)
The Brut	*The Brut, or the Chronicles of England, ed.* F.W.D. Brie (2 vols, Oxford: Early English Text Society, 1906–8)
Three Fifteenth Century Chronicles	*Three Fifteenth-Century Chronicles*, ed. J. Gairdner, Camden Society, new series 28 (London, 1880)
Six Town Chronicles	*Six Town Chronicles of England*, ed. R. Flenley (Oxford: Clarendon Press, 1911)

TNA	The National Archives
Wavrin	Jean de Wavrin, *Recueil des Croniques et Anchiennes Istories de la Grant Bretagne*, ed. W. and E.C.L.P. Hardy (5 vols, London: Rolls Series, 1864-91)
Whethamstede	*Registra Johannis Whethamstede, Willelmi Albon, et Willelmi Walingforde, Abbatum Monanasterii Sancti Albani*, ed. H. T. Riley (London: Rolls Series, 1873)

Acknowledgements

All books incur debts of gratitude in their writing and this is no exception. My academic colleagues have helped over the years with their thoughts and published work, but particular thanks are due to several individuals. Graham Evans and Dan Moorhouse have been the best of critical friends, and their comments and questions have enriched this book beyond measure. Helen Cox has been gracious in sharing her ideas and resources on the events at Wakefield in December 1460. Simon Marsh of the Battlefields Trust has offered a different perspective on various aspects of this book and been generous in his time and knowledge. Colleagues on the Research Committee of The Richard III Society, particularly Livia Visser-Fuchs, have also been very helpful and saved me from errors. Paul Dawson has been generous in sharing his own groundbreaking research on the career of Richard, Duke of York, and this book has benefitted enormously from my discussions with him on the period.

Introduction

Yet another book on the battles of the Wars of the Roses probably demands an explanation (or apology). The set-piece battles, skirmishes, raids and sieges which punctuated the long period of political instability in England between 1455 and 1487 have long fascinated historians, antiquarians and the public at large. The serious study of the battles and, more particularly, the places where they were fought, can probably be dated to Richard Brooke's pioneering *Visits to the Fields of Battle in England of the Fifteenth Century*, first published in 1857.[1] Yet the burgeoning interest in the fifteenth century among university-based historians in the late nineteenth and early twentieth centuries did not extend to the military aspects of the period, although Sir James Ramsey made some important comments on the battles in his epic two-volume *Lancaster and York*.[2] Indeed, it was not until the publication of Colonel Alfred Burne's *Battlefields of England* in 1951 that new thinking was systematically applied to battles such as Towton, St Albans and Bosworth. Unfortunately, Burne's essays did not contain much new research. Instead, he applied his theory of Inherent Military Probability to the battles of the fifteenth century. Where his sources left questions unanswered, Burne asked himself what a trained military commander would have done in those circumstances and filled in the blanks accordingly.[3] The pitfalls of applying Burne's methodology to medieval battles, where the weapons, training and military culture of the participants were so far removed from his own experience as an artillery officer in the First World War, are many and have been discussed by Mike Jones and other historians.[4] Yet Burne's methodology and his resulting conclusions have proved enormously influential and continue to shape interpretations of the battles of the Wars of the Roses to this day.[5]

It was not until the 1980s that the serious study of the military aspects of the Wars of the Roses gained pace. In 1981 two books, by John Gillingham and Tony Goodman, presented histories of the mid-fifteenth century that foregrounded the battles, the tactics and weaponry, and the military institutions of the time.[6] The stories of the individual battles have continued, however, to be

1 Richard Brooke, *Visits to Fields of Battle in England in the Fifteenth Century* (London: John Russell Smith, 1857).

2 James H. Ramsey, *Lancaster and York: A Century of English History, c. 1399–1485* (2 vols, Oxford: The Clarendon Press, 1892).

3 A.H. Burne, *The Battlefields of England* (London: Methuen, 1950).

4 Michael K. Jones, 'The Battle of Verneuil (17 August 1424): Towards a History of Courage', *War in History*, 4 (2009), pp.375–411.

5 See for example John Sadler, *Towton: The Battle of Palmsunday Field 1461* (Barnsley: Pen & Sword, 2011), pp.88–90, 112, 130–1, 199.

6 Anthony Goodman, *The Wars of the Roses: Military Activity and English Society, 1452–1497* (London: Routledge, 1981); John Gillingham, *The Wars of the Roses* (London: Weidenfeld and Nicolson, 1981).

written largely from the contemporary chronicle sources. This was the case with Philip Haigh's pioneering *Military Campaigns of the Wars of the Roses* and Andrew Boardman's in-depth study of the Battle of Towton.[7] It was not until the early 2000s that historians began to look at the battles of the Wars of the Roses with fresh perspectives, such as Michael Jones's 2002 study of the Battle of Bosworth.[8] Nevertheless, the range and depth of military history on the Wars of the Roses has not come close to the excellent work done on the battles of the Hundred Years War by the likes of Anne Curry, Clifford Rogers and, most recently, Michael Livingston.[9] The most important advances in our knowledge of the battles of the Wars of the Roses in recent years have probably come from archaeologists, exemplified by Tim Sutherland's work on Towton and Glenn Foard's on Bosworth.[10] The scarcity of archaeological evidence, nevertheless, has hindered attempts to apply their methodologies to other battlefields. By contrast, our understanding of the ways in which armies were raised, men supplied with weapons and victuals, and how battles were fought during the Wars of the Roses has advanced little since the 1980s, despite the huge amount of research that has illuminated almost every other aspect of mid-fifteenth-century England. This book, and the two other volumes that will follow, are an attempt to draw together those advances in our knowledge and understanding of the period, along with new methodologies and new archival discoveries, to reconsider the history of the battles of the Wars of the Roses.

Writing the Battle History of the Wars of the Roses

Michael Livingston has recently suggested four 'maxims of battle' when writing battle history of the Middle Ages. Once the historian has assembled all the available information – written sources, archaeological evidence and topographical data – they should apply certain principles as the 'starting point' for any analysis. These are: 'follow the roads'; 'no man is a fool'; 'a battle is its ground'; and 'men move like water.'[11] These work very well for the well-documented set-piece battles of the Hundred Years War, with their rich and often conflicting chronicle evidence and copious documentary remnants – even where there is a lack of archaeological evidence – but less well perhaps for the battles of the Wars of the Roses.

Probably the most important of these, at least for Livingston in his work on Crécy and Agincourt, is that 'a battle is its ground.'[12] 'This means,' he writes, 'that we have to *find* the ground. Reconstructing a battle in a featureless vacuum serves little purpose if the goal is to understand

7 Philip A. Haigh, *The Military Campaigns of the Wars of the Roses* (Stroud: Sutton Publishing, 1995); Andrew Boardman, *The Battle of Towton* (Stroud: Sutton Publishing, 1994).

8 Michael K. Jones, *Bosworth 1485: Psychology of a Battle* (Stroud: Sutton Publishing, 2002).

9 C.J. Rogers, *War Cruel and Sharp: English Strategy under Edward III* (Woodbridge: Boydell and Brewer, 2001); Anne Curry, *Agincourt 1415: A New History* (Gloucester: The History Press, 2024); Michael Livingston, *Crécy: Battle of the Five Kings* (Oxford: Osprey Publishing, 2022); *Agincourt: Battle of the Scarred King* (Oxford: Osprey Publishing, 2023).

10 Anne Curry and Glenn Foard, *Bosworth 1485: A Battlefield Rediscovered* (Oxford: Oxbow Books, 2013); Tim Sutherland, 'Conflicts and Allies: Historic Battlefields as Multidisciplinary Hubs – A Case Study from Towton AD 1461', *Arms & Armour*, 9 (2012), pp.40–53.

11 Livingston, *Crécy*, pp.166–8.

12 Michael Livingston, 'A Battle is its Ground: Conflict Analysis and a Case Study of Agincourt, 1415', *Journal of Medieval Military History*, 21 (2023), pp.227–57.

what happened in reality.'[13] Related to this is the notion that 'men move like water', following the path of least resistance and demanding of the historian 'a thorough understanding of the ground.' The merits of this approach for the civil wars of the fifteenth century have been shown by Glenn Foard's and Anne Curry's work on Bosworth, but the situation for 1455 to 1461 is altogether more complex. The precise site of the Battle of Mortimer's Cross, for example, has eluded extensive archaeological search. Whether the battle was fought near Mortimer's Cross and the River Lugg or further south in Kingsland parish has important consequences for how the armies were arrayed and how the battle was fought. Equally, the ground over which the two battles of St Albans, in 1455 and 1461, were fought is lost amid centuries of urban development and the contradictory nature of the written sources. Here, efforts to interpret the battlefield have led to undue significance being given to landscape features, such as the importance placed on Tonman Ditch in some accounts of the second battle.[14] I'm not convinced, however, that the lack of this information means we cannot reconstruct, at least to some degree, *what* happened even if we are not certain *where* it happened.

Where we can identify with some certainty through archaeological and placename evidence the ground over which a battle was fought, such as on Towton Dale, there is the danger that landscape features determine our analysis. Here there is more than a hint of 'Inherent Military Probability' as the landscape provides answers to questions unresolved by the documentary evidence. A case in point is the ridge, marked now by a single hawthorn tree, that dominates the traditional site of the Battle of Towton.[15] This is generally assumed to be the position of the Yorkist army on Palm Sunday. It is a commanding position, looking down upon Towton Dale, and by placing the Yorkists there, historians have assumed they arrived first, leaving the Lancastrians at a disadvantage, both having to advance uphill and with Cock Beck at their rear impeding any line of retreat. This analysis challenges the one presented later in this book, which is based primarily on the documentary and chronicle sources. If the Lancastrian army retreated from Ferrybridge, making stands at 'Dintingdale' and then at Towton, why did they not take up a more advantageous defensive position on the Hawthorn ridge? Was the main Lancastrian force, heavily defeated at Ferrybridge, then destroyed between Sherburn-in-Elmet and 'Dintingdale'? Was the Lancastrian army that fought on Towton Dale a separate one to that defeated at Ferrybridge? In truth, we don't have any conclusive evidence for the deployment of either the Yorkist or Lancastrian armies at Towton. Here the maxim that 'a battle is its ground' can lead to speculation where the perceived importance of landscape features or archaeological evidence dictates our analysis of the battle in the absence of other sources or, worse still, leads to interpretations not supported by the documentary record.

What the documentary evidence for Towton and other battles of the Wars of the Roses does confirm, however, is the importance of the 'follow the roads' maxim. Towton, both battles of St Albans, Northampton and Mortimer's Cross were all fought where they were – wherever that may be – because of the roads. The fighting at Towton appears to have followed the line of the Old Great North Road, while the ancient Roman road of Watling Street was instrumental to where and how the Second Battle of St Albans and Northampton were fought. There is a danger here, too, though. Wars of the Roses armies are usually characterised as being predominantly comprised of foot soldiers and the operational tempo of the campaigns determined by the estimated 12 to 15 miles

13 Livingston, *Crécy*, p.167.

14 Peter Burley, Michael Elliott and Harvey Watson, *The Battles of St. Albans* (Barnsley: Pen and Sword, 2007), pp.106–12.

15 Personal correspondence with Simon Marsh regarding his discussion of Towton with Bob Evans.

The view from the 'Hawthorn Ridge' on Towton Dale looking down towards Dintingdale. (Simon Marsh)

an army could march in a day. My feeling is that we have underestimated the proportion of troops in any army that were mounted and the importance and frequency of encounters fought by largely mounted troops, both archers and men-at-arms. In 1483 Domenico Mancini observed that while the English generally fought on foot, they rode to battle 'so as to arrive fresher and not fatigued by the hardships of the road.'[16] Thus the clashes of arms which developed, such as at Wakefield and Towton, may have been very different to and much more fluid than the set-piece battles that they are usually portrayed as.

That battles were not always planned and demanded that commanders and individual soldiers reacted quickly to events unfolding around them should make us note the final of Livingston's maxims: 'no man is a fool.' 'A battle reconstruction that requires one side to be stupid is,' he writes, 'frankly, probably pretty stupid itself.'[17] There are several examples of where alleged incidents of foolishness shape narratives of the battles of the Wars of the Roses. The idea, for example, that both Lord Clifford and Lord Dacre were killed at Towton by arrows when they had momentarily removed their visors is, at best, an unfortunate coincidence and, at worst, a startling show of

16 Domenico Mancini, *De Occupatione regni Anglie*, ed. Annette Carson (Horsham, 2021), p.71.

17 Livingston, *Crécy*, p.167.

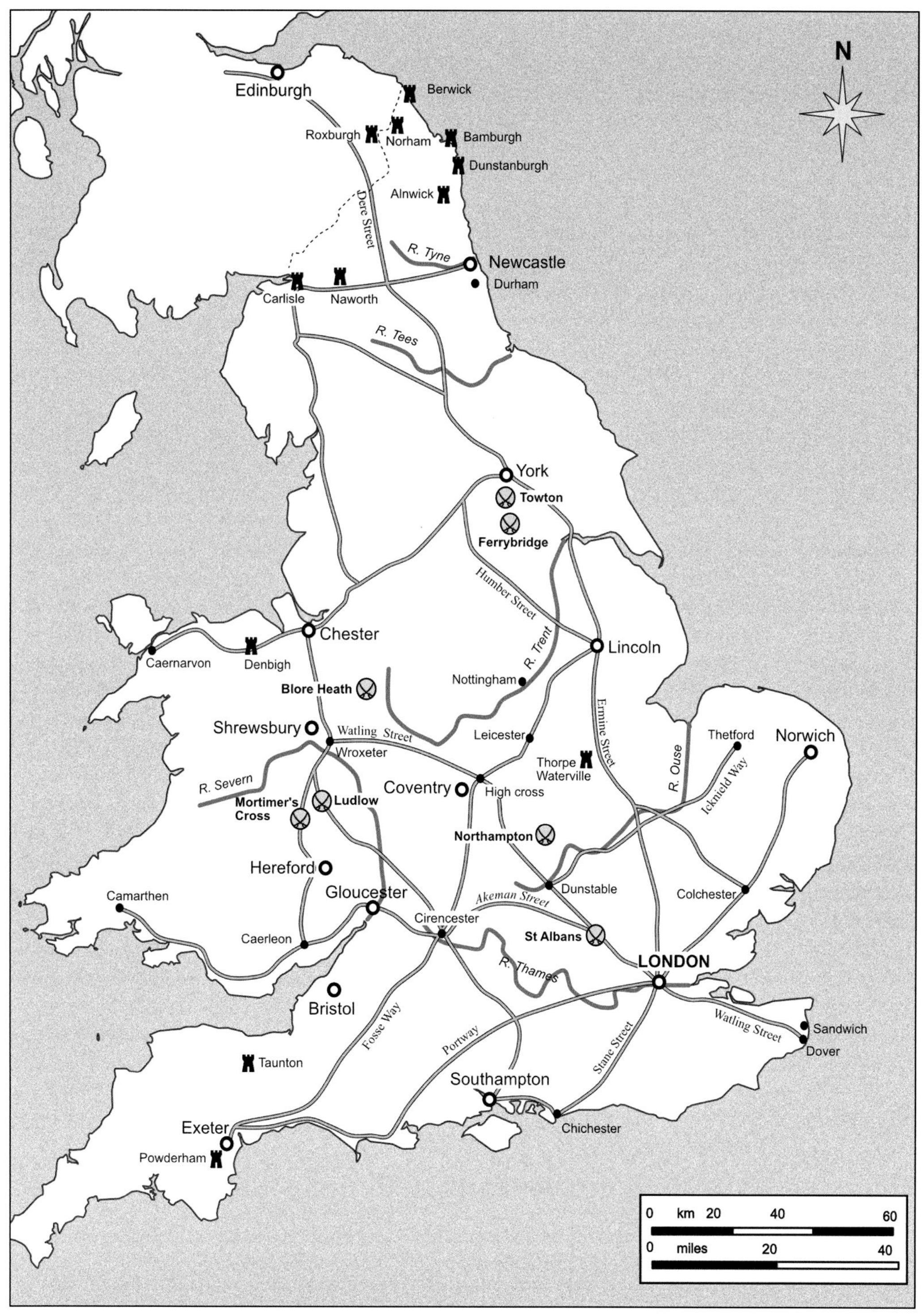

The principal roads of fifteenth-century England and the battlefields of 1459 to 1461.

stupidity on the part of the Lancastrian commanders. In fact, it was probably neither and the story was merely the repetition of a familiar trope in battle narratives.[18] One recurrent act of stupidity in modern accounts is the Yorkist lords' trust in Andrew Trollope. Already well known to them for his service to the Duke of Somerset's father in the 1440s and 50s, they nevertheless trusted Trollope with the most important part of their army, the men of the Calais garrison, at Ludford Bridge in 1459. His desertion to the Lancastrians was the prelude to the lords' flight into exile. York compounded the error, fatally, at Wakefield in 1460, where he inexplicably allowed Trollope entry to Sandal Castle, only to be tricked outside its walls and killed in a battle with the Lancastrians in which he was hopelessly outnumbered. In other accounts of Wakefield, York and Salisbury were the fools when they fell for the deception of John, Lord Neville. As we shall, even if he was not the most astute politician and military commander, not even Duke Richard was *that* stupid!

Sources and Methodology

The archaeological record is scant indeed for this first stage of the Wars of the Roses. Only three battles – Blore Heath, Northampton and Towton – are included in Historic England's Battlefield Register and among these, extensive archaeological study has only been carried out at Towton. Ludford Bridge was not a battle in any meaningful sense, while the precise locations and scale of Mortimer's Cross and the 'battle of Wakefield' are unknown. Any study therefore of the battles and military campaigns of this first stage of the Wars of the Roses is primarily dependent on written source material. These can be divided into two main categories: first, chronicle and literary sources, including letters, and second, documentary records including financial accounts, royal warrants and legal records. Compared to both earlier and later periods, the historian of the Wars of the Roses is relatively shortchanged in both. There are no fewer than 80 fourteenth-century accounts or brief notices of the Battle of Crécy, while there are a rich and varied collection of chronicle accounts, both English and French as well as Burgundian, of Agincourt. The newsletters and letters relating to the battles of the British civil wars of the mid-seventeenth century reach levels, in terms of both sheer numbers and detail, that medievalists can only dream of. The historian of the Wars of the Roses has no such advantages. Many of the newsletters that we know were circulated at the time are now lost. The vernacular English and French chronicles are relatively few and derivative, while the Latin chronicles are less useful than those of previous centuries. The records of government, so rich for reconstructing thirteenth and fourteenth-century armies and campaigns, are less useful and abundant for our period simply because of changes in administrative procedures and the accidental loss of records due to of fire, flood and neglect.[19]

Michael Hicks was optimistic when he wrote that 'battles are the best documented of events' in his survey of the sources relating to the Wars of the Roses.[20] In fact, the chronicles are usually laconic in their description, often only stating that a battle took place and who won. Although their authors frequently listed the lords they thought were present or who fell in action, their claims can often be shown to be wrong. Hicks concedes 'we are seldom clear about the strategy of both

18 For Jean de Wavrin's use of these literary devices see Livia Visser-Fuchs, *History as Pastime: Jean de Wavrin and His Collection of Chronicles of England* (Donington: Shaun Tyas, 2018), pp.483–92, 584–9.

19 Michael Prestwich, *Armies and Warfare in the Middle Ages: The English Experience* (New Haven, CT: Yale University Press, 1996).

20 M.A. Hicks, 'The Sources', in *The Wars of the Roses*, ed. A.J. Pollard (Basingstoke: Macmillan, 1995) pp.20–40.

sides, about the tactics and total casualties, or about the size or composition of the armies'. In fact, as we will see, the contemporary English chronicles of the Wars of the Roses rarely provide any meaningful detail of the fighting itself. The one exception is the vernacular English chronicle once attributed to the London alderman William Gregory, but even its author is frustratingly vague on the disposition of the armies and their commanders. Many of the contemporary chroniclers, most of whom were London-based, compiled their accounts from the same sources, interspersing rumours, the propaganda of newsletters, and familiar tropes with the occasional personal reflection. The continental sources are no different. The long and detailed account of the Burgundian chronicler Jean de Wavrin was not simply a personal account compiled through his own research and conversations with participants. He too copied, sometimes verbatim, from previous chronicle accounts, some of which may have drawn from newsletters circulated in the wake of the battles, but he also included stock battle descriptions and phrases used by chroniclers throughout the Middle Ages to describe the experience of battle. The lack of detail in the chronicles of the mid-fifteenth century had led historians to rely on the accounts of early Tudor writers such as Polydore Vergil and, especially, Edward Hall. Yet Vergil and Hall were not contemporaries. They did not compile their accounts by talking to the participants nor, as far as we know, did they visit the battlefields or have access to materials now lost. Both drew upon fashionable Classical precedents when compiling their battle narratives and spun stories which were principally exercises in the art of rhetoric, designed not to reveal the 'truth' of what happened but to show the moral fortitude or failings of their principal characters.[21]

In attempting to reconstruct the battles of the Wars of the Roses I have followed a simple and straightforward methodology. I have privileged the earliest chronicle sources over those of the later fifteenth century and early sixteenth century. Most of our information on the period 1455 to 1461 comes from a relatively small corpus of vernacular English chronicles, almost all London-based, written during the 1460s. They are broadly Yorkist in their sympathies and political allegiance. A very few, such as that copied by John Benet, the vicar of Harlington in Bedfordshire for a decade or so from the late 1450s, are written in Latin. Among these are the so-called *Annales*, long thought to be written by William Worcester and now generally accepted to have been written by an unknown Londoner.[22] This source contains information not corroborated elsewhere, which makes it significant but problematic.

The chronicles shared much in common, and they are also linked to a Franco-Burgundian vernacular chronicle tradition. These are to be found in a group of manuscripts of the so-called Monstrelet Continuator, written at the end of an earlier chronicle written by the Picard writer Enguerrand de Monstrelet (d. 1453), and in the work of Jacques du Clercq (d.? 1468), a citizen of Arras. They are little known by historians of the Wars of the Roses but are important for two reasons. First, they appear to have been compiled from lost newsletters distributed principally, it seems, by the Earl of Warwick from Calais to the Burgundian court in 1460 and 1461. We know of the existence of these newsletters because of the similarities between the information contained in the chronicles and that in the correspondence of the Milanese ambassador to the court of the Dauphin Louis, Italian merchants in London and Bruges, and Warwick's agents like Antonio

21 David Grummitt, *The Wars of the Roses: War and Martial Culture in England* (Oxford: Oxford University Press, 2025), pp.128–9, 195–204.

22 For the identity of the author of the *Annales* see K.B. McFarlane, 'William Worcester: A Preliminary Survey', in *England in the Fifteenth Century* (London: The Hambledon Press, 1981), pp.209–11.

de la Torre. Second, it was the chronicle of the Monstrelet Continuator and the tract known as 'Warwick's Apology' that, in part, shaped the narrative presented by the Burgundian chronicler, Jean de Wavrin. Wavrin's narrative, often confused and sometimes contradictory, is, nevertheless, our most detailed source for the military campaigns of 1459 to 1461. Much of his account of the events of 1460 and 1461, from Wakefield to Towton, seems to have been derived from a unique manuscript of the so-called Monstrelet Continuator, now Bibliothèque Nationale de France, Manuscrit Français 88 and entitled *Cronicques des guerres advenues entre France, Angleterre et Bourgoingne depuis l'an 1444 jusque en l'an 1471*. This was owned by Louis of Bruges, Lord of Gruythuuse, and may even have been written by Wavrin himself.[23] Identifying where Wavrin's narrative in his *Recueil* diverged from that of other Franco-Burgundian chronicle accounts of the 1460s thus provides an important tool in understanding the events of this period.[24]

As well as chronicles, correspondence is a vital source for this period. The value of the Paston letters, an unrivalled collection of correspondence by and to the members of a minor, albeit ambitious, Norfolk gentry family, has long been recognised by historians. In contrast, the correspondence relating to England in Milanese, Venetian and other European archives has not received the recognition it deserves. While its writers were often confused by English names and events, they reported information they had received first-hand from participants in the events they described. The correspondence contained in foreign archives is often the earliest reaction we have to events in England.

Battles are fought by people and affect them in a variety of complex and often unexpected ways. That is an obvious thing to say, but the personal experience of the political turmoil of the mid-fifteenth century and of battle itself has not always been the foremost concern of those who have written battle history. Yet the human stories offer a rich vein that can be mined to illuminate what happened both on the battlefield and in its immediate aftermath. Fifteenth-century England was a country that was both highly bureaucratised and highly litigious. Thus, the records of government, both royal government at a national level and the local administration of towns and villages, can shed much light on the planning, execution and consequences of war. That said, we know very little of how armies were recruited. We can only guess at their size, know little of how they were armed, and almost nothing of how they fought. What we do know, mainly from legal records, is how men and women dealt with the aftermath and consequences of battle. At times, as in the case with the events at Wakefield in December 1460 which led to the death of the Duke of York, this evidence suggests entirely new explanations and understandings of the battles of the Wars of the Roses.

Throughout this book it will be clear that is often easier to say what did not happen than to say with any certainty what did. In reviewing the written sources on each battle, we can reasonably apply some principles which have a relevance for writing premodern battle history more generally. First, wherever possible we need to go back to the primary sources themselves and be aware of any errors, biases or misinterpretations introduced by later editors. Fortunately, many of the key texts of the period have benefitted from the rigorous attentions of modern academic editors. Second, statements of fact or interpretations contained in only one contemporary source need to be treated with appropriate caution. The more sources that agree on a particular individual being at a battle, or of an event happening on a particular day, then the greater the probability of

23 *Manuscrits enluminés des anciens Pay-Bas méridionaux: I Manuscrits de Louis de Bruges*, ed. Ilona Hans-Collas and Pascal Schandel (Bibliothèque Nationale de France: Paris, 2009), pp.205–7.

24 Visser-Fuchs, *History as Pastime*, pp.397–423, 474–9.

that statement being truthful. Third, generally, sources written closer to the events they describe have been favoured over those written many years or even decades later. This, as Tony Goodman explained back in 1981, is why Edward Hall's chronicle or the work of Polydore Vergil cannot be considered as primary sources for the battles fought between 1455 and 1461.[25] Ultimately, however, it is impossible to recover and reconstruct the 'truth' of the military campaigns of the Wars of the Roses. As Malcolm Wanklyn has reminded us in his excellent explanation of how he approached writing the battle history of the English Civil Wars, 'most information to be found in the traces of the past is opinion, not fact'.[26] It is an obvious thing to say that when analysing these written traces of the past we need to be aware of their authors' biases, agendas and the simple fact that they themselves did not really know or understand what had happened in the events they described, even if they were eyewitnesses. As Jean de Wavrin wrote when describing the role of the Duke of Bedford at the Battle of Verneuil in 1424, a battle in which he had himself fought: 'Bedford, *as I heard say for I could not see or understand everything, because I was pretty well occupied defending myself*, performed marvellous feats of arms and slew many a man.'[27]

The battle histories presented in these pages are, then, works of interpretation and represent my attempt to place some order on the chaos of the past. I have tried to present the evidence as it appears in the sources from the time, subjecting it, I hope, to a rigorous and critical analysis. I have noted modern interpretations and showed how historians from the sixteenth century onwards have imposed their own frameworks over the contemporary evidence. In some cases, the historiography has completely obscured the explanations offered by the earliest commentators on the battle. I have not included battle plans of the type found in most books and articles on premodern battles simply because we have no reliable evidence of the disposition of armies for any of the battles of the period 1455 to 1461, with the possible exception of Northampton, and certainly not for those where we cannot be certain where the fighting took place! Nor have I included any of the insights claimed by others to have been gained through re-enactment or experimental archaeology. There are too many variables and too many unknowns for this to be anything other than speculation when analysing the battles from St Albans to Towton. Ultimately, though, this book remains one interpretation of the complicated and often chaotic events of these years. More evidence remains, I am sure, to be found and our understanding of the battles of the Wars of the Roses will continue to evolve as other historians, writing from a different perspective, study the period. I can only hope this book adds to that journey of discovery and understanding.

A Note on Sources

The main vernacular contemporary chronicle sources have been in print since the nineteenth and early twentieth centuries. The Middle English continuation of the *Brut* chronicle referred to here as *An English Chronicle* is often erroneously referred to as 'Davies' Chronicle' after its nineteenth-century editor (*An English Chronicle of the Reigns of Richard II, Henry IV, Henry V, and Henry VI*, ed. John Silvester Davies, Camden Society, old series 64 (1856)). I have used the excellent modern edition by William Marx (*An English Chronicle, 1377–1461: A New Edition,*

25 Goodman, *The Wars of the Roses*, pp.8–9.
26 Malcolm Wanklyn, *Decisive Battles of the English Civil War* (Barnsley: Pen and Sword, 2014), pp.7–32.
27 Wavrin, iii., p.76.

ed. W. Marx (Woodbridge: Boydell and Brewer, 2004)). Similarly, 'Gregory's Chronicle' was edited in the 1870s by James Gairdner who, almost certainly incorrectly, identified the London alderman William Gregory as its author (*The Historical Collections of a Citizen of London in the Fifteenth Century*, ed. James Gairdner, Camden Society, new series 17 (1876)). The continuation of the chronicle, which covers this period, has a new scholarly edition by Embree and Tavormina (*The Contemporary English Chronicles of the Wars of the Roses*, ed. D. Embree and M.T. Tavormina (Woodbridge: Boydell and Brewer, 2019)). The chronicle of another Londoner, Robert Bale, was first edited in 1911 and then, in 2013, a missing folio covering the Second Battle of St Albans was discovered in Trinity College Dublin (*Six Town Chronicles of England*, ed. R. Flenley (Oxford, 1911); Hannes Kleineke, 'Robert Bale's Chronicle and the Second Battle of St Albans', *Historical Research* 87 (2014), pp.744–750). Another important London chronicle is the 'Short English Chronicle', so named by its editor, James Gairdner, when published in 1880 (*Three Fifteenth-Century Chronicles*, ed. James Gairdner (Camden Society, new series 28, 1880)). The two most important Latin chronicles, the *Annales* previously thought to be written by William Worcestre and John Benet's chronicle, are available in edited form (G.L. and M.A. Harriss, 'John Benet's Chronicle for the Years 1400–1462', *Camden Miscellany*, 24 (1972), pp.151–223; *Letters and Papers Illustrative of the Wars of the English in France During the Reign of Henry the Sixth, King of England*, ed. J. Stevenson (2 vols in 3, London: Rolls Series, 1861-4)). Alison Hanham has recently translated Benet, but there is no full translation of the *Annales* (*John Benet's Chronicle 1399–1462* (Basingstoke: Palgrave Macmillan, 2016)). Similarly, the register of Abbot Whethamstede is only available in its nineteenth-century Latin edition (*Registra Johannis Whethamstede, Willelmi Albon, et Willelmi Walingforde, Abbatum Monanasterii Sancti Albani*, ed. H.T. Riley (London: Rolls Series, 1873)). The correspondence relating to English affairs contained in the archives of Milan was edited and published in shortened form in the early twentieth century (*Calendar of State Papers and Manuscripts in the Archives and Collections of Milan 1385–1618*, ed. A.B. Hinds (London: HMSO, 1912)). The original transcripts of the material in the archives of Milan still exist in The National Archives, but the collection is not complete (TNA, PRO31/1/1, 2).

The main series of records of English government of this period – those of the Exchequer, the common law courts and most of the records of Chancery – remain unedited and unpublished. Photographs of many of them, particularly the legal records, are reproduced on the Anglo-American Legal Tradition website (www.aalt.edu). In the early twentieth century, the Public Record Office made available calendars of the series of Patent, Close and Fine Rolls and these are invaluable for this period. The Parliament Rolls were first published in the eighteenth century, but here the excellent modern edition has been used (*The Parliament Rolls of Medieval England 1275–1504*, ed. Chris Given-Wilson et al. (16 vols, Woodbridge: Boydell and Brewer, 2005)). Much of the French manuscript and printed material cited here is available online through the Gallica website (www.gallica.bnf.fr). There is not a full modern translation of Jean de Wavrin, unfortunately, but Christopher Smith (www.twentytrees.co.uk) has recently made translated editions of portions of Wavrin and other medieval texts available as Kindle books (*Recueil des Croniques et Anchiennes Istories de la Grant Bretagne*, ed. W. and E.C.L.P. Hardy (5 vols, London: Rolls Series, 1864–91)). The chronicle of the so-called Monstrelet Continuator has existed in English translation since Thomas Johnes's edition of 1867 (*The Chronicles of Enguerrand de Monstrelet* (2 vols, London: Routledge, 1867)), but has been little used by historians of the Wars of the Roses. The Paston Letters are without doubt the richest source for many aspects of mid-fifteenth-century English politics and society. They are widely available online and in print. The best printed edition was for a long time Gairdner's six-volume edition first published in 1908 (*The Paston Letters*, ed. James Gairdner

(6 vols, London: Chatto & Windus, 1908)). This has largely been superseded by Norman Davis's two-volume modern edition, with a third supplementary volume edited by Colin Richmond and Richard Beadle. That edition has been used here wherever possible (*Paston Letters and Papers of the Fifteenth Century*, ed. Norman Davis, Colin Richmond and Richard Beadle (3 vols, Oxford: Early English Text Society, 1971–2004)).

1

The Road to War

Historians have long debated the causes of the Wars of the Roses. For the first generation of professional historians, writing in the second half of the nineteenth century, it was a result of quarrels between the greatest noble families and the local disorder caused by their unruly retinues. This analysis held sway into the mid-twentieth century, when the influential Oxford historian K.B. McFarlane stressed that local disorder arose from a vacuum of power and leadership at the heart of government. This was principally due to the inadequacy of King Henry VI. While Henry's personal failures must remain at the heart of any explanation of the conflict from 1455 to 1461, more recent scholars have questioned whether there were not more deep-rooted issues – fiscal problems and the inherent weakness of the Lancastrian dynasty which had usurped the throne in 1399 – which made the political crisis inevitable. Henry V's decision to relaunch the Hundred Years War in 1415, while amazingly successful to begin with, set England upon a path that was both costly and politically fraught with danger. It imposed what would prove to be an unsustainable burden on the Lancastrian polity. Indeed, some of the most recent accounts of the Wars of the Roses have stressed the devastating impact that defeat in France had on the Lancastrian monarchy's ability to govern effectively at home.[1]

'Woe Betide the Land whose King is a Child': England 1422–1450

The untimely death of Henry V on 31 August 1422 and the accession of his infant son as Henry VI placed great strain on the English crown, both at home and in those parts of France under English control.[2] Less than two months later, Charles VI of France died, and the infant English King became ruler of the dual monarchy of England and France according to the terms of the Treaty of Troyes negotiated in 1420. England was ruled by a council of the great lords and leading churchmen. Its politics were dominated by the squabble between the King's uncle, Humphrey, Duke of Gloucester, and Cardinal Henry Beaufort, Bishop of Winchester. In Lancastrian France, the King's other uncle, John, Duke of Bedford, ruled as regent. By the middle of the decade, the conquests of Henry V were becoming increasingly untenable. In 1429 Joan of Arc galvanised French resistance to the

1 David Grummitt, *A Short History of the Wars of the Roses* (2 edn., London: Bloomsbury, 2025), pp.xii–xxvi; Christine Carpenter, *The Wars of the Roses* (Cambridge: Cambridge University Press, 1995), pp.4–26.

2 For what follows see David Grummitt, *Henry VI* (Abingdon: Routledge, 2015), pp.52–157.

Lancastrian dual monarchy, and the Dauphin, the disinherited son of Charles VI, was crowned Charles VII of France in a lavish ceremony at Reims. In 1436 the Burgundian ruler, Duke Philip the Good, abandoned his alliance with Henry VI and attempted to capture the English-held town of Calais. The Burgundian siege was lifted in the most successful English campaign in France of this latter stage of the war. The momentum could not be maintained, however, amid a continuing shortage of money and squabbles among the young Henry VI's councillors. The war settled into a pattern of attrition and the English were again forced to the negotiating table.

Despite the King's minority and the occasionally public disputes between Gloucester and Beaufort, England during the 1420s and 30s was a remarkably stable polity. The Lancastrian regime commanded a majority among the lords who were willing to support the legacy of Henry V, both at home and abroad. Although the English Parliament was reluctant to fund the Lancastrian war effort in France, this was a consequence of the Treaty of Troyes and the understanding that England and France remained two distinct kingdoms. The King's long journey towards adulthood and personal rule was carefully managed. In May 1426 Henry himself was knighted by his uncle, Bedford. After Bedford had dubbed his nephew, Henry repeated the honour for the 36 other young men and boys. Among those knighted were the heirs to several magnate families (Mowbray, Percy, Ormond and Talbot), young magnates (the Duke of York and the earls of Oxford and Westmorland among others), and several young men who had already distinguished themselves in France (including Robert Hungerford, Ralph Boteler and the younger Richard Woodville). The aim of this ceremony was twofold: first, it reaffirmed the young King's primacy at the heart of public life for the assembled lords and commons; second, it created a body of men whose personal loyalty to Henry himself would become a defining feature of the reign in the decades to come. In November 1429 Henry was crowned King of England in Westminster, and in April the following year he crossed the Channel at the head of a large army in preparation for his coronation as King of France in Notre Dame, Paris, on 16 December 1431. He arrived back in Dover in February 1432. Despite having been out of the country for nearly two years, the government of England continued without any breakdown of royal authority in the King's absence. From 1436, Henry began to take on more of the functions and responsibilities of an adult king, and in November 1437, just days shy of his sixteenth birthday, he formally began his personal rule.

In 1445, Henry VI married the French princess Margaret of Anjou, a match designed to bring an end to the long war between England and France. While not abandoning his French kingdom, Henry had secretly agreed to cede some Lancastrian territories in France to Charles VII in return for a truce. Although unpopular among some, especially those who had served in the Lancastrian garrisons in Normandy and elsewhere in France, the truce was supported by the English lords and commons in Parliament. In March 1449, however, the truce was broken when the English were implicated in the capture of the key Breton fortress of Fougères, and by May the following year Normandy, the principal Lancastrian conquest, had been entirely lost. This sparked unrest in England, with the King's chief counsellor, William de la Pole, Duke of Suffolk, murdered and a popular uprising throughout the south of England, beginning in Kent, erupting in June 1450. The rebels called for the lords of the King's blood, naming the dukes of York, Buckingham, Exeter and Norfolk, to take the lead in counselling the King and banish the corrupt courtiers who had been responsible for the English defeat in France. The rebels made their camp at Blackheath and marched on London, where they were defeated on London Bridge by the city levies during the night of 6–7 July. The rebels retreated into Kent, where they were pursued by royal forces. Eventually the King issued a general pardon to all except their leader, Jack Cade, who was captured and killed in Sussex on 12 July. York did not arrive in England until the last week in August and demanded to be named as the King's chief counsellor. Henry resisted and instead promoted York's great rival and the last commander of the English forces in Normandy, Edmund Beaufort, Duke of Somerset.

Somerset and York: A Deadly Rivalry

The rivalry between York and Somerset, which arose largely from the latter's conduct as Henry VI's lieutenant and governor-general of France between 1447 and the fall of Normandy, defined the politics of the early 1450s.[3] Richard, Duke of York (1411–1460), was the greatest magnate of his age. He was descended from Edward III through the paternal and maternal line, enjoyed the largest baronial income of the mid-fifteenth century (some £5,000 p.a.), and had been a key supporter of the Lancastrian regime, especially in France. Moreover, he was a man acutely aware of his own status and lineage. More importantly for the politics of the 1450s, others too were aware of York's pedigree. To Cade's rebels he was the 'hye and myghty prince' who, along with the other 'trewe lordes,' would restore good government.[4] In April 1450 Henry VI had been confronted on his way to the Leicester Parliament by John Harries, a Yorkshire shipman. Threshing the air with a flail, Harries had announced that 'the Duke of York then in Yreland shold in lyke manner fight with traytours at Leicester parliament and so thrashe them downe as he had thrashed the clods of erth in that towne'.[5] Harries was hanged, drawn and quartered for his ill-considered outburst, but he revealed an apparently widely held opinion among the commons that York was the champion of reform. In 1450 Duke Richard found himself, at first reluctantly, thrust forward as the saviour of the commonweal and antidote to the disastrous government of Henry VI.

Up to the point at least of his departure as lieutenant-general of Ireland in June 1449, York had been a loyal and integral part of the Lancastrian regime. His birth had guaranteed him a position close to the throne, and in 1436 he had been appointed the King's lieutenant in France. He relied on his elder brother-in-law, Richard Neville, Earl of Salisbury, and the experienced commander John, Lord Talbot (from 1442 Earl of Shrewsbury) for both advice and practical assistance, but his first period of office was reasonably successful. A second period in command (from 1441 until 1445) was less auspicious militarily, but the Duke proved himself a capable administrator and diplomat. He was fully complicit in the negotiations for the truce of Tours in 1444, the prelude to the marriage treaty between Henry VI and Margaret of Anjou, and he received the backing of his peers the following year when Bishop Moleyns accused him of embezzlement.[6] From 1446 he was among the leading figures in domestic government and benefitted personally, in terms of land and office, from the demise of Humphrey, Duke of Gloucester, during the Parliament of February 1447. In the late 1440s, however, York's position was becoming increasingly difficult. By 1450 the crown owed him the arrears of wages and other sums totalling more than £26,000. Although he had not fared worse than many of the crown's other creditors – indeed, he had fared much better than some – the Duke's own financial problems may have confirmed for him the more widely held sense of crisis in 1449–50. There is also evidence that York may have left England for Ireland under

3 M.K. Jones, 'Somerset, York and the Wars of the Roses', *English Historical Review*, 104 (1989), pp.285–307.

4 I.W.M. Harvey, *Jack Cade's Rebellion of 1450* (Oxford: Oxford University Press, 1991), p.191.

5 R.A. Griffiths, 'Duke Richard of York's Intentions in 1450 and the Origins of the Wars of the Roses', in *King and Country: England and Wales in the Fifteenth Century* (London: Hambledon, 1991), pp.281–2.

6 Paul Johnson, *Duke Richard of York, 1411–1460* (Oxford: Oxford University Press, 1988), pp.28–50.

something of a cloud. It was certainly not the exile that Cade's followers were later to claim. Yet when he returned the following year, York claimed that certain members of the King's household had planned to ambush him when he landed in North Wales.[7] In Ireland York was worried about the lack of money to fund his campaign against the rebellious Gaelic chieftains and that the same accusations of incompetence and treason levelled against those in charge of the war in Normandy would be made against him.[8]

In the summer of 1450 York thus found himself reacting to a series of events over which he had little control and which threatened to destroy his power and influence around the King. Cade's rebels and others had identified him as an antidote to the 'traitors' around the King who were subverting the commonweal; the King's household and the other targets of the commons' anger similarly identified the Duke as their chief enemy; York himself feared he would be indicted for treason for giving support to Cade (who claimed kinship with the Duke and took the alias John Mortimer) and that his position as heir presumptive would be undermined or worse. It was into this atmosphere of suspicion and rumours that York returned to England, probably in the last week of August. One contemporary reported that the King's household were 'aferd right sore' of the Duke's return.[9] This fear lay behind the failed attempt by some members of the King's household to waylay him on his route from North Wales and the Duke's protestation of loyalty to the King in September. York's 'first bill', as it has become known, challenged those who had spoken out against the Duke to confront him publicly before the King. He protested his loyalty and declared himself 'a true Knighte'. Henry appears to have accepted York's protestations of good faith at face value, the two were reconciled and the King admitted him 'as oure trew faithful subiecte and as oure weel bilovid cosyn'.[10] Shortly afterwards, however, in early October, York moved from being a private petitioner, seeking a confirmation of his own loyalty, into a public spokesman calling for reform of the commonweal. In a second bill, addressed to the King but circulated widely as a public statement of his position, the Duke offered his services to ensure 'justice be had a yenst alle suche that [have] ben so endited or openly so noysed' of treason.[11] It was a damning indictment of the King's incompetence and York's bill justified the commons' calls for justice on the traitors. Henry's response was forthright. He did not accept the Duke's offer; instead the problems were to be addressed by a 'sad and so substantial council' to which York was invited but in which he was to have no special importance. York was disappointed but not defeated. A third bill, addressed to the King and the lords, outlined the need for reform and introduced a new angle of attack. Duke Richard introduced the defeat in France as a result of the greed and evil counsel of those 'broughte up of noughte' and called, in language taken directly from Cade's manifestos, for counsel to be given by 'the trewe lordes and inespeciall the lordes of the mighti roiall blood'.[12] This bill seems to have been met with the same response as his previous complaint. York's campaign sought its legitimacy in two contradictory ways: first, by an appeal to his position as chief magnate and (implicitly) as heir presumptive and, second, by an appeal to the commons. It failed because the Duke badly misjudged the mood of his fellow peers and the

7 R.A. Griffiths, 'Richard of York and the Royal Household in Wales', in *King and Country*, pp.265–76.

8 J.T. Gilbert, *History of the Viceroys of Ireland* (Dublin: James Duffy, 1865), p.361.

9 *Paston Letters and Papers*, ed. Davis, ii., p.47.

10 Griffiths, 'Duke Richard's Intentions', pp.299–301.

11 Griffiths, 'Duke Richard's Intentions', pp.301–2.

12 *The Politics of Fifteenth-Century England: John Vale's Book*, ed. M. Kekewich et al. (Stroud: Alan Sutton, 1995), pp.187–9.

King's steadfast loyalty to those around him. On 6 November 1450 a new Parliament assembled at Westminster and the dynamics of politics shifted again.

Duke Richard arrived in Parliament in great pomp, with a sword carried before him and at the head of a large retinue. One of his leading servants, Sir William Oldhall, was elected speaker. A Parliamentary petition called for the banishment of 31 individuals, led by Somerset, from court. Duke Edmund was promptly imprisoned in the Tower (albeit briefly), Parliament enacted a more effective Act of Resumption than that passed in 1450, and York seemed in the ascendancy.[13] However, during the following months whatever support he could command among his fellow peers appears to have drifted away; the excluded courtiers returned to their posts and the inquiries in Kent failed to satisfy the commons or punish the 'traitors'. In May 1451 one of the MPs for Bristol, Thomas Young, called for York to be formally recognised as heir to the throne. His call appears to have been backed by the Commons but rejected out of hand by the lords and the King, who responded by immediately dissolving Parliament.[14] Whether this was a desperate attempt by York to recover his position or an unsolicited intervention by one of his supporters, its effect was to eclipse the Duke's political power and return the control of the government to the King, his household and the peers in attendance upon him.

York's interventions in politics had now lost all semblance of legitimacy. His armed involvement on behalf of Thomas Courtenay, Earl of Devon, in his dispute with Lord Bonville in Somerset in September 1451 confirmed the Duke's growing reputation among his peers as a disruptive and self-interested individual. While York might have considered his actions as restoring law and order, the King disagreed. While other peers were imprisoned for their parts in the disturbances, York and his new ally, Devon, refused the King's summons to attend a council meeting in the Midlands.[15] In London and elsewhere attacks on his servants and proceedings for treason against Sir William Oldhall gathered pace. The King's household doubled the guard around Henry's person in the winter of 1451–52 amid fears of a rising and an attempt on the King's life by York's supporters. Duke Richard now attempted to repeat the events of 1450. He dispatched open letters to the King protesting his loyalty and called for the removal of Somerset as a danger to the commonweal. In February 1452, joined by the Earl of Devon and Lord Cobham, York assembled a large force – one chronicler gave the unlikely number of 20,000 – from his friends and tenants to demand redress of his grievances. On this occasion the King's party was organised in its resistance to the opposition. Duke Richard was faced by the King, most of the temporal lords and an army estimated at the equally unlikely number of 24,000. The two sides faced off at Brent Heath, between Crayford and Dartford. York was forced to back down in the face of a concerted show of loyalty to the King from his peers. He agreed to submit to royal arbitration in his dispute with Somerset. The following month the Duke was compelled to take an oath at the high altar of St Paul's cathedral that he would not seek to use force again against the King or any of his subjects.[16]

Significantly, for all his display of armed might, York's actions were not considered as treasonable at the time. The 1459 Act of Attainder would later state that the Duke planned to 'raise a general insurrection on the pretext of the common weal, planning to give battle to you, sovereign

13 *Parliament Rolls of Medieval England*, Parliament of November 1450, items 6, 16 and 17.

14 *Letters and Papers*, ii (part 2), p.770.

15 *John Benet's Chronicle*, p.32.

16 R.L. Storey, *The End of the House of Lancaster* (Stroud: Alan Sutton, 1996), pp.93–104; R.A. Griffiths, *The Reign of Henry VI* (London: Ernest Benn,1981), pp.693–700; Johnson, *Duke Richard of York*, pp.107–24.

lord, beside Dartford in the county of Kent, and so destroy your most noble person.'[17] Indeed, there is plenty of evidence that the Duke was raising men for an armed confrontation in the autumn of 1451. There were armed congregations in favour of York in Hereford, Caxton near Oswestry and in other towns and villages where the Duke held sway.[18] Even after York's surrender at Dartford, risings in his name continued to occur in the Welsh Marches, Kent and London and continued until May.[19] It is doubtful, however, that these incidents were directed by York, and they reveal how potentially damaging the commons' actions were for the Duke. It seems, however, that the lords who had stood with the King at Dartford, including the Duke of Buckingham and the earls of Salisbury and Warwick, were reluctant to punish York, even if they did not support his vendetta against Somerset. Indeed, the indictments brought against his servants for their part in 'the Dartford incident' merely stated their offences were 'contrary to the statutes and ordinances of the realm' without being explicit that their actions may have constituted treason.[20] The Earl of Devon was indicted for rising with Lord Cobham, for which he was pardoned in September 1453. A charge of treason was then brought against him in Parliament the following March, but he was acquitted by his peers. York took this as a deliberate slight against his honour and made a declaration himself of his own loyalty in front of his peers in the same session.[21]

Henry VI's Illness and York's First Protectorate

The Parliament that assembled at Reading on 6 March 1453 represented the high watermark of Henry VI's kingship. The King had seen off the challenges to his authority by rebellious subjects and troublesome magnates and he had agreed to an Act of Resumption to rescue the royal finances. Expectations were high that he would lead an expedition to recover Normandy in person, following the Earl of Shrewsbury's remarkable success in recapturing much of Gascony during the previous autumn. A grateful Commons made a life grant of the customs of tunnage and poundage (recalling the grant made to Henry V after Agincourt) and devised a generous subsidy to equip 20,000 archers for six months' service overseas, as well as attainting Sir William Oldhall and denouncing Jack Cade as a traitor. The Duke of Somerset was back in the ascendancy, while his rival York was conspicuous by his absence from the first two sessions of Parliament (6–28 March and 25 April–2 July 1453). However, on 17 July the English commander in Gascony, John Talbot, Earl of Shrewsbury, was killed leading an ill-advised attack on French gun emplacements laying siege to the town of Castillon.[22] The English defeat did not lead to an immediate military collapse in the duchy and, although Castillon itself fell two days later, Bordeaux held out until late October. Shrewsbury's death and defeat nevertheless had a catastrophic effect on the King. On hearing the news in early August Henry, then on progress in the Savernake Forest in Wiltshire and attended

17 *Parliament Rolls of Medieval England*, Parliament of November 1459, item 8.

18 TNA, KB9/7/2/35; 26/12, 14; 34/1/5; 85/10.

19 TNA, KB9/9/26/1/25; 34/1/5, 8, 48; 48/1/6–11, 13–14, 18; 103/1/15; 130/1.

20 *Parliament Rolls of Medieval England,* Parliament of November 1459, item 7; TNA, KB9/15/1/23, 34. The term 'Dartford Incident' is from Griffiths, *Henry VI*, p.693.

21 J.G. Bellamy, *The Law of Treason in England in the Later Middle Ages* (Cambridge: Cambridge University Press, 1970), p.136; *Parliament Rolls of Medieval England*, Parliament of March 1453, items 34 and 49.

22 Peter Hoskins, *The Battle of Castillon, 1453* (Warwick: Helion & Co, 2023).

only by his riding household, collapsed into a stupor, totally unable to speak, act or even at first to eat. He was to remain in this state for over a year.

If Henry had failed to live up to contemporary expectations of kingship for much of his adult reign, he had nonetheless been seen to go through the motions, listening to and responding to counsel and exercising his prerogative powers. On key occasions, such as the decision to release the Duke of Orléans in 1439, to press for peace in 1444–5, or when deciding to banish Suffolk or dismiss York's complaints against Somerset in 1450, Henry's active royal presence is the most convincing explanation of events. The situation in August 1453 was entirely different: when, in March the following year, a delegation of lords visited him to seek the appointment of a new chancellor following the death of Cardinal Kemp, they met a King who could not respond to their entreaties in any way. After three attempts to communicate with the King they left 'in a state of hopelessly, unproductive, sorrowful embarrassment'.[23] By the autumn of 1453 a Great Council was effectively in control and in October York was summoned to London to attend its meetings. Immediately York's ally, the Duke of Norfolk, launched a fierce attack against Somerset, who was again accused of responsibility for the loss of Normandy and Gascony. Somerset was committed to the Tower on 23 November and York set about building a new regime. This new regime was, ostensibly at least, built on consensus and compromise. Duke Richard promised to do all 'that sholde or might be to the welfare of the king and his subgettes', and there was to be no repeat of the attempted household purges of 1450.[24] The birth of a son, Edward, to the King and Queen in October had raised the spectre of Margaret of Anjou ruling as regent, something which most of the lords had been keen to dismiss. York's passage to pre-eminence among his fellow councillors was eased by his acceptance on 15 March 1454 of the young Prince Edward as heir to the throne, and on 27 March it was agreed in Parliament that the Duke should assume the title and duties of 'protector and governor of the realm' during the King's incapacity. York protested that this had arisen not from his own ambitions but from his acceptance of the necessity of the situation and in response to pleas from his fellow peers. As Ralph Griffiths has observed: 'To make him protector in the constitutional uncertainty of 1454 might be deemed by some a dynastic challenge on York's part and the Duke may have regarded it in precisely the same light.'[25] In any case it seems certain that the protectorate was something arrived at only reluctantly by the lords, evidenced by the numerous protestations of infirmity, old age or youthfulness which several peers offered as excuses not to serve on the council.

Indeed, the expressions of unity made in Parliament and council masked deepening and dangerous divisions among the nobility, some of which had already escalated into violent feuds by the winter of 1453/4. The Bonville/Courtenay dispute in the West Country, in which York had intervened in September 1451, rumbled on, complicated by the involvement of the Earl of Wiltshire, a nobleman close to the court, on the side of Lord Bonville. In 1452 the feckless Henry Holland, Duke of Exeter (who was also York's son-in-law), had seized Ralph, Lord Cromwell's manor of Ampthill in Bedfordshire. Cromwell's attempt to recover the property at law had met a violent response from Exeter, who had attacked his rival in Westminster Hall in July 1453. Cromwell now looked for help and allied himself, through marriage, to the powerful Neville family. Maud Stanhope, Cromwell's niece and joint heiress, was betrothed to the Earl of Salisbury's second son, Sir Thomas Neville.

23 B.P. Wolffe, *Henry VI* (New Haven, CT: Yale University Press, 2001), p.272.

24 *Calendar of Patent Rolls, 1452–61*, p.143.

25 Griffiths, *Reign of Henry VI*, pp.7–25.

In August, having celebrated their nuptials at Tattershall Castle in Lincolnshire, the couple and their wedding party were attacked on their way north by Thomas Percy, Lord Egremont, the somewhat unstable younger son of the Earl of Northumberland, and his brother, Sir Richard Percy. The Percy/Neville feud, between the two greatest magnate families in the north, had its origins in the 1440s over the families' respective influence on the Anglo-Scottish marches but it had reached a crisis because Lord Cromwell held some former Percy lands that the current Earl now hoped to recover. This hope was now seriously threatened by the alliance between Cromwell and the ambitious Nevilles.[26]

The Nevilles' ambitions caused problems elsewhere too. In the Midlands Salisbury's eldest son, Richard Neville, had married Anne, the sister and principal heiress of Henry Beauchamp, late Duke of Warwick. This worsened his existing dispute with the Duke of Somerset, who was married to one of Anne's half-sisters, Eleanor. Richard, now Earl of Warwick in the right of his wife, clashed with Somerset over custody of the Despenser lands in Glamorgan, South Wales. Warwick had held these during the minority of his cousin, George Neville, Lord Abergavenny, but in June 1453 the King had granted the custody to Somerset. By the autumn Warwick was holding them by force against Somerset and John Sutton, Lord Dudley, to whom the Earl had been ordered to surrender them.[27] While tensions simmered in the Midlands, South Wales and the West Country, it was in the north that matters came to a head. Early in 1454 the Duke of Exeter allied himself with Lord Egremont and in the spring, having opposed York's appointment and claimed the office of protector for himself, he went north to join his Percy allies. The renegade lords attempted to seize the city of York in May but fled as the Duke of York travelled north with a large retinue to enforce justice. Exeter claimed sanctuary in Westminster Abbey, but the judicial proceedings failed to punish the Percies and their servants. Instead, they were defeated by Sir Thomas and Sir John Neville at Stamford Bridge at the end of October; Egremont and his brother, Sir Richard Percy, were captured and imprisoned in Newgate in London, while Exeter was taken from sanctuary and incarcerated, under Salisbury's guard, in Pontefract Castle.[28]

The King's illness, and York's protectorate, had thus been marked by an alarming breakdown in order. While later Yorkist chroniclers would conclude that York had governed 'most admirably, and wonderfully pacifying all rebels and malefactors according to the law, and without undue rigour', the fact remains that a significant proportion of the political nation probably regarded the protectorate as partisan government at its worst, driven by self-interest rather than the good of the commonweal.[29] In part this was the inevitable conclusion of any government that was not led by the impartial authority of an active king, but it was also an impression reinforced by York's activities and the decisions made during his protectorate. On 2 April 1454 he secured the appointment of the Earl of Salisbury as chancellor of England to replace the recently deceased Archbishop of Canterbury, Cardinal John Kemp. Kemp was a stalwart of the Lancastrian regime, a churchman who had served Henry V and been a voice of moderation throughout the 1440s and early 1450; the contrast with Salisbury could not have been lost on the regime's opponents. York's record at dealing with local disorder was mixed. Although he moved quickly and forcefully to quell

26 Simon J. Payling, 'The Ampthill Dispute: A Study in Aristocratic Lawlessness and the Breakdown of Lancastrian Government', *English Historical Review*, 104 (1989), pp.881–907.

27 Michael Hicks, *Warwick the Kingmaker* (Oxford: Blackwell, 1998), pp.94–125.

28 R.A. Griffiths, 'Local Rivalries and National Politics: The Percies, the Nevilles and the Duke of Exeter, 1452–1454', in *King and Country*, pp.321–64.

29 *John Benet's Chronicle*, p.37.

disorder in Yorkshire, elsewhere he was less successful. The Derbyshire gentry who had sacked Walter Blount's manor of Elvaston simply refused to answer the protector's summons, making the unfortunate messenger eat the writ, seal and all, while in Wales York failed to control Gruffyd ap Nicholas, whose violent behaviour made a mockery of the protector's authority.[30] Even where he did intervene forcefully, such as in the West Country, where he bound over his erstwhile ally, the Earl of Devon, to keep the peace, York's policies backfired and lost him much-needed support. More damning perhaps was the long imprisonment of Somerset without a trial. In autumn 1454 the protector attempted to instigate proceedings against his rival, but he found little support among the other lords.

The end of York's first protectorate was signalled by the recovery of the King around Christmas 1454. The basis for the Duke's government dissolved and calls for the release of Somerset grew. On 26 January Duke Edmund was released from the Tower on condition that he remained at least 20 miles distant from the King. This was probably small consolation to York, who surrendered his office, possibly at the same council meeting that settled terms for Somerset's release. Power now passed back to the King and his household. On 4 March the council, with the King present, lifted the restrictions on Somerset's movement and repudiated the charges against him. York was forced to submit the matters between him and his rival, now reduced to a private squabble rather than a fundamental question of public government, to the arbitration of his fellow peers. Moreover, the office of captain of Calais, granted to York in July 1454, was taken back into the King's hands only to be bestowed on Somerset two days later. This was a deliberate affront to York, who had accused Somerset of military incompetence and worse only to see the most important command in the realm given to his rival, but it also demonstrated a reassertion of the royal authority. York's influence at court evaporated: on 7 March Salisbury resigned the Great Seal; a week later Exeter was released from Pontefract Castle; and on 15 March Somerset's ally James Butler, Earl of Wiltshire, replaced the Earl of Worcester as treasurer of England. Grants of office and patronage that had been made to York and his allies during the protectorate were now cancelled and redistributed among men close to the King. In mid-April Henry and his council resolved to summon a Great Council to meet at Leicester. York and his Neville allies, perhaps justifiably, feared a repeat of the events of February 1447 when Humphrey, Duke of Gloucester, had been summoned to the Bury Parliament only to be arrested on charges of treason and soon afterwards die in mysterious circumstances. They decided to withdraw from Westminster, probably in the third week of April, leaving without apparently asking permission of the King.[31]

* * *

The politics of the early 1450s were dominated by two related concerns: the illness and obvious inability of Henry VI to exercise effectively the office of kingship, and the bitter rivalry between the dukes of Somerset and York. The first made the second intractable, while the second threw the first into sharp relief and transformed a situation that must have been increasingly apparent during the 1440s into a crisis that threatened to destroy the foundations of Lancastrian kingship and

30 Helen Castor, '"Walter Blount was Gone to Serve Traytours": The Sack of Elvaston and the Politics of the North Midlands in 1454', *Midland History*, 19 (1994), pp.21–39; R.A. Griffiths, 'Gruffyd ap Nicholas and the Fall of the House of Lancaster', in *King and Country*, pp.201–19.

31 Hicks, *Warwick the Kingmaker*, pp.112–13; Griffiths, *Reign of Henry VI*, pp.738–41.

royal government. The defeat in France, and the loss of Normandy and Gascony, was due to this paralysis at the centre of power as much as it was due to the military reforms and leadership of the French King Charles VII. Furthermore, the failure of Henry VI to maintain peace among his lords and the notorious instances of aristocratic violence further destabilised the realm. The role of the commons and the popular identification of the Duke of York with the agenda of reform demanded by the rebels in 1450 also complicated matters further. Duke Richard was forced to defend himself from accusations that he was a rabble-rouser lest he alienate himself from the majority of moderate lords who hoped that the façade of Henry VI's kingship could be maintained. York overplayed his hand, however, and in 1452 and 1454 he overestimated the support he enjoyed among his peers. By the spring of 1455 York was backed into a corner and the resort to violence which had been avoided at Blackheath three years earlier seemed inevitable.

2

The First Battle of St Albans

The First Battle of St Albans, fought in the town's streets on 22 May 1455, was not only the opening clash of the series of conflicts we now know as the Wars of the Roses. It is also the best documented battle of the wars, with several contemporary newsletters surviving alongside the Parliamentary and later chronicle accounts. The newsletters, the first written within hours of the end of the battle, survive in both English and French. Several versions exist of more than one English newsletter, and at least one other newsletter was circulated on the continent. Except for the so-called 'Fastolf Relation', the newsletters represent the initial attempt by York and the Neville earls to explain and justify their conduct in the days after the battle. They were superseded by the 'official' Yorkist narrative of the battle, enrolled in the form of a pardon issued to York, Warwick, Salisbury and their adherents by the King during the Parliament that met at Westminster on 9 July. This account also contained the text of two letters sent by the Yorkist lords, the first to Archbishop Bourchier on 20 May and the second to the King the following day, explaining why they had travelled to St Albans arrayed for war. These letters, they claimed, were not shown to the King, which explained why they had been forced into violence. Other contemporary documents, such as the casualty list in the register of the Archdeacon of St Albans, shed light on different aspects of the battle, but none present a Lancastrian account of events. John Whethamstede, Abbot of the Benedictine monastery of St Albans, may have been an eyewitness to the battle, but his account probably owed more to his love of Classical tropes than any desire to accurately record the events of the day. The first (and only) surviving Lancastrian account of the battle was that contained in the 1459 Act of Attainder of the Yorkist lords. Subsequently, the pro-Yorkist chronicles of the 1460s would add other details and fully incorporate the First Battle of St Albans into their explanations of the collapse of Henry VI's kingship.[1]

The Road to St Albans

As soon as York and his allies had left London in April 1455, both the Lancastrians and their opponents began making active preparations for armed conflict. York's movements in the month or so leading up to St Albans are unclear. The Duke probably retired to Sandal Castle near

1 C.A.J. Armstrong, 'Politics and the Battle of St Albans, 1455', *Bulletin of the Institute of Historical Research*, 33 (1960), pp.1–72; Michael Hicks, 'Propaganda and the First Battle of St Albans, 1455', *Nottingham Medieval Studies*, 44 (2000), pp.167–83.

Wakefield. Towards the end of the month a royal delegation comprising the Earl of Worcester, the Bishop of Coventry and Lichfield, and the prior of the Hospitaller Order in England were sent to ascertain York's intentions. One hostile chronicler claimed the Duke detained the delegation to hide his military preparations from Henry VI and Somerset.[2] York's fear that Somerset was back in control and planning action against him may not have been unfounded. The King's recovery may have been fitful at best, and he is not recorded as signing any official documents between 3 February and 21 April.[3] According to Abbot Whethamstede, after withdrawing from London, York, Salisbury and Warwick met and decided to move against Somerset. It is impossible to know what sources Whethamstede based his account upon – other than his paraphrasing of the letter St Augustine of Hippo wrote to Boniface in the fifth century about the trials of the Biblical King David – but its sentiments sound entirely plausible in the circumstances of 1455. York allegedly told the Neville earls that although Henry was 'a simple and just man' (*simplex et rectus*), he had allowed Somerset, 'that impious and seditious man', to subvert the laws of the realm. 'Peace and tranquillity' could not exist while Duke Edmund, who 'endeavours to erase the three of us from the book of life', lived. York urged Salisbury and Warwick to 'thrust our three spears into his vitals, for he is not only odious to us but also to the common people and many nobles.'[4] Whethamstede captured the real fear that York may have felt and his belief that Somerset wished him dead. Yet he also captured the Duke's awareness of the commons and their perception of the struggle between him and Duke Edmund.

By contrast, the King and Somerset appear dilatory in their response to the Yorkists' mobilisation. On 14 May the King instructed commissioners to raise loans throughout the realm, ostensibly for the defence of Calais against a French army. 'The notable nombre of men of werre' to be assembled and paid with the money raised could as easily be used against York as they could be sent across the Channel.[5] It was not until 22 May, however, that the mayor and citizens of Coventry received the King's signet letter, written at Westminster four days earlier, asking them to send as many men as they could to attend upon the King 'wheresoeuer we be in all hast possibull.' The council quickly assembled 100 'goode-men defenseably with bowes & arowes, Jakked & saletted arayd' and sent them to meet the King. The letter did not direct them to Leicester but instructed them to meet the royal party on the road to Westminster, suggesting that the King knew that York intended to prevent him and Somerset from reaching the Midlands town. In Coventry's case, their contingent did not reach the King in time and hearing Henry 'was remeued to London ageyne', they returned home.[6] Yet the Lancastrian court was prepared for confrontation. In preparation for their departure for Leicester three new brigandines had been ordered for Henry VI. They were tested with 'shot' and the one that emerged unscathed from the proofing was covered in purple velvet and delivered to the King. Five hundred bows were also purchased to equip men of the royal household, while the Tower of London armoury appears to have been reorganised and old stuff,

2 *Incerti Scriptoris Chronicon Angliae de Regnis Trium Regum Lancastrensium Henrici IV, Henrici V et Henrici V*, ed. J.A. Giles (London: D Nutt,1848), part 3, pp.47–8.

3 J.R. Lander, 'Henry VI and the Duke of York's Second Protectorate 1455–6', in *Crown and Nobility 1450–1509* (London: Hodder and Stoughton, 1976), pp.78–80.

4 Whethamstede, pp.164–5.

5 *Proceedings and Ordinances of the Privy Council of England*, ed. Sir Harris Nicolas (6 vols, London: Record Commission, 1831–37), vi., pp.234–44.

6 *The Coventry Leet Book or Mayor's Register*, ed. M.D. Harris, Early English Text Society, original series, pp.124–5, 138, 146 (1907–13 in 1 vol.), 282–3.

some dating back 20 years or more, was disposed of.[7] The King certainly left Westminster with a sizeable force and one Italian observer related that 'they went armed because they suspected that the Duke of York would also go there with men at arms'.[8] The contemporary newsletters differed in their estimation of the size of the king's party from 2,000 'and more' to 3,500.[9] Henry was accompanied by an impressive assemblage of the peerage: various sources list the dukes of Buckingham and Somerset, the earls of Devon, Northumberland, Pembroke, Stafford and Dorset, and lords Berners, Clifford, Dudley, Fauconberg, Roos and Sudeley in the royal party. On 19 May the King directed the chancellor, Archbishop Bourchier of Canterbury, to draw up royal letters chastising York and the others for illegally arraying the King's subjects. The Duke was ordered to dismiss all but 200 of his men, while the Neville earls and the Duke of Norfolk were commanded to have no more than 160 men each in their retinues.[10]

By 20 May the Duke of York was at Royston. We do not know where he was previously to this or whether he had travelled towards London from Sandal Castle or Fotheringhay. There is no way of knowing whether York had initially planned to march on London, travel to Leicester, or to intercept and stop the royal party. By the time he reached Royston, he was accompanied by the Earl of Salisbury, and he may have had his young sons, the earls of Rutland and March, with him, along with his old ally, John, Lord Clinton. Later chroniclers, writing in the 1460s, would add Henry, Viscount Bourchier, and his son, Humphrey, later Lord Cromwell, to those that accompanied York, but their presence at St Albans in the Duke's party is not noted by any contemporary. Warwick had been recruiting men in Warwickshire in April and May, and, in common with York, he may have drawn from his servants and tenants in Wales.[11] The contemporary newsletters were coy about how many men York and the Neville earls had assembled: 'The Dijon Relation' ventured 5,000 men, the figure also given by 'The Phillipps Relation.' Writing in Arras before 1467, Jacques du Clercq had heard that York had gathered a thousand men himself, while another 4,000–5,000, presumably the force gathered by the Nevilles, followed behind. While the King and Somerset were aware of York's force, he wrote, they were ignorant of the larger army assembled by the Nevilles. Other lords and knights were en route to St Albans but, like the men of Coventry, they only arrived after the battle. 'The Philipps Relation' claimed that the Duke of Norfolk, an ally of the Duke of York, was accompanied by 6,000 men and arrived 'a day aftyr the jurney', as did the Earl of Oxford, while the Earl of Shrewsbury, Lord Cromwell and Sir Thomas Stanley 'were comynge' with 10,000 men.[12]

It was from Royston on 20 May that York, Salisbury and Warwick wrote the first of two letters that would provide the cornerstone of their account of the events at St Albans. According to the narrative enrolled on the Parliament Roll, they sent their first missive to the chancellor, presumably a response to his letter of the previous day. They wrote to assure him of their peaceful but resolute intentions, 'because we hear that there is great rumour and wonder at our coming, and at the manner of it' put into the minds of Henry and others by 'various people who … have not done all they should to advance the honour and prosperity' of the King. They continued that they

7 TNA, E404/70/3/22, 34; *Calendar of Patent Rolls, 1452–1461*, pp.247–8.

8 *Calendar of State Papers, Milan*, p.17.

9 2,000 'and more' ('The Stow Relation': *Contemporary English Chronicles*, p.93); 3,000 ('The Phillipps Relation: *The Paston Letters*, ed. Gairdner, iii., p.29); 3,500 ('The Dijon Relation': Armstrong, 'St Albans', p.63).

10 TNA, C81/770/10079.

11 Hicks, *Warwick the Kingmaker*, pp.114–15.

12 Armstrong, 'St Albans', pp.17–18, 63; *The Paston Letters*, ed. Gairdner, iii., p.30; *Mémoires de Jacques du Clercq*, ed. Frédéric Baron de Reiffenberg (3 vols, Brussels: Arnold Lacrosse, 1823), ii., pp.237–8.

believed the Great Council at Leicester had been convened for malicious purposes and promised to do 'whatever accords with our duty for the security' of the king's person. They had assembled an armed force to protect themselves against their enemies and demanded to know who had defamed them to the King. York and his allies called for proclamation of excommunication to be made 'in as rigorous and fearful a manner as the church will allow, upon and against those who plan any disloyalty, prejudice, harm or damage to the welfare of our said sovereign lord or his land.' They asked Archbishop Bourchier to make representations on their behalf to the King and the lords of the council and assured him they only wished for the 'removal and overthrow of the seditious blasphemy and defamation, untruly … laid upon us.'[13]

By the next day the Yorkist lords were at Ware. From there they wrote a second letter, this time addressed to King Henry himself. They related 'their greatest earthly sorrow', namely that their 'proven enemies' sheltered under the king's protection, spreading lies about them and impugning their loyalty. Their enemies had done their best 'to estrange us from your noble presence and from the favour of your good grace'. While they hoped that the King would give credence to their complaints, they nevertheless made their intentions clear: 'we at this time are coming … as your true and humble liegemen … to do that which may advance or promote the honour and welfare of your said majesty, and the security of your most noble person'. The lords stated that they had not been 'ascertained whether our intentions [contained in the letter to Archbishop Bourchier] were shown … to your good grace or not', and for convenience enclosed another copy. The message was clear: while loyal subjects of the King, they nevertheless could not allow their enemies – in the other words, the Duke of Somerset – to remain in positions of authority about the King. York and the Neville earls would go on to claim in their Parliamentary declaration that neither of these two letters had been delivered. Instead, Somerset, Thomas Thorpe, a royal councillor and one of the barons of the exchequer, and William Joseph, one of the ushers of the King's chamber, 'intending … the hurt and destruction' of the three lords, had kept their letters from reaching the King. The first letter was received by Archbishop Bourchier and sent to the King, then at Kilburn. It was carried by the Archbishop's servant, John Say, and given to Thomas Manning, a clerk of the royal household, who showed it to Somerset, Thorpe and Joseph. The second letter, addressed directly to the King, was delivered by Master William Williflete, York's confessor, and received by the Earl of Devon at 2 a.m. on 22 May. It too was kept from the King by the machinations of Somerset, Thorpe and Joseph. When York, Salisbury and Warwick arrived at St Albans on the morning of the 22nd they approached the King's party asking for a response to their letters. At midday, 'on the advice of the said [Duke] Edmund, Thomas Thorpe and William Joseph', they were told, without the King's knowledge, that their letters had not been received. Thus, the Parliamentary declaration concluded, the King could not know 'the true and faithful disposition of our same cousins towards and our estate'. York, Salisbury and Warwick were forced to enter the town by force to make their declarations of loyalty in person to the King, but Somerset, Thorpe and Joseph were there 'with a great multitude of people … defensibly arrayed planning to prevent our said cousins coming into presence, and destroy and slay them, openly calling them false traitors to us'. Somerset and his allies then 'greviously assaulted our said cousins' but Duke Edmund was himself killed in the fighting. It was a convenient story that exonerated York and his allies, blaming the whole sorry affair on Somerset, who, of course, could no longer refute the charges against him.[14]

13 *Parliament Rolls of Medieval England*, Parliament of July 1455, item 19.
14 *Parliament Rolls of Medieval England*, Parliament of July 1455, items 20 and 21.

The First Battle of St Albans

The Parliamentary process, the subsequent declaration of York's loyalty, and the pardon extended to him, the Nevilles and those who fought with them at St Albans were obviously partisan pieces of political theatre. As one well-informed contemporary observed, once the declaration attributing blame to Somerset had passed through Parliament, 'many a man groged full sore'.[15] Indeed, the newsletters written in the battle's immediate aftermath, their Yorkist origins and bias notwithstanding, suggest a somewhat different account of what happened at St Albans on 22 May. The royal party had left Westminster early in the morning of the 21st, with the expectation that they would arrive in St Albans around 9 a.m. the following day. Henry was at Watford on the night of Wednesday, 21 May and in the morning, according to one anonymous chronicler, a council meeting had been held where the King had dismissed Somerset as constable of England and replaced him with the Duke of Buckingham. Buckingham had rejected calls to meet the Yorkists in battle and instead decided to push onto St Albans.[16] What happened next is far from clear, but when the royal party arrived in the town, they were probably surprised to learn that York was camped in Key Field, to the east of St Albans. Several exchanges of heralds followed, with York repeating his demand that Somerset be delivered to him. Buckingham may have requested that York and his followers retreat to Barnet or Hatfield while the King considered his response. An alternative explanation is that Henry simply refused to hand over Somerset and when this became clear, York attacked. A third possibility, suggested by du Clercq, is that York and the Neville lords mounted a pre-emptive attack on the royal party aimed at removing Somerset once and for all.[17]

The so-called 'Stow Relation', written hours after the battle, is probably the account closest to the truth of events on 22 May. York demanded that the King 'deliver suche as we wull accuse, and thei tahave like as thei have deserved'. Henry's response was unambiguous: he demanded to know 'what traitor dare be so bolde tareise any people in myn owne reaume'. He continued: 'rather thane they shall have eny lorde that is here with at thys tyme, I shall this day for theire sake in this quarrel my selfe lyve and dye'. It was a rare display of resolve from Henry VI, but one that forced the hand of York and his Neville allies. York addressed his men, concluding that their enemies were gathered 'in full purpose to destroye us all'. There was no option but to move against their enemies, 'sethe it will noon be otherwise to be but that we shall be utterly dye, bettir it is to us to dye in the felde, than kowardly tobe put unto utter rebuke and shamefull detthe'. York's attempt to intimidate the King had failed. It is unclear whether Buckingham, commanding the royal troops, was aware of the full extent of the force arrayed against him, but he seems not to have expected to have to fight in the town. He seemed confident that York would continue to negotiate, and that the crisis could be solved as it had been three years earlier at Blackheath.

The 'Stow Relation' related how York and the Neville earls began their attack between 11 a.m. and midday; the 'Dijon Relation' had the fighting begin an hour earlier. St Albans was not a walled town and was instead protected by a town ditch. Three main roads from the east – Cock Lane, Shropshire Lane, and Sopwell Lane – led to the market square, where the King and Buckingham took up residence in the Moot Hall ('the place of Edmond Westby, hundreder of the seid towne'). Long wooden 'bars' could be used to block the main routes into the town centre, and the

15 *Paston Letters and Papers*, ed. Beadle and Richmond, iii., p.158.

16 *Incerti Scriptoris Chronicon Angliae*, part 3, p.48.

17 Armstrong, 'St Albans', pp.63–7; *Mémoires de Jacques du Clercq*, ii., pp.227–8.

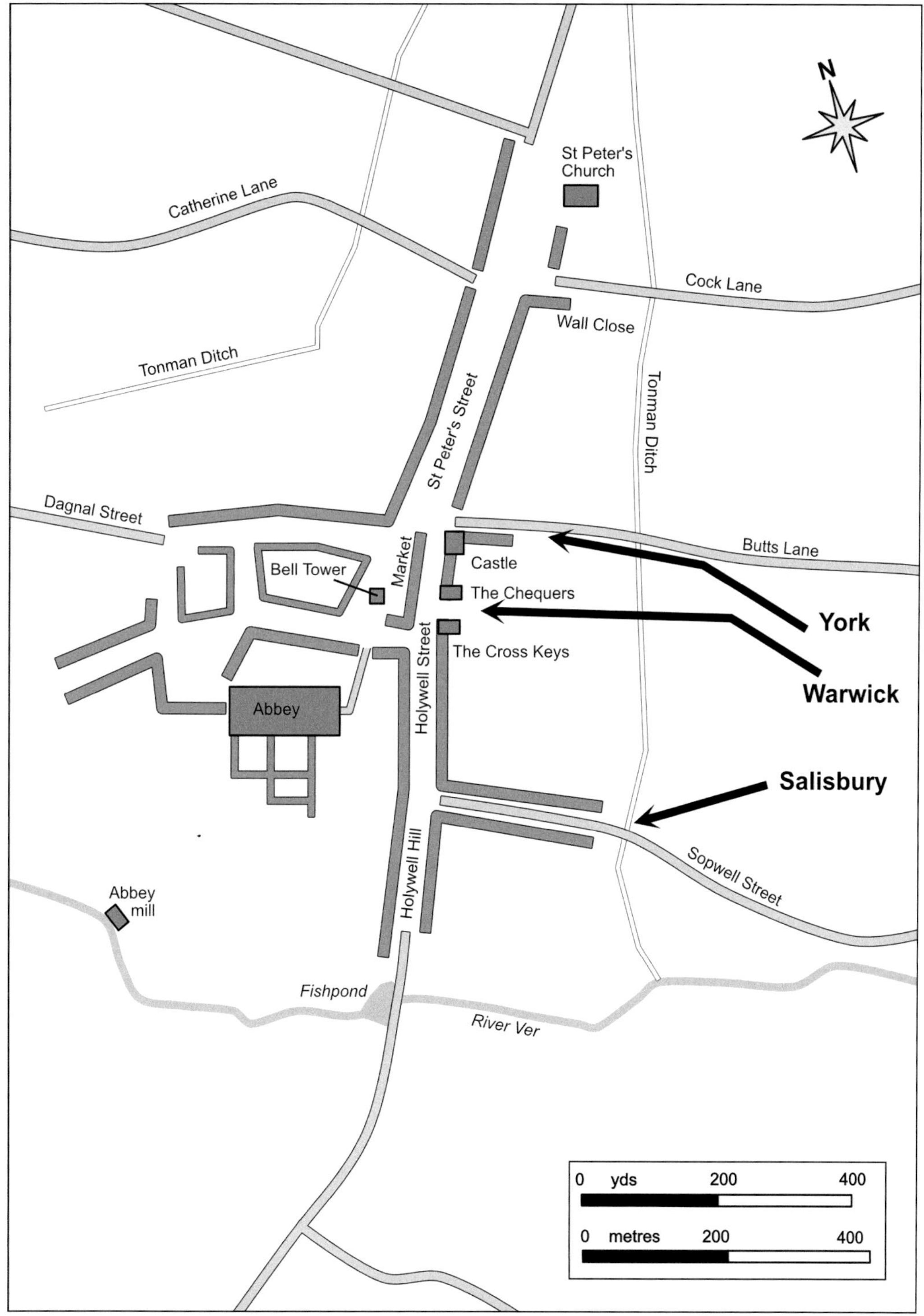

The First Battle of St Albans was fought in the centre of St Albans on the morning of 22 May 1455.

Lancastrians had put these in place early on the morning of the 22nd. Thomas, Lord Clifford, was tasked with defending these and it was here that York began his assault. Clifford resisted stoutly, so 'the seyde Duke of York myyght not ony wyse, with all the powere that he hadde, entre ne breke into the toun'. It was at this point that the Earl of Warwick made a critical intervention. Aware of Duke Richard's difficulties at the bars, he led his men to the gardens that backed onto the town ditch. They crossed the ditch and then made an audacious 250-yard dash through the gardens to burst into the market square between two inns, the Sign of the Key and The Chequer, in Holywell Street. There they blew their trumpets and 'sette a cry with a shout & a grete voyce "A Warrewe, A Warrewyk! A Warrewyk"'.[18] According to the 'Phillipps Relation', Warwick's 600 men were led by Sir Robert Ogle, an experienced soldier from the Northumberland marches with Scotland and long-time associate of the Nevilles of Middleham.[19]

The appearance of Warwick's men in the market square caused panic among the royal party. The town's bell, 'Gabriel', in the clock tower rang out, calling the King's men to arms, many of whom had apparently yet to don their armour. A flurry of arrows caused mayhem. King Henry himself was lightly wounded by an arrow in the neck or shoulder, while the 'Dijon Relation' claims four of his bodyguard were killed by archery.[20] Abbot Whethamstede described the scene in his usual mixture of hyperbole and Classical allusion:

> So savage was the fighting that you could see one man lying there with his brain exposed, another with his arm severed, a third with his throat slashed, a fourth with his chest pierced, and the entire street further filled with corpses, both from their side and from every direction.

He attributed the success of Warwick's partly to the savagery of the northerners, but also to the character of the King's household men. They fled in terror, 'whether innate or induced', and, being 'men of fair appearance', acted more like Paris than Hector, preferring the comfort of 'a soft bed' to the rigours of combat![21] Faced with the turmoil in their rear, the Lancastrians manning the bars similarly faltered, allowing York and Salisbury to 'brake up the barreres' and join the fray in the market square.[22]

The fighting cannot have lasted long, only half an hour according to the 'Phillipps Relation', although the 'Dijon Relation' stated it continued until half past two. Contemporaries noted the relatively light casualties. John Crane, writing to John Paston senior on 25 May, noted that although there was a 'grete multytude' of people at the battle, 'ther was at most slayn vj score'.[23] The 'Stow Relation' named 23 individuals killed on the king's part and a further 25 whose names were not known. The 'Dijon Relation' judged the number of dead to be 200, while the 'Phillipps Relation' doubled that to more than 400 (a figure also repeated by Jacques du Clercq).[24] More significant than the simple number of casualties was the identity of those who died. There seems little doubt York and the Nevilles

18 *Contemporary English Chronicles*, pp.93–5; Armstrong, 'St Albans', p.64.
19 *Paston Letters*, ed. Gairdner, iii., p.30. For Ogle see *The House of Commons, 1422–1461*, v., pp.711–16.
20 Armstrong, 'St Albans', p.64.
21 Whethamstede, p.168.
22 *John Vale's Book*, p.192.
23 *Paston Letters and Papers*, ed. Davis, ii., p.116.
24 Armstrong, 'St Albans', p.64; *Contemporary English Chronicles*, pp.95–6; *Paston Letters*, ed. Gairdner, iii., p.30; *Mémoires de Jacques du Clercq*, ii., p.228.

The clock tower in the market square in St Albans. It was from here on the morning of 22 May 1455 that the bell 'Gabriel' rang out to signal the Yorkist attack on the royal party. (Simon Marsh)

intended to kill their political rivals once they had chosen to attack. According to the 'Dijon Relation', the Duke of Somerset found himself trapped in an inn in the market square. He attempted to fight his way out, killing four of his assailants, until he was himself overpowered.[25] A Milanese observer, writing from Bruges on 3 June, had heard differently: he informed the Archbishop of Ravenna that Somerset had been taken and beheaded.[26] The fate of the Earl of Northumberland and Lord Clifford was not described in detail by any of the contemporary sources. They merely noted their deaths, but as the author of *An English Chronicle* would later note, 'when þe seyde Duke Edmond and þe lordes were slayne, the batayle was ceased'.[27] Several other prominent Lancastrians were killed: the Yorkshire knight Ralph Babthorpe and his son, the veteran of the Hundred Years War Sir Bertram Entwistle, and various members of the King's household. Others were badly injured. The Duke of Buckingham and his son, the Earl of Stafford, were both wounded with arrows, as were the Earl of Devon, Somerset's son and heir, the Earl of Dorset, and Lord Sudeley. Sir John Wenlock was carried away in a cart, seriously hurt, while Sir John Fastolf's nephew, Henry Fillongley, although he fought 'manly, was shet thorwe the armys in iij and iij placys'.[28] Others managed to escape unharmed, including the Earl of Wiltshire. 'The Stow Relation' relates that he and Thomas Thorpe fled, casting their harness in the town ditch, while the later continuator of 'Gregory's Chronicle' adds the detail that Wiltshire was charged with the King's banner, but abandoned it propped up against a gable end, fleeing for his life because 'he was aferyd of lesynge of beute, for he was namyd the fayryd knyght of this londe'.[29] The Norfolk knight Sir Philip Wentworth was similarly disgraced. He allegedly bore the royal standard and 'kest it down and fled'. 'Myn Lord Norfolk', William Barker told William Worcester at the beginning of June, 'seyth he shal be hanged therefore.'[30]

According to Whethamstede, the King was first led to the safety of a cottage, presumably one of the workshops on the market square. He remained there until the Duke of York arrived. The words Whethamstede puts into York's mouth – 'Rejoice, illustrious Prince ... for now that impious accuser, who accused me and my brothers, your lords present with me here ... is now cast down' – seem unlikely, and the King could have been under no illusion as to the weight of the events that day. From the market square, Henry was conveyed the short distance to the abbey, where he spent the night. He may have been unaware of the pillaging that followed the Yorkist victory. We might doubt how widespread 'the plundering, looting, and rapine' actually was, as Whethamstede's description is tinged by his familiar disdain for northerners, but certainly some Lancastrians were despoiled.[31] One later chronicler claimed that Richard Percy, Bishop of Carlisle, the only ecclesiastic present and a son of the Earl of Northumberland, was robbed of his jewels and horse and had to travel to the Percy manor of Isleham in Cambridgeshire on foot. Thomas Gascoigne claimed that no one was robbed unless it was directly on York's orders. Equally we might question Whethamstede's claim that the dead remained unburied as 'no one, lest it incur the wrath of the said Duke [of York], dared to prepare graves and bury them'.[32]

25 Armstrong, 'St Albans', p.64.
26 *Calendar of State Papers, Milan*, p.17.
27 *An English Chronicle*, p.73.
28 *Paston Letters*, ed. Gairdner, iii., pp.29–30.
29 *Contemporary English Chronicles*, pp.60, 96.
30 *Paston Letters*, ed. Gairdner, iii., p.33.
31 Whethamstede, pp.169–73.
32 *Three Fifteenth Century Chronicles*, p.152; Thomas Gascoigne, *Loci e Libro Veritatum*, ed. James E. Thorold Rogers (Oxford: Clarendon Press, 1931), p.204; Whethamstede, p.175.

The victors, accompanied by King Henry VI, left St Albans for London on Friday, 23 May. Henry was flanked by York on his right and Salisbury on his left, with Warwick ahead of them bearing the sword. Once they had arrived within the city, there was a 'general procession', underlining the political significance of events the previous day, before the King was lodged at the Bishop's Palace, on the north-west side of St Paul's. Two days later, York placed the crown on Henry's head in a solemn crown-wearing ceremony at the cathedral, and on 26 May the King despatched writs summoning a Parliament for 9 July. The mood was ostensibly one of conciliation. All discussion of the battle was, as the one Milanese observer wrote, quickly forbidden and among the King's men, only Lord Dudley and the Duke of Exeter were arrested.[33] A major redistribution of offices followed that demonstrated that political power had been transferred to York, at least temporarily. York replaced Somerset as constable of England and was given command of castles in Wales formerly held by his rival. Most importantly, Somerset's captaincy at Calais was granted to Warwick. On 24 July the assembled lords each took a personal oath to Henry VI. As John Armstrong noted, it was an attempt to move on from the events of 22 May and sought to emphasise the unity of the peers through their individual responsibility to uphold royal government.[34] One final piece of business, enacted before the first session of Parliament closed a week later, testified to the partisan agenda of the assembly. The Commons introduced a petition rehabilitating Humphrey, Duke of Gloucester, and asking that proclamation be made to the effect that he had been the King's faithful liegeman until the day of his death.[35] By associating himself with Gloucester, fast emerging as the erstwhile champion of reform and leader of the opposition to Henry VI's corrupt counsellors, York staked his own claim to lead the commonweal to better things.

* * *

The events of 22 May 1455 were an extraordinary display of political violence that sowed the seeds for the conflict that would ignite again four years later. The murder of Somerset, Northumberland and Clifford was a sore that would fester in the English polity until its bloody resolution at Wakefield in December 1460. It seems unlikely that York had planned the death of his rival Somerset from the onset. York merely hoped for his removal from the King's counsels and, as Thomas Gascoigne ventured, for Somerset to 'be lawfully led into the Tower of London'.[36] It seems very unlikely that York would have wished the death of Northumberland and Clifford. That was the Nevilles' doing and York would ultimately pay the price for allowing their regional rivalry to spill over into national politics. Later Yorkist chroniclers would stress that the commons welcomed the death of Somerset. He was a malign presence who had 'principally gided and gouerned' the King 'as he had be[en] before by þe the Duk of Suthfolk'. It was Somerset, they said, who had taken the King to Clarendon two years earlier, where he had fallen sick.[37] In these accounts York was forced into action by a stubborn King, guided by evil counsel, to save himself and the realm. Whatever York's motive, his actions had nevertheless crossed a line. He had broken the oaths made at Dartford, had drawn the King's blood, and he had acted without the support of most of his peers, taking control of the government by force of arms.

33 *Calendar of State Papers, Milan*, pp.16–17.
34 *Parliament Rolls of Medieval England*, Parliament of July 1455, item 25; Armstrong, 'St Albans', p.62.
35 TNA, C49/30/18.
36 Gascoigne, *Loci e Libro*, p.201.
37 *An English Chronicle*, p.72; *Contemporary English Chronicles*, p.60.

Further Reading

John Armstrong's 'Politics and the Battle of St Albans, 1455', *Bulletin of the Institute of Historical Research* 33 (1960), pp.1–72, remains the seminal study of the battle. The 'Dijon Relation' and 'Fastolf Relation' are only printed in Armstrong's article. Michael Hicks, 'Propaganda and the First Battle of St Albans, 1455', *Nottingham Medieval Studies* 44 (2000), pp.167–83, provides more context and a critical analysis of the contemporary sources, tracing the development of the Yorkist narrative. A more accessible account of the battle that places it firmly within its local context can be found in Peter Burley, Mike Elliott and Harvey Watson's *The Battles of St Albans* (Barnsley: Pen and Sword, 2007).

3

The Battle of Blore Heath and Ludford Bridge

If Richard, Duke of York, thought that the Battle of St Albans would restore him to his rightful place in the King's counsels and as the foremost peer of the realm he would soon be disappointed. His government appears to have enjoyed little support among his fellow peers, at least if their parlous attendance at Parliament is any measure of their commitment to the new regime. The second session of the Parliament of 1455 assembled at Westminster on 12 November amid news of further, violent disorder in the localities. In the West Country the Courtenay Earl of Devon continued his feud against William, Lord Bonville, while trouble also flared up in the Midlands and in London. In the King's absence York was named as his lieutenant in Parliament, but the Commons demanded that the Duke once more be appointed protector to deal with the disorder; the hearing of petitions for justice, they argued, 'shuld be overe grevous and tedious to his highnesse'.[1] It seems unlikely that Henry had suffered a relapse of the condition that led to York's first appointment as protector. This time it was the Duke and his followers in the Commons who pressed for York's reappointment as protector. The Commons' request, communicated not by the speaker, John Wenlock, but by York's servant William Burley, one of the knights of the shire for Shropshire, was at first refused by the lords. Yet on 17 November, they reluctantly agreed to the Duke's appointment as protector until such time as the King, with the advice of the lords in Parliament, ended it. The Duke's ability to govern was circumscribed by the presence of the King. In all matters touching 'the honour, wurship and suertee' of the King's person, the council was to notify Henry of its decisions, presumably so he might, if he chose to, alter them.[2] On 13 December Parliament was prorogued to allow York to travel west to deal with the Courtenays and the Bonvilles. Both parties were soon under arrest and, although York himself never made it as far as Devon, he had, on the face of it at least, restored order.

When Parliament resumed on 14 January 1456 the limits of York's authority were laid bare. The Duke threw his weight behind the Commons' call for the resumption of royal lands and offices granted by the profligate King. The lords failed to back the demands despite the presence of large armed retinues brought to Westminster by York and the Earl of Warwick. On 25 February, in accordance with the terms of his grant, the Duke was removed by the King in person, acting upon the advice of his lords spiritual and temporal. Although he was compensated financially, this may have been designed to placate him and remove a potential source of grievance rather than as a genuine expression of thanks for his service. York, however, may have read his dismissal in

1 *Parliament Rolls of Medieval England*, Parliament of July 1455, item 32.
2 Ibid., item 41.

other ways. His support for the Commons' call for resumption had failed, and he had been unable to establish the type of political ascendancy his victory at St Albans had promised. According to one source, the Duke and King argued soon after his dismissal from office and York had left Westminster before the Parliament ended on 9 March.[3]

Queen Margaret and the Lancastrians

Discussions of the period following York's dismissal as protector in February 1456 and the outbreak of renewed conflict in September 1459 are often dominated by the role that Queen Margaret of Anjou played in galvanising a 'Lancastrian' opposition to the ambitions of the Duke of York.[4] Margaret (b. 1430) was the younger daughter of René, Duke of Anjou and King of Naples, a direct relation of the kings of France. As such her espousal to Henry VI in 1444 was a vital part of the diplomatic rapprochement between England and France, culminating in the truce of Tours, sealed just four days after their formal betrothal. Until 1453 she appears to have played a conventional role as queen consort, acting as mediator and patron, as well as developing close connections to the Duke of Suffolk and other leading members of the Lancastrian affinity. The King's illness in the summer of 1453 and the birth of their first son, Edward (created Prince of Wales on 15 March 1454), transformed her situation. Her attempts to establish a regency in January 1454 were thwarted by a lack of support among the lords, probably a reflection of her inability to provide the necessary military leadership, and led to the establishment of York's first protectorate. There can be little doubt that from this time Margaret considered York to be a threat to the Lancastrian dynasty in general and to her son in particular. These fears can only have been exacerbated by the death of her close ally, the Duke of Somerset, at St Albans and the deliberately meddlesome offer made by the Scottish king, James II, in May 1456 to support Duke Richard's claim to the throne. Contemporaries recognised her importance in the opposition to York's second protectorate. This centred upon defeating the Commons' demands for resumption, and one observer characterised her as 'a grete and stronge laboured woman, for she spareth noo peyne to sue hire thinges to an intent and conclusion to hir power'.[5] Perhaps more important than Margaret's perception of York was Duke Richard's perception of her. In the second half of the 1450s, there can be little doubt that York and his followers increasingly identified Margaret and her allies as their inimical enemies.

By the spring of 1456 what little authority still resided in the person of Henry VI was rapidly disappearing. Although government was naturally carried out in the King's name and he continued to sign council warrants and other instruments of government until 1460, real power was widely assumed to lie with Margaret. The Queen and Prince retired to her dower lands in the Midlands shortly after the dissolution of Parliament. Thereafter, Lancastrian influence was centred upon the duchy of Lancaster honours of Tutbury, Leicester and Kenilworth, and the city of Coventry emerged as the Lancastrian 'capital'. In the middle of August Henry moved to join his queen. Bertram Wolffe characterised this retreat to the Midlands as 'the actions of the rash and despotic queen',[6] but it can equally be seen as a desperate attempt to secure what remained of Henry's authority and

3 Johnson, *Duke Richard of York*, pp.171–3; Grummitt, *Henry VI*, pp.185–6.
4 For much of what follows see Grummitt, *Wars of the Roses*, pp.56–65.
5 *Paston Letters and Papers*, ed. Beadle and Richmond, iii., p.161.
6 Wolffe, *Henry VI*, p.302.

protect Lancastrian interests from the increasingly aggressive designs of the Duke of York. Henry, despite his increasingly evident shortcomings, was still king and control of his person and the process of counsel was of paramount importance. The summer and autumn of 1456 were characterised by fear and rumour. Rumours spread of an armed clash in which Viscount Beaumont had been killed and the Earl of Warwick injured, while the violent actions of York's servants and supporters in Wales only served to justify the defensive measures taken by the Lancastrian court. The defences of Kenilworth Castle were strengthened, and in December the crown commissioned the purchase and manufacture of ordnance and other weapons of war.[7]

It was almost certainly to further secure the reins of royal government that a Great Council was summoned to meet at Coventry on 7 October 1456. York and Warwick did attend, but key changes in the major administrative offices signalled that they had been sidelined by individuals more closely associated with the Queen and the Lancastrian court. On 26 September the King appointed Margaret's chancellor, Lawrence Booth, the new dean of St Paul's cathedral, as the new keeper of the privy seal, the prime instrument of government business (especially in matters of finance and the distribution of patronage). On 5 October the Earl of Shrewsbury replaced York's brother-in-law, Henry, Viscount Bourchier, as treasurer, and six days later Archbishop Bourchier surrendered the Great Seal to William Waynflete, Bishop of Winchester, the King's confessor and a man devoted to the personal service of Henry VI. Further institutional changes sought to protect the interests of the Lancastrian royal family. In February 1457 the newly established council of the Prince of Wales was given formal control of his patrimony. It included Booth, his brother Archbishop William of York, Waynflete, Humphrey Stafford, son and heir of the Duke of Buckingham, the earls of Shrewsbury and Wiltshire, Viscount Beaumont, and Lords Dudley and Stanley. There can be little doubt that this body sought to extend Lancastrian control at the expense of the Duke of York and his followers. In April, for example, the disputed castles of Aberystwyth and Carmarthen were taken from York and granted to the King's half-brother, Jasper Tudor.

Money remained an overriding concern for the Lancastrians. The Parliament of 1455 had not granted supply, and the royal households were forced to rely on their prerogative of purveyance (the compulsory purchase of foodstuffs and other supplies below their market price). This, of course, risked engendering popular opposition and it may be these fears that explain why the King spent at least a third of his time between August 1456 and July 1460 enjoying the hospitality of various religious houses. In many ways the normal mechanisms of public, royal finance broke down in these years. The Lancastrian court retreated into itself, the volume of government business diminished and the court depended increasingly on the private resources of the duchy of Lancaster and palatinate of Chester to finance the diminished royal household. A good example of this is the increased importance of William Grimsby, the treasurer of the King's chamber and keeper of his jewels, who from the autumn of 1456 until September 1457, when Henry returned to the Home Counties and London, regularly travelled between the Midlands and the Exchequer at Westminster with cash for the private use of the King. In October 1458 he became deputy treasurer of England, an indication of how ostensibly public offices were being subjugated to the private needs of the Lancastrian royal family. When the King returned to the Midlands in May 1459 Grimsby emerged as the principal messenger between the government at Westminster and the court in Coventry.[8]

7 Dan Spencer, 'The Lancastrian Armament Programme of the 1450s and the Development of Field Guns', *The Ricardian*, 25 (2015), pp.61–70.

8 For Grimsby's career see *The House of Commons*, iv., pp.687–90.

It is, however, too simplistic to assume that power had passed completely to the Queen and the group of committed Lancastrians who now emerged to support her and her son, the Prince of Wales. The Queen and her allies failed to mobilise the resources, both financial and in terms of the manpower, of the Prince's patrimony in Cheshire and Wales.[9] Many, if not most, of the lords remained uncommitted to either the Duke of York or to the Lancastrian party solidifying around the Queen. The council at Westminster continued to meet regularly and transact business, even if this had contracted in volume. Judicial business seems to have continued under the guidance of the council, with special commissions of inquiry attempting to dispense impartial justice on a range of local disputes. The Earl of Salisbury, absent from the council since the middle of 1456, had returned in November, while York also played a prominent part in its deliberations. In February or March 1457, a large and representative Great Council met at Coventry. It was the occasion for a concerted attack on the Yorkist lords, led by Chancellor Waynflete, perhaps at the Queen's instigation. Nevertheless, the French raid on the Kentish port of Sandwich at the end of August that year put the brake on any immediate slide into faction. The French attack coincided with the King's return to London and the issue of commissions of array for most of the southern and Midland counties. It was most likely the broadly based, inclusive council of nobles and leading churchmen then gathered at Westminster who initiated the attempt at reconciliation between the Yorkist lords on the one hand and the Queen and the relatives of those lords killed at St Albans on the other.[10] This process culminated in the so-called 'Loveday' of March 1458. In November 1457 the Percies had already been persuaded to submit their dispute with the Nevilles to the arbitration of the council, and this prepared the ground for a further Great Council meeting on 28 February 1458, attended by both the Yorkist lords and their enemies, where a settlement was brokered.[11]

If the majority on the council had high hopes for the projected reconciliation, they were soon to be disappointed. One reason for this, as we shall see, was the continued fear and suspicion of each other that dominated the thoughts and actions of the principals. A more immediate reason was that both the settlement brokered by the lords (and encouraged, it seems, by the King himself) and its formal recognition at the 'Loveday' ceremony at St Paul's on 25 March 1458 highlighted the essentially private and personal nature of the dispute between the rival camps. This in turn further undermined the King's government, which had conspicuously failed to offer the higher authority to which both sides were willing to submit. The council's award in effect attributed blame to York and his adherents, going some way to reversing the account presented in the Parliament of 1455. The Yorkists had been the first to draw blood and the award required them to make amends by endowing a chantry chapel at St Albans for the souls of the deceased. Both Somerset's heir and widow and Clifford's heir were compensated, while the damages due to the Nevilles from the Percies for their actions in 1453–54 were forgotten in an attempt to end that dispute. While the Earl of Salisbury seems to have acquiesced in the council's decision, for York it represented his failure to convince his fellow lords of the justice of his cause. His platform for reform, his stand against Somerset as a traitor, and his defence of the commonweal were reduced to a petty, personal squabble. The symbolism of the 'Loveday' itself was telling. Salisbury processed to St Paul's hand-in-hand with the new Duke of Somerset, and York likewise with Queen Margaret. This charade

9 Tim Thornton, 'Lancastrian Rule and the Resources of the Prince of Wales, 1456–61', *Journal of Medieval History*, 42 (2016), pp.382–404.

10 John Watts, *Henry VI and the Politics of Kingship* (Cambridge: Cambridge University Press, 1996), pp.342–5.

11 TNA, E28/88/9.

both explicitly recognised the existence of two, rival armed camps and ignored the public nature of York's grievances, presenting the political crisis purely and simply as one of private feud. It was a triumph for Queen Margaret and the Lancastrians in as much as it upheld the legitimacy of Henry VI's government and its ability to resolve conflicts between the King's greatest subjects.[12] Ironically, however, this reconciliation also ended once and for all any prospect of a peaceful resolution of the crisis.

Yorkist Fears and Failure

Since his return from Ireland in the autumn of 1450, one consistent motive had dominated Richard, Duke of York's decisions and actions: fear. He had initially returned from Ireland to counter any allegations of wrongdoing on his part and refute the rumours that connected him to Cade's Rebellion. The attempted coup at Dartford two years later was motivated by his failure to remove the Duke of Somerset from the King's confidence, and a justified fear that his political eclipse would lead to financial ruin or worse. York's first protectorate and Henry VI's mental collapse allowed him to fulfil his own perception of himself as the King's leading subject, but it also provided his enemies with more grievances against him once the restraining hand of the King was removed. When Henry recovered his limited faculties, however, York's fortunes were even more tied to the idiosyncratic behaviour of an increasingly enfeebled monarch. The attack on the royal party at St Albans was out of sheer desperation. Duke Richard simply could not allow the unfavourable settlement of his dispute with Somerset which the Great Council due to meet at Leicester threatened. The position of the Neville earls of Salisbury and Warwick was equally threatened by the territorial ambitions of Somerset and, more importantly, their Percy rivals in the north. While York may have been heralded by some at the time (and by many more after his death) as the champion of reform, it was his failure to achieve his ends by 'constitutional' means and a genuine fear of his own security that led him to take up arms against the house of Lancaster.

Once the King and Queen had moved to Coventry in the autumn of 1456 the perception grew of their hostility towards the Duke of York and his allies. Even if Duke Richard did not at first respond himself with violence, the actions of his servants could certainly be construed as direct assaults on royal authority. The most notorious incident came in South Wales. By the summer of 1456 the King's half-brother, Edmund Tudor, Earl of Richmond, had successfully wrested control of several key Welsh strongholds from the notorious ruffian Gruffyd ap Nicholas. The problem was that command of two of these, Carmarthen and Aberystwyth, had been granted to York. In August two of the Duke's retainers, Sir William Herbert and Sir Walter Devereux, assembled a force of some 2,000 men and took both castles by assault, imprisoning Richmond (who died while incarcerated on 3 November, possibly from plague). Both men were summoned to answer to the King for their actions, but Herbert escaped and attempted to raise men from York's and the Nevilles' marcher lordships in the winter of 1456–57. It was not until June 1457 that Herbert finally submitted himself to the King. How far York was behind his servants' actions is unclear, but events in South Wales certainly heightened tensions between the Yorkist lords and their rivals. There were rumours that both York and the young Duke of Somerset, Henry Beaufort, would be 'distressed'

12 Grummitt, *Henry VI*, pp.190–1; Whethamstede, pp.298–308.

at the Great Council meeting in October 1456.[13] In November the dukes of Exeter and Somerset and the Earl of Shrewsbury allegedly tried to ambush Warwick as he rode to London, while the following month the Mayor of Coventry had to intervene to prevent Somerset attacking York. It was Herbert's continued resistance that almost certainly led to York's summons to a further Great Council meeting at Coventry in February 1457. Although the evidence for its proceedings comes principally from the later attainder of the Yorkist lords in the Parliament of November 1459, there is no reason to doubt that it was anything other than a concerted attempt to humiliate and punish the Duke of York. The new chancellor, Bishop Waynflete, accused York of jeopardising the safety of both the realm and the King's person. The Duke of Buckingham and the other lords pleaded with the King to intervene and warn York and any other lord who again resorted to violence that they would be punished 'aftre ther deserte'. Duke Richard and the Earl of Warwick (whose father, Salisbury, did not attend the meeting) swore on the gospels not to attempt anything in future by 'wey of fayt'.[14]

For the Yorkist lords the message was clear: their enemies at court were gathering their resources for a final attack. For York himself it was particularly dangerous as groups and individuals unconnected to him continued to advance his name as the champion of reform and a rival to Henry VI for the throne itself. In May 1456 a new uprising in Kent, led by one John Percy of Erith, had again linked the Duke with the Mortimer claim to the throne, while James II's mischievous offer to help him gain the throne of England can only have poured fuel on the fire. In September, while York stayed in London, a particularly grisly comment was made on his political ambitions: five dogs' heads were impaled on stakes outside the Bishop of Salisbury's house, where he lodged. Each had a verse held in its jaws, suggesting that York, the son of a traitor, was 'that man that all men hate/ y wolde hys hede were here for myne/ ffor he hath caused all the debate.'[15] The Yorkist lords faced a dilemma: they could either absent themselves totally from the processes of government and counsel, leaving the field clear for their enemies, or they could attempt another coup along the lines of that initiated at St Albans in 1455. Although Warwick could, and did, retire to his command at Calais, absence from the political spotlight was not really an option for the Duke of York. He may have genuinely believed his rhetoric that the King was surrounded by traitors and corrupt counsel who planned his destruction and the subversion of the commonweal, but his wealth and 'worship' as a great lord and his ability to command the obedience of his servants also depended on his position at the centre of government. To do nothing was not an option.

In November 1458 an attempt on Warwick's life by members of the royal household appears to have almost succeeded. The Earl had finally acceded to royal demands that he appear before the council to answer charges of piracy in the English Channel. A brawl broke out, perhaps as members of the King's household attempted to arrest him, perhaps because of a perceived slight, but Warwick would later claim he barely escaped with his life. The Earl returned to Calais convinced of his enemies' determination to remove him by whatever means necessary.[16] At the beginning of the month, according to a later source, Warwick's father, the Earl of Salisbury, committed himself formally to the Duke of York. He met his counsellors and retainers at his seat of Middleham in

13 *Paston Letters and Papers*, ed. Davis, ii., p.168.

14 *Parliament Rolls of Medieval England*, Parliament of November 1459, item 1.

15 *Historical Poems of the XIVth and XVth Centuries*, ed. R.H. Robbins (New York: Columbia University Press, 1959), pp.189–90.

16 A.J. Pollard, *Warwick the Kingmaker: Politics, Power and Fame* (London: Hambledon Continuum, 2007), pp.37–8, 201–2.

Yorkshire and agreed that they 'sholde take ful partie with þe ful noble prince the Duke of York'.[17] Whether this meeting took place or not on this particular date, at some point, probably towards the end of 1458, Salisbury committed himself and the Middleham affinity to York's cause. His reasoning is not difficult to fathom. On 10 June 1458 Henry VI had agreed to hand the disputed castle and manor of Wressle near Hull to Henry Percy, Lord Egremont. Wressle, a former Percy manor forfeited when the first earl had rebelled against Henry IV in 1403, had passed to the Nevilles after the marriage of Salisbury's second son, Sir Thomas Neville, to Maud Stanhope, the widow of Robert, Lord Willoughby, five years earlier. The previous year, Humphrey Neville of Brancepeth, a member of the senior branch of the family and nephew of Ralph Neville, Earl of Westmorland, had been made steward of the Honour of Richmond, replacing Salisbury's brother Lord Fauconberg. The honour was held by Jasper Tudor, Earl of Pembroke during the minority of Edmund Tudor's son, Henry (the future Henry VII), but the stewardship gave the Nevilles of Raby effective control over its financial and military resources.[18] The restoration of Wressle to the Percies and the grant to Humphrey Neville was a clear sign that the Nevilles' ascendancy in the north would not be allowed to continue under Henry VI and Queen Margaret. The prominence of the new Percy Earl of Northumberland in the Queen's counsels and the attempts on the lives of both Warwick and York were enough to convince Salisbury that only York's eventual victory could safeguard his own position and power.

The Battle of Blore Heath

If the Nevilles had indeed committed themselves to York's cause towards the end of 1458, they were not called upon immediately to rally to his side. Indeed, in the first months of 1459 the concern may have been more with a rumoured French attack on Calais than on tensions between rival English lords. Fears of a Scottish attack were also raised. In Calais, Warwick's diplomacy worked overtime to prevent a rapprochement between Charles VII of France and the Duke of Burgundy. Amidst these concerns, there is some evidence of a return to some sort of normality in royal government. In late January or February, however, the Duke of Exeter assaulted one of the King's justices in Westminster Hall and was temporarily imprisoned. On 20 February the lords were summoned to attend a great council meeting on 2 April to appoint a delegation to the church council to be held in Mantua the following June. When violence broke out between London apprentices and the men of the King's household, it was Archbishop Bourchier and Lord Fauconberg along with the Earl of Wiltshire, Viscount Beaumont and Lord Sudeley who calmed tempers.[19] The King, it seems, divided his time between Westminster, Windsor and St Albans, with no indication of the drastic turn in events that would soon follow.

In May 1459, Henry VI joined Queen Margaret in the Midlands. By the 9th of that month, he was at Coventry. Royal letters were sent to several counties ordering the gentry to attend upon the King at Leicester on 10 May with as many men defensibly arrayed as they could muster. Three days earlier, the King had ordered the purchase of 3,000 bow staves 'considering thennemies on

17 Thomas Dunham Whitaker, *An History of Richmondshire in the North Riding of the County of York* (2 vols, London; Longman, 1823), i. 2., pp.261–2.

18 *Calendar of Patent Rolls, 1452–1461*, pp.335, 428.

19 *John Benet's Chronicle*, p.44.

every side aproching upone us, as welle upon the see as on lande'.[20] This may have been the prelude to another Great Council meeting. There are no documentary records of this assembly and our knowledge of it derives entirely from the pro-Yorkist chronicles of the following decade. According to John Benet's chronicle, the council convened on 24 June. York, Salisbury, Warwick, the Earl of Arundel and Viscount Bourchier, as well as the bishops of Ely and Exeter, were excluded and 'all the aforesaid were indicted' of treason. On hearing this, York, Salisbury and Warwick purposed 'to go to the king, because the king had amassed a great army'.[21] The Act of the Attainder passed against the Yorkist lords in the Coventry Parliament of November 1459 accused them of failing to answer several summons to attend a council meeting, but the precise dates of their refusals were not recorded and there was no specific mention of a council meeting in Coventry the previous June.[22] In 1455 the Duke of York had mobilised quickly when he perceived an immediate threat to his safety; in the summer of 1459 the Yorkist lords' military preparations seemed altogether more planned and deliberate. The Coventry Parliament would later attaint York's servants Sir William Oldhall and Thomas Vaughan, along with Alice, Countess of Salisbury, for plotting and assisting the Yorkist lords to raise men and commit treason in London in July and at Middleham the following month.[23] Nevertheless, either the crown was ignorant of Salisbury's machinations in Yorkshire, or the extent of the Earl's planning was exaggerated. At the end of August, the King commissioned a group of Yorkshire gentry, led by the Earl's retainer Sir Thomas Harrington and his ostensible foe, the steward of the duchy of Lancaster honour of Knaresborough, Sir William Plumpton, to investigate 'opprobrious words spoken against the king's person and majesty' by Henry Walron, bailiff of the Neville manor of Bawtry, who was then languishing in jail in Coventry.[24]

It was not until September, however, that York and his allies revealed their hands. On 18 September the Earl of Salisbury was mustering men at Boroughbridge near Knaresborough, where he had been actively retaining men throughout the previous year.[25] The Duke of York may also have been at his castle of Sandal near Wakefield in September, and some of his retainers, such as Roger Kynaston and members of the Ashton family of Fryton in the North Riding, fought with Salisbury at Blore Heath. While it has been argued recently that the composition of Salisbury's army revealed the limitations of his lordship when it came to persuading his retainers and tenants to commit treason, there seems little doubt that the Earl assembled a sizeable force which contained many prominent knights and gentry from Yorkshire and elsewhere.[26] He was accompanied by his two younger sons, Sir Thomas and Sir John, his retainers Sir Thomas Harrington and his son James, Sir John Conyers and Sir Thomas Parr. Thomas Meryng of Tong, Shropshire, a former member of the King's household, who had married a Nottinghamshire heiress, was also prominent enough to be among the seven named individuals attainted in the Coventry Parliament for fighting with Salisbury. Other men identified as probably serving at Blore Heath came from Yorkshire, the

20 TNA, E403/819, m. 3; E28/88/49; E404/71/3/77.

21 *John Benet's Chronicle*, p.45. For an alternative assessment of this Coventry meeting and the argument that it was attended by the Yorkist lords see Hicks, *Warwick the Kingmaker*, pp. 157–9.

22 *Parliament Rolls of Medieval England*, Parliament of November 1459, item 13.

23 *Parliament Rolls of Medieval England*, Parliament of November 1459, item 21.

24 *Calendar of Patent Rolls, 1452–61*, p.518.

25 A.J. Pollard, *North-Eastern England During the Wars of the Roses* (Oxford: Oxford University Press, 1990), p.271.

26 TNA, DL29/560/8899, m. 2; Tim Thornton, 'The Battle of Blore Heath: Sources, Historiography and the Implications for the Outbreak of Conflict', *Midland History*, 49 (2024), pp.1–20.

Midlands and the Welsh marches.[27] The 1459 Act of Attainder claimed Salisbury's army was 5,000 men strong, which is a large if not unreasonable estimate given the geographically wide area which the Earl appears to have recruited from. English chroniclers' estimates of its size ranged from Abbot Whethamstede's 'small band of commoners', the unlikely 400 in one of Jean de Wavrin's accounts and 500 given in 'Gregory's' chronicle, to a more plausible 3,000 men given by John Benet and the London chronicles of Robert Bale and British Library, Cotton MS Julius B.i, 4,000 in the 'Short English Chronicle', and the 7,000 ventured by the writer of *An English Chronicle*.[28]

One notable individual to fight alongside Salisbury was William Stanley, younger brother of Thomas, Lord Stanley. William's sister-in-law was Eleanor, one of the daughters of the Earl of Salisbury. Their father, also Thomas, who had first been summoned to the Parliament as Lord Stanley in 1455, had died on 11 February 1459, and this had probably encouraged Salisbury to think he could rely on the new Lord Stanley, his son-in-law, to lend his considerable resources in Lancashire to the Yorkist cause. Stanley played a careful game, but according to a petition presented by the Commons in the 1459 Parliament calling for his impeachment, he had actively encouraged and assisted Salisbury in the build-up to Blore Heath. The petition claimed that Lord Stanley had ignored the King's summons to arms, as well as a similar request sent in the name of Prince Edward, with the excuse that he was 'not then ready.' Eventually, Stanley had sent a message to the Queen and Prince, then lodged at the Bishop of Coventry and Lichfield's palace at Eccleshall in Staffordshire, offering to lead the royal vanguard against Salisbury, but the Queen and Prince had ordered him to join the Lancastrian army led by Lord Audley. Stanley, with his 2,000 men, had instead waited at Newcastle-under-Lyme while Audley was defeated by Salisbury. It was further alleged that Stanley had sent a letter to his father-in-law at Market Drayton on the night of the battle, congratulating him on his victory and promising to support the Earl in the future. Salisbury shared this letter with Sir Thomas Harrington, saying, 'Sirs, be merry, for yet we have more friends.' Stanley had also prevented his tenants in the Wirral and Maxfield Hundred in Cheshire from being arrayed for the King, while men wearing his livery had served with William Stanley in Salisbury's army. The Commons asked the King to imprison Stanley, which he appears to have ignored. Indeed, Lord Stanley was present at the Coventry Parliament and was among those peers who swore oaths of allegiance in December to the King, Queen and Prince of Wales. He was unable, however, to prevent his brother William from being attainted of treason for his part in the Battle of Blore Heath.[29]

The extent of the Lancastrian preparations is unclear. We have seen how weapons and military supplies were being assembled as early as May, but it is not clear when the Lancastrians began actively recruiting soldiers. Commissions of array had been issued throughout the country in September 1458 and February 1459, but this had most likely been in response to fears of French and Scottish attacks.[30] Traditionally, the Lancastrian army at Blore Heath has been characterised as 'the quene's partie', predominantly recruited from the Prince of Wales's patrimony in Cheshire and Lancastrian estates in the north Midlands. This perception drew from the pro-Yorkist chronicles

27 *Parliament Rolls of Medieval England*, Parliament of November 1459, item 15; Thornton, 'Blore Heath', pp.13–17.

28 Wavrin, v., p.269; Whethamstede, p.388; *Contemporary English Chronicles*, p.65; *A Chronicle of London from 1089 to 1483*, ed. E. Tyrell and H. Nicholas (London: Longman, 1827), p.140; *Three Fifteenth Century Chronicles*, p.72; *Six Town Chronicles*, p.148; *An English Chronicle*, p.78; *John Benet's Chronicle*, p.45.

29 *Parliament Rolls of Medieval England*, Parliament of November 1459, items 26 and 38.

30 *Calendar of Patent Rolls, 1452–1461*, pp.489–90, 494–5.

of the 1460s and was firmly established in the work of the mid-Tudor chronicler Edward Hall. 'Gregory' described how Salisbury faced the 'quenys galentys', while *An English Chronicle* described the 'notable knyghtis and squyers of Chesshyre that had resceued the lyuerey of the swannes'. By the time Hall came to write in the 1540s, Blore Heath had become synonymous with the tragedy of civil war, pitting neighbour against neighbour. Hall described how some 2,400 men were killed 'but the greatest plague lighted on the Chesshire men, because one half of the shire, was the one part, and the other on the other part'. [31] In fact, as recent research has shown, only a minority of the Cheshire gentry were engaged at Blore Heath and the Lancastrian army in fact drew its ranks from across the north-west and the north Midlands.[32] Most sources suggest that the Lancastrian army was larger than the Yorkist, but this in part may have been to emphasise the drama of Salisbury's victory. Estimates ranged from the 14,000 men mentioned in several London chronicles and 12,000 in Robert Bale's chronicle, to the 10,000 put forward by Abbot Whethamstede, and 6,000 to 8,000 given by Wavrin, *An English Chronicle* and John Benet. It seems likely that there was a discrepancy between the two forces, although perhaps not so marked as to prompt the reflection on Seneca that Whethamstede attributed to Henry VI after the battle: 'It is not the number of people, but rather the virtue of the few, that wins battles and overthrows enemies.'[33]

Command of the Lancastrian force was in the hands of James Tuchet, Lord Audley. Audley is sometimes characterised as an old man, and he was 61 at the time of Blore Heath. He had served with distinction in France, first crossing the Channel in Henry V's retinue in 1420, aged only 12. He had been chamberlain of South Wales early in Henry VI's reign, but in 1447 he was granted an exemption for life from attending Parliament, perhaps suggesting ill health. Audley may seem an odd choice to lead such a key component of the Lancastrian response to the Yorkist lords. He did, however, hold extensive lands in Shropshire, Staffordshire and Derbyshire. Audley, along with John Sutton, Lord Dudley, had accompanied Queen Margaret on her peregrination from Coventry to Chester and onto Eccleshall and the duchy of Lancaster estates in the Honour of Tutbury. Dudley was a staunch Lancastrian and important landowner in Cheshire, Staffordshire and Derbyshire, having carried the royal standard at Henry V's funeral, as well as serving extensively in France during the 1420s and 30s and on various diplomatic embassies. Dudley had been wounded at St Albans in 1455 and then imprisoned in the Tower of London by the Duke of York, but he had returned as a royal councillor at the end of York's second protectorate. In February 1459 he had succeeded Lord Stanley as chamberlain of North Wales, and he may have used this office to recruit men for Blore Heath.[34]

The fifteenth-century English sources are laconic to say the least on what happened at Blore Heath on 23 September 1459 and provide no details of the course of fighting other than to note

31 *Contemporary English Chronicles*, p.65; *An English Chronicle*, p.79; Charles Lethridge Kingsford, *Chronicles of London* (Oxford: Oxford University Press, 1905), p.276; *Hall's Chronicle*, p.240.

32 Thornton, 'Blore Heath', pp.6–13; J.L. Gillespie, 'Cheshiremen at Blore Heath: A Swan Dive', in *People, Politics and Community in the Later Middle Ages*, ed. J. Rosenthal and C. Richmond (Gloucester: Alan Sutton,1987), pp.77–89; D.J. Clayton, *The Administration of the County Palatine of Chester, 1442–1485*, Chetham Society, 3rd series, 35 (1990), pp.79–90.

33 Whethamstede, pp.338–9; *Three Fifteenth Century Chronicles*, p.72; *Chronicle of London*, p.140; *Six Town Chronicles*, p.148; Wavrin, v., pp.269, 319; *John Benet's Chronicle*, p.45; *An English Chronicle*, p.78.

34 Hugh Collins, 'Sutton, John [John Dudley], First Baron Dudley (1400–1487)' in *OBND*; *The House of Commons 1422-1461*, iii., pp.118–26; G.E. Cokayne, *The Complete Peerage*, ed. V. Gibbs et al. (13 vols, London: The St Catherine Press, 1910–59), i., p.341; iv., pp.479–80.

The monument to John, Lord Audley, commander of the Lancastrian forces at Blore Heath, erected in 1765 on the site of an existing memorial, marks the site of the battle. (Battlefields Trust used with permission)

Salisbury's victory and Audley's death in the field.[35] Most modern accounts are derived from two sources: the Burgundian chronicler Jean de Wavrin and the Tudor writer Edward Hall.[36] Both are deeply problematic sources, not only for Blore Heath but for any of the battles fought between 1459 and 1461. Hall's sources for Blore Heath are unclear, but his main purpose, as throughout his *Union of the Two Noble and Illustre Famelies of Lancastre & York*, was to illustrate the perils of civil war and tell a good story. There is no real evidence that his account of the battle was compiled partly by 'drawing on local sources', and he used familiar tropes from medieval battle histories, such as the feigned retreat, to show that Salisbury knew 'the slaightes, stratagems, and the pollecies of warlike affaires'.[37] Wavrin's provenance is more difficult still to establish. His *Recueil des croniques* contains two separate and contradictory accounts of Blore Heath. The first appears out of chronological order and is very short, simply stating the Yorkist lords encountered the Queen's army, led by Lord 'Audelay'. The Yorkists were victorious, leading to the death of Audley and 'Lords Charinten and Kindreton' and the capture of Lord Dudley and the Cambridgeshire knight Sir Thomas Finderne. Wavrin's English editor suggested that 'Lord Chariten' was probably Sir James Harrington, while 'Kindreton' was Sir Hugh Venables of Kinderton, Cheshire, who we know from

35 Whethamstede, p.388; *Contemporary English Chronicles*, p.65; *A Chronicle of London*, p.140; *Three Fifteenth Century Chronicles*, p.72; *Six Town Chronicles*, p.148; *An English Chronicle*, pp.78–9; Kingsford, *Chronicles of London*, pp.169, 276; *John Benet's Chronicle*, p.45; *Parliament Rolls of Medieval England*, Parliament of November 1459, item 15.

36 Hugh Bicheno, *Battle Royal: The Wars of the Roses 1440–1462* (London; Pegasus), pp.199–209; John Sadler, *The White Rose and the Red: The Wars of the Roses, 1453–1487* (London: Routledge, 2009, pp.72–5; Haigh, *Military Campaigns of the Wars of the Roses*, pp.15–22.

37 *Hall's Chronicle*, p.240; Thornton, 'Blore Heath', pp.6–7.

other sources died at Blore Heath. The origin of Wavrin's first account was probably a lost newsletter which was 'York-centred', as opposed to much of Wavrin's work, which drew upon sources which lauded the Earl of Warwick's role in the events of 1459 to 1461. The same account was probably used by Jacques du Clercq in his brief account of the battle.[38]

Wavrin's second account, which was not copied into the earliest manuscript of the *Recueil*, probably produced in the early 1470s, follows on from the insertion of a pro-Warwick text, the so-called 'Warwick's Apology', in the manuscript from which the edited version was taken.[39] This too is out of chronological sequence, following on from a section describing events in Calais in 1460, York's return from Ireland, and the Act of Accord of October that year. The narrative is terribly confused: the Lancastrian army is commanded by the Duke of Exeter and Viscount Beaumont, while Salisbury is accompanied by the Earl of Warwick. It contains details, such the Yorkists spotting the Lancastrians by the 'tips of their pennons' poking over a great hedge, that have formed the substance of many accounts of Blore Heath.[40] Crucially, Wavrin is the only source to provide any indication of how Salisbury may have arrayed for battle:

> They assembled on foot at the back of a forest which gave them protection on one side, and on the other side they put their wagons and their horses tied together, and made a good trench behind them for security, and in front of them they had set up their archers' stakes in the English fashion.[41]

The Yorkists then 'kissed the ground' and met the first Lancastrian cavalry charge with a storm of arrows that left 500 or 600 Lancastrians dead for the loss only 20 of so from Warwick's army. A second cavalry charge by Exeter led to similar results before Beaumont, seeing 'that fighting on horseback brought little honour and even less advantage, dismounted about 4,000 men who joined the battle against Warwick'. After half an hour's fighting, a cry of 'Warwick, Warwick' went up from among Beaumont's men and some 500 changed sides, signalling the rout of the Lancastrians. Wavrin concluded by saying that Beaumont and Lord Welles were captured. So much of this account is clearly nonsense, and Wavrin may have conflated events at Blore Heath with those at Northampton in July the following year (especially the supposed switching of sides, something not mentioned in any other accounts). In the manuscripts of the *Recueil* the account of Blore Heath is followed by those of Ludford Bridge and Northampton, before returning to its chronological sequence. It is unclear what Wavrin's sources were. This account of Blore Heath does not appear in Bibliothèque Nationale de France, Manuscrit Français 88, from where Wavrin took his account of Wakefield, the Second Battle of St Albans and Towton, and it may have been based upon his

38 Wavrin, v., p.269; *Mémoires de Jacques du Clercq*, i., p.455.

39 Visser-Fuchs, *History as Pastime*, pp.408–9, 474–5. The earliest surviving manuscript is probably BNF, Ms Français 20358, which omits the second account of Blore Heath, Ludford Bridge and Northampton.

40 Francis Randle Twemlow, *The Battle of Blore Heath* (Wolverhampton: Whitehead Brothers, 1912), pp.25–8.

41 'Ilz se misrent a pie a larriere dune forest qui leur faisoit cloture a ung coste, et de lautre avoient mis leur charroy et leurs chevaulz lyez les ungz auz autres, et par derriere eulz avoient fait ung bon trenchis pour sceurete, et devant eulz avoient fichie leurs peux a la fachon dAngleterre': Wavrin, v., p.320. The English Heritage Battlefield Report translates this passage: 'They assembled on foot *in front* of a wood which gave them protection on one side, and on the other side they put their wagons and their horses tied together, and made a big trench for security, and in front they fixed their archers' stakes in the English manner.' English Heritage Battlefield Report, *Battle of Blore Heath 1459* (1995), https://historicengland.org.uk/content/docs/listing/battlefields/blore-heath/, accessed 20 March 2025.

garbled understanding of conversations with the Earl of Warwick's men a decade or so after the event.[42] Whatever its provenance, Wavrin's account cannot be verified with other written sources and thus should be used with caution in reconstructing the Battle of Blore Heath.

Even if the course of the battle is obscure, we can be reasonably confident of where Blore Heath was fought. The battlefield straddles the A53, some three miles to the east of Market Drayton. The battlefield location is largely based upon the presence of 'Audley's Cross', an eighteenth-century stone monument erected to mark the spot where Lord Audley was supposedly killed. There had been some sort of battlefield memorial to Audley since at least the mid-sixteenth century. The current Rowney Wood, where Salisbury may have anchored the left of his line, was much larger in the fifteenth century than today, and apart from some ridge-and-furrow land on the southern and eastern edges of the battlefield, Blore Heath was probably fought over uncultivated heathland. The valley which runs through the centre of the Registered Battlefield contains a small brook, which would have been dammed due to the nearby Hempmill in the later Middle Ages and would have proved a more formidable obstacle for any army wishing to cross it then than it does today. The English Heritage Battlefield Report proposes that the Yorkist army occupied a frontage of perhaps 1,000 yards, 'anchored in the former woodland near Oaklands Farm to the south-east and extending north-westwards beyond Audley Cross Farm'. The Lancastrian line, with their larger army, ran for about a mile along the ridge above the Hempmill Brook from near Blore in the south-east to the Mucklestone road in the north-west. In the absence of further archaeological or documentary evidence, this sounds a plausible description of the opening positions of each side.[43] Ultimately, as Tony Goodman concluded, 'there are no detailed accounts of Blore Heath' and any description of the fighting remains conjecture.[44]

There seems little doubt, however, that the battle was hard fought. Few chroniclers ventured an estimate of the casualties, but most agreed that 'many' died.[45] As well as Lord Audley, there were several prominent casualties on the Lancastrian side, including the Cheshire knights Sir John Done, Sir Thomas Dutton, Sir William Troutbeck, Sir Hugh Venables, Sir John Legh and Sir John Egerton (who died of his wounds a few days after). 'Gregory' also names 'Sir Thomas Hamdon' as the most prominent Lancastrian alongside Audley among the dead, but it is unclear to whom the chronicler was referring. 'Gregory' also named seven men who were knighted by Audley before the battle, five of whom were killed. These included Sir John Done and probably Sir Thomas Dutton mentioned above, but also Sir John Bromley of Cheshire. The list of identified dead on the Lancastrian certainly seems to confirm the sense that the bulk of the gentry killed at Blore Heath came from Cheshire.[46] Other Lancastrians, including Lord Dudley, were taken prisoner on the field.[47]

Salisbury's army, by contrast, seems to have suffered few battlefield casualties. We can probably discount 'Gregory's' curious tale of an Austin Friar who shot guns during the night to cover the Yorkists' retreat. Blore Heath was a resounding victory for the Earl of Salisbury and his Yorkist allies. From Blore Heath, Salisbury and the rest of his army spent the night of the 23rd encamped

42 Wavrin, v., pp.319–21 from BNF, MS Français 84, fos. 150–1; BNF, MS Français 15491, fos. 89v–91.

43 English Heritage Battlefield Report, *Battle of Blore Heath 1459*.

44 Anthony Goodman, *The Wars of the Roses: Military Activity and English Society, 1452–1497* (London, 1981), p.27.

45 *John Benet's Chronicle*, p.45 states 2,000 Lancastrians were killed or captured, while Hall, with his usual certainty, gave a figure of 2,400: *Hall's Chronicle*, p.240.

46 Thornton, 'Blore Heath', pp.7–11; *Contemporary English Chronicles*, p.65; Wavrin, v., p.269.

47 *Parliament Rolls of Medieval England*, Parliament of November 1459, items 15, 38; *The Brut*, i., p.601.

near Market Drayton. At some point, however, the Earl's sons, Sir Thomas and Sir John, and Sir Thomas Harrington were captured. *An English Chronicle* suggests their capture took place at Blore Heath, but 'Gregory' provides a different explanation. The chronicler relates how the son of Sir John Done had heard his father had been slain at Blore Heath and raised his tenants to march into the Midlands. Between 'the fylde and Chester ... bysyde a lytyl towne inamyd Toperlay [Acton Bridge near Taporley, Cheshire]', he captured the Nevilles and Harrington and imprisoned them in Chester Castle, where they remained until the Yorkist victory at Northampton. However, a later petition and John Benet's chronicle suggest they were captured near Ludlow on 14 October, following the Yorkist retreat from Ludford Bridge.[48]

Ludford Bridge

The Earl of Warwick arrived in London on 20 September, three days before his father's victory at Blore Heath. He was accompanied by 300 to 600 men from the Calais garrison, probably between a third and a quarter of its total strength, led by the veteran of the Hundred Years War and porter of Calais, Andrew Trollope.[49] His arrival in the capital coincided with a manifesto, issued in the name of the Yorkist lords, outlining their grievances. It contained a litany of familiar complaints: justice was not administered impartially, crimes went unpunished, the crown was impoverished, and, crucially, the King was counselled by men driven not by their concern for the commonweal, but by their 'owne covetise'. The Yorkist lords were marching to the King to offer him their service to right these wrongs.[50] Warwick may have hoped to recruit more men from his estates in the Midlands but may have been prevented from doing so by the Duke of Somerset, and instead made for Worcester, where he met with his father and the Duke of York.[51]

Salisbury himself had pressed onto Worcester after Blore Heath, where he was joined by the Duke of York. There the three Yorkist lords entered into a solemn agreement, an indenture signed and sealed in the cathedral, the contents of which are now unfortunately lost but which presumably bound them to assist one other saving only their allegiance to the King. This agreement, along with their demands, was now taken to the King by the prior of Worcester cathedral priory and other churchmen. Further letters were taken to Henry by Garter King of Arms. Their final letter to the King, written on 10 October, again professed their loyalty in the face of the declaration of treason apparently made against all three lords in the wake of Blore Heath. They stated that they had been forced to resort to taking up arms against the King because of the malice of their enemies and committed their cause to God and 'to the trouthe and dutee to your seyde hyghnesse, and to the sayde commone wele'. [52] Henry, it seems, was willing, once again, to extend his pardon to York and Warwick but not on this occasion to Salisbury, who had waged war against him at Blore Heath. Warwick, according to Abbot Whethamstede, urged his uncle to refuse the King's pardon, arguing that it was meaningless in the face of a hostile council and Parliament.[53]

48 *Contemporary English Chronicles*, p.65; *An English Chronicle*, p.79; *John Benet's Chronicle*, p.46; *The House of Commons*, iv., pp.798–9.
49 *Six Town Chronicles*, pp.147–8.
50 *John Vale's Book*, pp.208–10.
51 Hicks, *Warwick the Kingmaker*, p.163.
52 *An English Chronicle*, pp.79–80.
53 Whethamstede, pp.339–41.

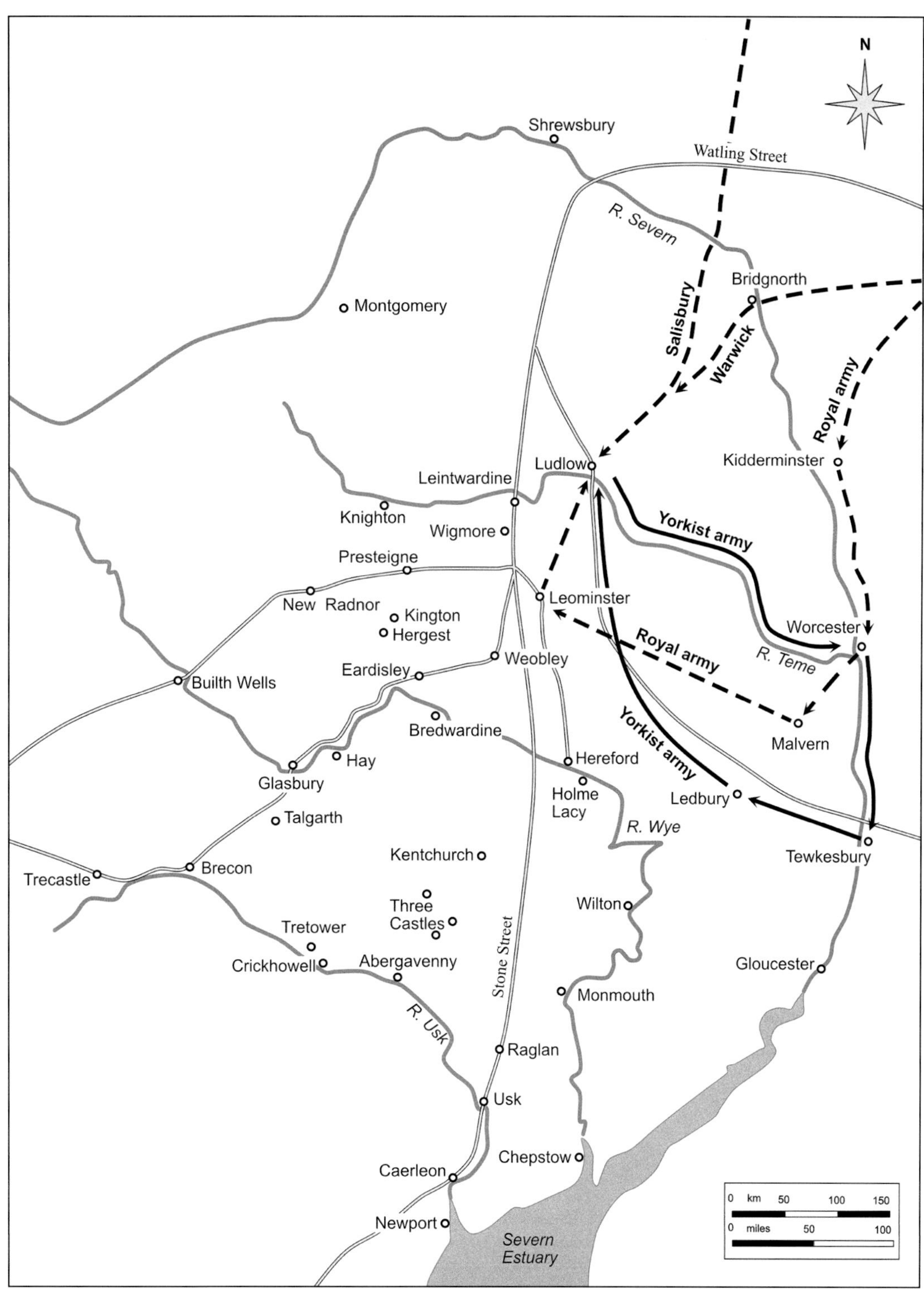

The Ludford Bridge campaign, September–October 1459.

York and Warwick declined the offer of a royal pardon, and the three lords retreated to the Duke's stronghold of Ludlow, via Tewkesbury.[54] Now there could be no hope of compromise. The Yorkists had now played their hand, yet despite their military successes their cause had attracted little support from their fellow peers. As they marched cross-country to Ludlow they were accompanied only by York's two sons, the earls of Rutland and March, and lords Clinton and Grey of Powis. On 9 October writs went out summoning a Parliament to gather at Coventry on 21 November. York, Salisbury and Warwick, as well as Lord Stanley, were not summoned, and it seems certain that the intention was to attaint them and their followers as traitors.

The King's actions in this period are more obscure as, with the exception of the Parliamentary record, most of the sources were written subsequently from a Yorkist perspective. From Coventry, Henry's party moved to Coleshill and from there through Kidderminster to Worcester to confront the Yorkist lords. From Worcester, they probably marched to Malvern and then to Leominster, where the writs to summon Parliament were issued on 9 October.[55] The Act of Attainder praised the King's 'princely manner', remembering how Henry had pursued the Yorkist lords and

> followed as swiftly as you could, not deterred by any obstruction or difficulty in the way, or by any bad weather, danger to your most royal person, or by the fact that this lasted for about thirty days, with you not resting two nights in the same place except on Sundays, and sometimes and when necessary you camped in a bare field, sometimes two nights in a row, together with all your host, in the cold season of the year.[56]

Quite how large the King's host was, or precisely which lords accompanied him, is unclear. 'Gregory' claimed an unlikely 30,000 'harneysyd men beside nakyd that were compellyd for to come whythe the kynge', while 'A Short English Chronicle' gave an even more outlandish 50,000.[57] Henry was almost certainly accompanied by the dukes of Buckingham, Exeter and Somerset, as well as the earls of Pembroke, Northumberland, Shrewsbury and Wiltshire. There is no way of knowing, however, just how many of the three dukes, five earls, two viscounts, and 22 barons who swore the oath of allegiance at the Coventry Parliament were with the King when he arrived at Ludford Bridge, across the River Teme, south of Ludlow, on the morning of 12 October.[58]

The Yorkists had made 'a grete depe dyche and fortefyde it whythe gonnys, cartys and stakys', but they were hopelessly outnumbered.[59] Whethamstede claimed that at this point the three lords sent a final letter to the King, explaining their actions, which was rejected. Turning to their followers, Henry offered a pardon to those who would submit themselves within six days. Many of the Yorkist rank and file gladly accepted this, realising the peril they were in and aware that their lords had run out of money and options.[60] The Act of Attainder recalled how Henry made a speech to his host 'in so witty, so knightly, so manly and so cheering a style, with such a princely bearing and assured manner' and arrayed his men for battle and displayed the royal banner. York's response, it continues, was to have 'falsely and traitorously raised war against you in the field there,

54 *John Benet's Chronicle*, p.45.
55 Wolfe, *Henry VI*, p.371; TNA, C219/16/5.
56 *Parliament Rolls of Medieval England*, Parliament of November 1459, item 15.
57 *Contemporary English Chronicles*, p.66; *Three Fifteenth Century Chronicles*, p.72.
58 *Parliament Rolls of Medieval England*, Parliament of November 1459, item 26; Wavrin, v., p.322.
59 *Contemporary English Chronicles*, p.66.
60 Whethamstede, pp.341–4.

The bridge over the River Teme connecting the village of Ludford and the town of Ludlow was newly built in the fifteenth century and is today a scheduled ancient monument. (John Clift CC BY-NC 2.0)

and fired their said guns then and there, and fired at your most royal person, as well as at your lords and people then and there with you'. Faced with a resolute King, the Yorkists wavered and, 'Almighty God, who sees into the hearts of people and from whom nothing is hidden, suddenly struck the hearts of the said Duke of York and earls from that most presumptuous pride into the most shameful cowardice imaginable, so that at about midnight that night they stole away from the field.' Some of York's followers, Richard Grey, Lord Powis, Walter Devereux and Sir Henry Radford, instead of fleeing with the Duke, instead sought out the King and sought pardon. Although their estates were forfeited, the King graciously spared their lives.[61]

Some pro-Yorkist chroniclers told a different story, however. In what would become a familiar trope to both explain Yorkist failure and success, the rout at Ludford Bridge was ascribed to treachery. Most of the English chroniclers merely stated that York and his allies chose to retire, but John Benet noted that 'certain men on the duke's side proposed to betray the duke and his lords'.[62] The fullest account is to be found in a version of the *Brut* chronicle:

61 *Parliament Rolls of Medieval England*, Parliament of November 1459, items 17–19, 23.

62 *John Benet's Chronicle*, p.45; *An English Chronicle*, p.80; *Three Fifteenth Century Chronicles*, p.72; *Six Town Chronicles*, p.148; *Chronicle of London from 1089 to 1483*, p.140.

> bot in þe night Andrew Trollop & al tholde soudioures of Caleys, with a gret felasship, sodenly departed out of þe Dukes oost & went strayt vnto þe Kinges feld, wher þei were received joyously, for þei knew þe entent of þe othir lordes, & also þe maner of þer felde. And þen þe Duke of York, with þe oþer· lordes, seyng þame so descevyd, toke a councel shortly þat same night, & departed fro þe felde, levyng behynde þame þe moste parte of þer peple to kepe þe feld til on þe morne.[63]

'Gregory' claims that Trollope had deserted Warwick earlier, as soon as he realised the Earl was not marching to join the King, and that York was 'fulle sore afrayde when he wyste that sum olde soudyers went from hym unto the kynge'. Once again, Wavrin provides two separate accounts of events at Ludford Bridge, but he made misplaced loyalty and trickery the centre of both narratives, claiming Andrew Trollope 'had undertaken to deliver these lords to the king'. Trollope had received a letter from Somerset, warning him against committing treason by arraying for war against the King. Trollope was able to persuade his fellow Calais soldiers to follow him. It is likely that the story originated in Yorkist newsletters designed to exculpate the Yorkist lords, and especially Warwick, and that it was the King's offer of a pardon that led to desertions from the Yorkist ranks. The Burgundian writer Jacques du Clerq noted that pardons were offered 'provided they left the Duke of York and retired to his [i.e. Henry's] side. Which thing was very burdensome to the Duke of York; for the greater part of his army left him and retired with the Queen, and even those of the garrison of Guines [i.e. Trollope and soldiers from Calais].' Wavrin claims that the 600 soldiers from Calais were, nevertheless, forced to strip to their shirts to beg for the King's grace and that five were executed.[64] There may have been some substance to this narrative. The previous year Warwick had refused to pay a £20 annuity from the revenues of Calais granted to Trollope by the King, and this may have been enough to persuade him and his fellow soldiers of the garrison not to commit treason.[65] Equally, as we shall see, Trollope became something of a bogeyman of Yorkist propaganda and his prominent role in some Yorkist narratives of Ludford Bridge may have been designed simply to mask the Yorkist lords' failure to gain widespread support for their rebellion.

* * *

Whatever the truth of Trollope's defection, it provided a convenient distraction (as did tales of the sack of Ludlow and the shameful treatment of York's wife, Duchess Cecily) from the Yorkist lords' utter failure in the autumn of 1459.[66] York, Salisbury and Warwick may have felt, perhaps rightly, that their opponents had left them with no choice, but their actions in raising war against the King were unmistakably treasonable and were not supported by the majority of their fellow lords. In the four and a half years that had followed the First Battle of St Albans, York and his allies had been offered several chances to redeem themselves, and even in the summer of 1459, as far as the King was concerned at least, the opportunity of reconciliation remained. After Blore Heath and Ludford Bridge, there was no realistic chance of peace, although that did not stop

63 *The Brut*, i., pp.526–7.

64 *Contemporary English Chronicles*, p.65; Wavrin, v., pp.276, 322; *Chroniques d'Enguerrand de Monstrelet*, ed. J.A. Buchon (14 vols, Paris: Verdiere Libraire, 1826), xiv., p.2.

65 TNA, E101/195/7, fo. 38v.

66 *An English Chronicle*, p.80.

efforts to find compromise. But for York, Salisbury and Warwick, as well as probably for Queen Margaret, the Duke of Somerset and the Earl of Northumberland, the coming months could only offer renewed conflict.

Further Reading

The period from York's second protectorate to Blore Heath is covered in all the major studies of the period but see the contrasting arguments in Tony Pollard's and Michael Hicks's books on Warwick the Kingmaker. For Blore Heath, Tim Thornton's article ('The Battle of Blore Heath: Sources, Historiography and the Implications for the Outbreak of Conflict', *Midland History*, 49 (2024), pp.1–20) is a very thorough introduction to the sources and analysis of the historiography. Blore Heath is only one of three battlefields (along with Northampton and Towton) of this period on Historic England's Battlefield Register. The English Heritage report on the battlefield has a good overview of the sources, but its reconstruction of the battle is ambitious in the confidence of its conclusions.

4

Calais and Ireland: The Forgotten War

After Ludford Bridge the Yorkist lords went their separate ways. The Duke of York and his second son, the Earl of Rutland, fled to Ireland, while the earls of Salisbury and Warwick and York's eldest son, the Earl of March, travelled, via Devon and the Channel Islands, to Calais. York's journey to Ireland appears almost leisurely: he first went south to Devon, possibly with the other lords, before sailing to North Wales and from there he crossed the Irish Sea. Duke Richard arrived in Dublin and was received there as 'if a Messiah had descended among them'.[1] Warwick, Salisbury and March's journey to Calais was altogether more eventful. They were assisted by the Devon gentleman John Dynham and his redoubtable mother, Lady Joan. Warwick used money lent to him by Dynham to buy a ship, which then probably departed from the Dynham manor of Hartland, pursued by the Lancastrian Earl of Devon. They may have intended to join York in Ireland but ended up, either by design or the vagaries of the weather, in the Channel Islands. From Guernsey they waited for a fair wind and from there sailed to Calais. The fugitive earls eventually landed in Warwick's stronghold on 2 November.[2]

The Lancastrians had wasted no time in moving against their enemies. On 9 October the King had issued writs for a Parliament to meet at Coventry on 20 November. It was summoned to condemn the Yorkist lords and their allies, yet it was not a narrowly partisan gathering. Most of the remaining peers attended in person and, while many of the known 156 members of the Commons were later to emerge as supporters of the house of Lancaster, a significant minority remained neutral or even supported the Yorkists. It was decided to proceed against the rebellious lords by way of attainder: they were to be stripped of their estates and their heirs disinherited without any chance to put their case or appeal to their peers. In all 24 rebels were attainted, an unprecedented use of this extra-judicial form of punishment. This was certainly fewer than had originally been planned and several notable Yorkist supporters, including Lord Stanley, Sir Walter Devereux, William Herbert and William Hastings, were pardoned. Perhaps the King, whose professed willingness to pardon all those willing to submit was well known, tempered the mood.[3] There may also have been disquiet about the process of attainder itself. Although not unknown previously, its use on this scale was unprecedented, and this may have unnerved many among the Lords and Commons.

1 Whethamstede, pp.367–8.
2 Whethamstede, p.345; *Contemporary English Chronicles*, p.66.
3 *Parliament Rolls of Medieval England*, Parliament of November 1459, items 7–23.

It was probably to counter growing disquiet over the process of attainder that the tract known as the *Somnium Vigilantis* was written. It set out the case against York and his allies in no uncertain terms. No matter how grave the problems facing the realm, rebellion against the King could never be justified. Its author pointed out that the Yorkist lords had broken their oaths of allegiance to Henry on more than one occasion. Failure to punish them severely would now dangerously undermine royal authority. The author of the *Somnium* is unknown – although Lawrence Booth, Bishop of Durham, is one candidate – but its intended audience may well have been moderate lords or even the King himself. The beginning of the text is lost, but it took the form of an imagined conversation between representatives of the Yorkist lords who had come to court seeking clemency and a royal spokesman. The Yorkist lords claimed legitimacy by representing the commonwealth and stressed the royal virtue of mercy. The Lancastrian rebuttal of these claims was unambiguous. The Yorkist lords had forfeited their right to mercy as they had acted out of 'pure malice', bent on the 'final destruction of this gracious king'. It rejected their claims to act for commonwealth, arguing instead that the Yorkist lords' actions were driven by their own ambition. Significantly, the tract also dismissed the 'foolish commons' who still sympathised with the Yorkist lords' call for reform despite their broken oaths and rebellion.[4] Although the Yorkist lords were duly attainted, Henry reserved the right to pardon freely those who would submit to his grace in the future. Indeed, some who had turned out for the Yorkists at Ludford Bridge had already submitted themselves 'in hyr schyrtys and halters in hyr hondes, fallyng before the kynge', thus escaping the rigours of Parliamentary justice.[5] As a final act of the Parliament, on 11 December, 66 lords, bishops and heads of religious houses swore solemn oaths of allegiance to the King, as well as to Queen Margaret and Prince Edward.[6]

Calais and the Keeping of the Seas

The strategic importance of the Calais Pale – the area around the town and port of Calais under English control – cannot be underestimated. Not only was it home to the largest permanent military force in the realm, but Calais was also the centre of the English wool export trade to the Low Countries and thus closely tied to London. The town had been in English hands since it had been captured by Edward III in 1348 and the Treaty of Brétigny 12 years later confirmed it as English land, held in full sovereignty and not part of the kingdom of France. Since 1360, however, the area of English occupation had shrunk from that captured by Edward III. Nevertheless, by 1455 it was still substantial and stretched some 18 miles from near Wissant in Picardy to Gravelines in Flanders. Besides Calais, its castle and the nearby fortress at Rysbank Tower which overlooked the harbour, there were fortresses at Hammes and Guînes. Guînes' strategic position – it controlled the road from the French town of Ardres to Boulogne and was visible from the other English outpost at Hammes – made it almost as important a fortress as Calais itself.[7]

4 J.P. Gilson, 'A Defence of the Proscription of the Yorkists in 1459', *English Historical Review*, 26 (1911), pp.512–25.
5 *Contemporary English Chronicles*, p.67.
6 *Parliament Rolls of Medieval England*, Parliament of November 1459, item 26.
7 David Grummitt, *The Calais Garrison: War and Military Service in England 1436-1558* (Woodbridge: Boydell and Brewer, 2008), pp. 5-10; Susan Rose, *An English Town in France, 1347-1558* (Woodbridge: Boydell and Brewer, 2008), pp.135-40.

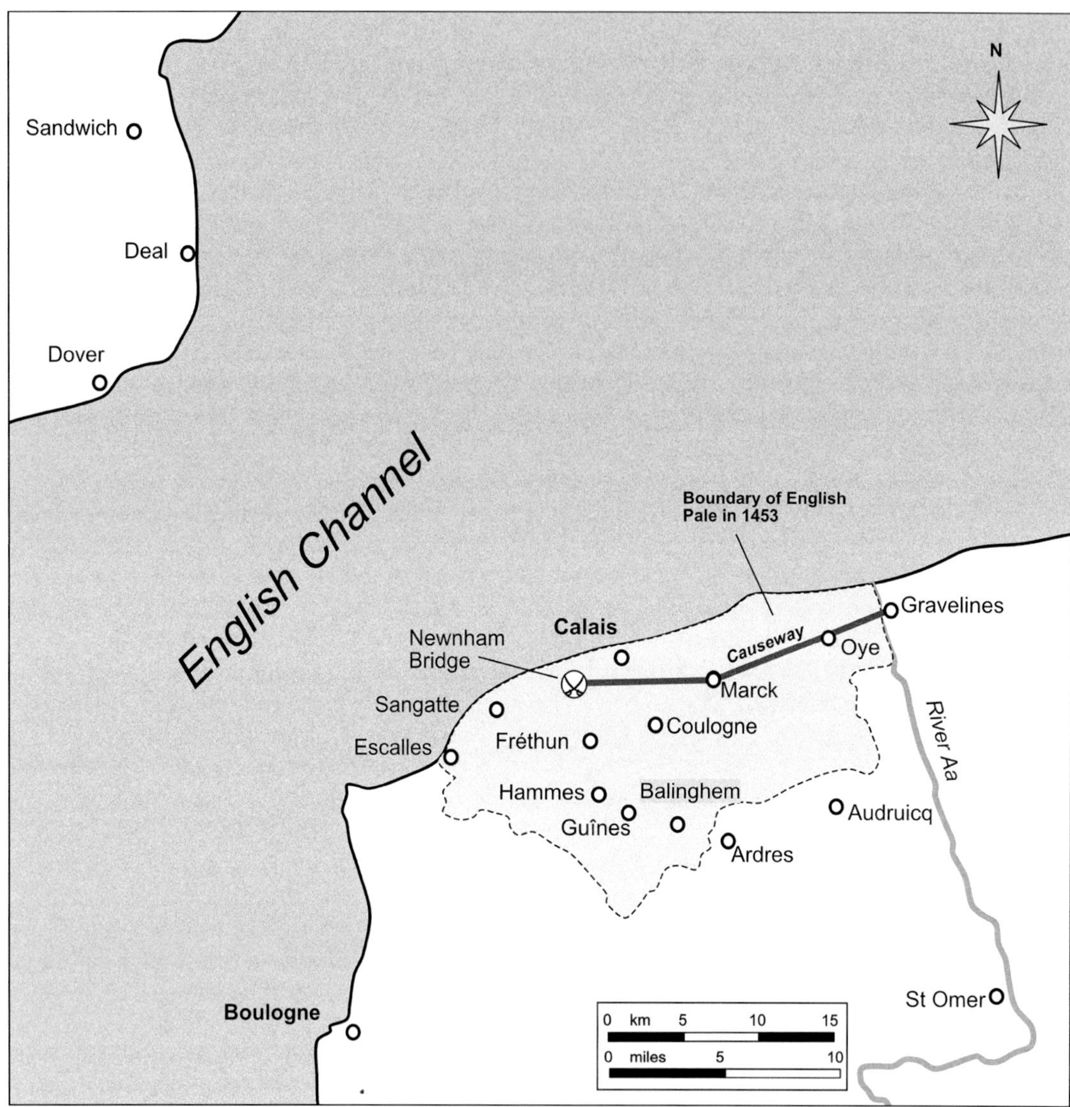

The Calais Pale, the area under English control, in the middle of the fifteenth century.

The English garrison at Calais was commanded by its captain. The captain was usually a royal prince or one of the greatest magnates of the realm. Henry V had been captain of Calais when Prince of Wales and his brothers, the dukes of Bedford and Gloucester, had both served earlier in Henry VI's reign. The size of the garrison was set down in indentures sealed between the King and the captain. When Edmund Beaufort, Duke of Somerset, indented on 14 September 1451, he agreed to serve with 30 mounted men-at-arms, including himself and his deputy, 30 mounted archers, 200 men-at-arms and 200 archers on foot. The captain also received wages for 40 crossbowmen, 20 carpenters and 15 masons. In the outlying fortresses the captains usually made their own indentures with the King. At Calais Castle there was the captain or lieutenant, 29 men-at-arms and 20 foot archers. At Rysbank Tower the captain or his lieutenant served alongside a man-at-arms and 16 men-at-arms or crossbowmen. At Guînes the captain or his lieutenant had 49 men-at-arms and 50 archers on foot, while at Hammes the captain or his deputy served alongside a single archer-on-horseback, 17 men-at-arms on foot and 22 foot archers. The only surviving muster roll for this period, made in 1466, lists a total of 527 men serving in Calais, Calais Castle and Rysbank Tower. Perhaps a third of these soldiers served in named retinues, either of the captain or his leading men-at-arms, but most, it seems, were appointed directly by the captain of Calais. The men-at-arms were frequently retainers and long-time servants of the captain or other leading office holders. At times of crisis, as in 1450, large 'crews', additional soldiers above the garrison's establishment, were contracted for service in Calais. These forces could become almost permanent additions to the captain's retinue. In June 1452 the Duke of Somerset's indenture as captain was revised to allow him to retain a further 160 men-at-arms and 511 archers. As well as these men 'in wages', there were an indeterminate number of men in 'petty wages.' They were privately sub-contracted by other members of the garrison and paid by them rather than by the treasurer of Calais. They may have served as household servants, as well as fulfilling military roles. In June 1473 Sir John Paston wrote to his brother asking him 'iff ye knowe any lykly men and fayre condycioned and good archerys, sende hem to me, thowe it be iiij, and I wyll have them and they shall iiij marke by yere and my levere'.[8] Although it is impossible to say with certainty, it is likely that these men in 'petty wages' boosted the total number of soldiers serving in Calais, Guînes and Hammes from some 700 in regular wages to nearer 1,000 in total. On top of the reinforcements sent earlier in the 1450s, it is likely that there were as many as 1,500 men serving in the garrison in 1455.[9]

It is tempting to think that when the Yorkist lords crossed to Calais in November 1459 they arrived at a place of safety. Yet the loyalty of the town and marches could not be taken for granted.[10] Edmund Beaufort had been appointed as captain in September 1451 and crossed the Channel a month later. He appointed two of his long-serving and most trusted captains – Andrew Trollope and Osbert Mountford – to positions in the garrison, but many of the other men-at-arms appear to have continued their service from previous captains. The outlying castles of Hammes and Guînes were commanded by Sir John Marney and Sir Thomas Fynderne respectively. Both were experienced soldiers yet had no previous connections to Somerset. The Duke managed to secure the garrison's loyalty by guaranteeing the regular payment of their wages. The garrison's wages had fallen badly into arrears under the previous captain, the Duke of Buckingham, and the debts amounted to over £19,000 when the total peacetime cost of the garrison was some £11,000 per annum. Somerset was able to use his influence at court and on the King's council to secure preferable treatment for the garrison among the crown's many creditors and ensured a regular assignment upon the wool customs to meet future wage bills.

York's relationship with Calais throughout the 1450s had been a troubled one. When Richard, Duke of York, became protector in April 1454 he moved quickly to secure his own appointment as captain of Calais. Sealing new indentures, however, was one thing; gaining access to the town and marches and winning the favour of the garrison was another. York began by insisting that patents of appointment to positions of command in Calais were surrendered, and on the residence of the men

8 *Paston Letters and Papers*, ed. Davis, i., p.463.

9 Grummitt, *Calais Garrison*, pp.44–9, 56–9.

10 For much of what follows see G.L. Harriss, 'The Struggle for Calais: An Aspect of the Rivalry between Lancaster and York', *English Historical Review*, 75 (1960), pp.30–53.

he intended to appoint. The real sticking point, however, was money. York overturned the arrangements made by Somerset and began negotiations with the merchants of the staple to underwrite his captaincy. However, in early May the garrison, who had received no payment of their wages since the previous summer, took matters into their own hands and seized the staplers' wool in Calais. In taking this action, the soldiers may have been encouraged by Lionel, Lord Welles, and Richard Woodville, Lord Rivers, appointed by Somerset as his deputies in the autumn of 1451 and effectively commanding the garrison in Duke Edmund's absence. York sent his ally Henry, Viscount Bourchier, to the town to negotiate a settlement and his entry into the town. By the middle of July, the negotiations had progressed sufficiently for Duke Richard to indent as captain of Calais, but instead of crossing the Channel he remained in London preparing formal charges against Somerset and seeking reform of the royal household. As a result, a final settlement in Calais was stalled and soldiers retained the staplers' wool. In November, York ordered Somerset to relinquish his command of Calais, also licensing the garrison to sell the wool to discharge their arrears. This forced the staplers' hand, and they finally agreed to finance York's assumption of command. Yet, just as his victory seemed assured, the King recovered from his illness and the Duke's authority as protector effectively ended. On 26 January 1455 Somerset was released from the Tower and the end of York's first protectorate soon followed. In March, York was obliged to surrender the captaincy of Calais, which was initially retained in the King's own hands before being regranted to Somerset. His rival soon set about re-establishing his control over the garrison, shored up by a national loan campaign for the defence of the Pale.

Somerset, of course, died at his enemies' hands at the First Battle of St Albans. In its aftermath, York was determined not to repeat the mistakes and delays that had thwarted his plans for Calais the previous year. In June he sent a commission, led by his brother-in-law William Neville, Lord Fauconberg, to Calais. By 4 August, talks with the garrison and the staplers had progressed enough to allow the Earl of Warwick to indent as captain of Calais. In October the staplers agreed to lend £12,000 in cash, secured by repayment from the customs which they themselves would pay on future sales of wool, to discharge the garrison's arrears of pay. Further promises of cash from the Yorkist-controlled government helped secure the soldiers' compliance. On 13 December 1455 the King's council implored the garrison to give no credence to claims made by Rivers and Welles of bad faith and of wholesale dismissals. The council asked them to admit Warwick in return for 20,000 marks in cash. Despite the end of York's second protectorate in February 1456, the plan was accepted and ratified in the new Parliamentary session. The staplers agreed to immediately pay some £20,000 for the garrison's arrears and for the first quarter-year wage payment for Warwick and his retinue. In May the garrison was pardoned of any offences arising from their seizure of the staplers' wool, and, sometime in mid-July, Warwick finally crossed the Channel to take up his post as captain of Calais.[11]

The staplers' cash had not discharged the garrison's arrears totally. In April 1456, the total amount owed to them had been calculated at no less than £65,444 16*s.* 9¾*d.* (although much of that was written off by crediting the value of the wool seized and sold by the soldiers). Lords Rivers, Welles and Stourton (captain of Rysbank Tower since March 1450) were discharged and Lord Fauconberg, himself an old soldier and veteran of the wars in France, installed as Warwick's de-facto deputy. The old campaigners Marney at Hammes and Fynderne at Guînes were allowed to remain in post, however, and there is little evidence of widespread change among the men-at-arms and archers

11 Hicks, *Warwick the Kingmaker*, pp.138–42; Pollard, *Warwick the Kingmaker*, pp.129–31.

of the garrison. Warwick now set about securing the loyalty of the garrison. He also sought to build diplomatic and military relationships with the neighbouring Burgundian garrisons at Saint-Omer and Boulogne. In May 1458 a *pas d'armes* was held between the Calais garrison and the Burgundians.[12] It is frequently said by historians that following his arrival in Calais, Warwick 'exploited his command of the straits by flagrant piracy', winning the loyalty of the rapacious garrison by enriching them at the expense of foreign merchants, while also discrediting Henry VI's government and its ability to protect trade.[13] The evidence for this, however, especially between Warwick's three-year appointment as keeper of the seas in December 1457 and his attainder two years later, is far from clear.[14]

In 1458 Warwick's ships operating out of Calais were involved in two major confrontations with foreign merchants. First, in late May there was a major sea battle between the Earl's ships and a Castilian fleet. The latter consisted of 22 ships, including 16 armoured great ships. The Calais fleet in contrast had only five ships of the forecastle, three carvels and four pinnacles. The ensuing six-hour battle was a close-run thing for the outnumbered English. John Jerningham, a correspondent of Margaret Paston and one of Warwick's soldiers in Calais, explained how he and 23 of his men had boarded a 400-ton ship and were captured by its crew. He was kept prisoner aboard the ship for the duration of the battle and freed in a prisoner exchange. By the end of the battle – the greatest seen in the Channel for forty years according to Jerningham – six foreign ships had been captured, 240 sailors killed and another 500 injured. Warwick had lost 80 dead and some 200 injured.[15] It was a high price to pay, but presumably one thought worthwhile by those who participated as the Earl's actions seem to have been fêted in London and Kent. More importantly, it added valuable ships to the Earl's naval power. The second encounter, shortly after, was an even more consequential event. Warwick intercepted the Hanseatic fleet returning from its annual journey to the Bay of Bourgneuf on the Loire estuary to collect salt. In the late summer, ships from Calais also attacked a Castilian-Genoese flotilla, capturing two Genoese carracks and three Castilian ships. The angry merchants immediately complained to the King's council and demanded redress.[16] On top of this, there were another eight recorded instances of individual ships or smaller flotillas being seized by men from Calais which elicited protests to the King's council that year.[17]

Yet Warwick's activities in the Channel in 1458 had some basis in both law and political expediency. It was customary for foreign vessels to 'strike' or lower their sails when called upon to do so in English waters by an officeholder such as the keeper of the seas or one of his deputies. They were also expected to submit their ships to search for uncustomed goods. This caused tensions when the same rights were demanded on the high seas and could lead to major diplomatic incidents, as it did in 1449 when the Hanseatic Bay Fleet had been attacked by an English fleet in the Narrow Seas. As keeper of the seas, Warwick was empowered to seize and requisition ships and mariners for the King's use. This practice had been widespread in the 1450s during periods of crisis. In 1454, for example, compensation was paid to the owner of a Portuguese ship which had been seized by Andrew Trollope for the King's service. Three years later, in March 1457, amid fears of a French

12 Archives Départementales du Nord, B.2034, *Registre* of the Receiver General of the Duke of Burgundy, Jan. 1458–Sept. 1459, fo. 141.
13 Harriss, 'Struggle for Calais', p.48.
14 Penny Tucker, 'The Earl of Warwick's Use of Sea-Power in the Late 1450s', *Southern History*, 42 (2020), pp.1–20.
15 *Paston Letters and Papers*, ed. Davis, ii., p.340.
16 *Three Fifteenth Century Chronicles*, p.71.
17 *Calendar of Patent Rolls, 1452–1461*, pp.437–40.

descent upon the Pale, Trollope had seized three Italian ships in the Thames. Uncustomed wool had been found in one ship (the reason why this case came before the Exchequer court), but it seems the Calais men had originally impressed the ships for the King's service, not impounded them because of a search for contraband goods.[18]

Nevertheless, in 1458 Warwick's activities on the high seas were causing widespread alarm among the foreign mercantile community in England and providing his enemies at court and in the council with an opportunity to move against him. In April and May Warwick was named to several commissions appointed to inquire into accusations of piracy against foreign ships. On 9 May he provided bail for his uncle and effective deputy at Calais, Lord Fauconberg, who had been imprisoned on some unknown charge (which could well have been related to an accusation of piracy made by the Spanish merchant, John de Sigure).[19] On 9 August commissioners, led by Lord Rivers, held an inquisition in Rochester into Warwick's attack on the Bay Fleet. Its outcome is unknown, but in November a council meeting was called to discuss, among other things, 'the taking of the Shippes of lubyke'. Warwick had not attended council meetings in September, where his conduct on the high seas was discussed, but he did attend to answer the charges against him, with almost fatal consequences, on 9 November. On leaving the session he was attacked in Westminster Hall, probably by men of the royal household. He narrowly escaped with his life, fleeing by barge to the Greyfriars and from there, with royal permission, returning to Calais. In January 1459 a Great Council assembled, probably with the intention of removing Warwick from his post as captain of Calais. Yet the meeting was called to a sudden end when the Duke of Exeter was arrested for striking a lawyer.[20] Perversely, Warwick's great rival for the keepership of the seas had probably saved his position. On 26 January the Earl's secretary paid for his master's indenture as keeper of the seas to be enrolled at the exchequer, presumably as protection for any legal challenge to his authority on the high seas. He and his wife, Countess Anne, also had their general pardon enrolled at the exchequer, a protection perhaps against more serious charges.[21] With Warwick safe in Calais and with a large fleet to patrol the Channel and Narrow Seas, there was little prospect of his enemies replacing him as captain of the town and marches. In late June or early July ships from Calais made another attack on foreign merchantmen, capturing five Genoese and Castilian ships and adding further strength to Warwick's fleet.[22]

The Battle for Calais

King Henry had in fact appointed Henry Beaufort, Duke of Somerset, captain of Calais on 9 October, three days before the events at Ludford Bridge.[23] Immediately after the rout of the Yorkist lords, the Duke gathered the soldiers of the garrison that had deserted Warwick and 'made him redy in al haste to go to Caleys, & take possession of his office'.[24] Unfortunately for the Lancastrian cause, it took Somerset some three weeks to organise his expedition, during which time Warwick

18 TNA, E159/233, *Recorda*, Easter 35 Hen VI, rots. 12–13.
19 TNA, SC8/332/15729.
20 *Letters and Papers*, i., pp.367–9; Tucker, 'Warwick's Use of Sea-Power', pp.10–11. See above p.39.
21 E159/235, *Recorda*, Easter 37 Hen VI, Hilary rots. 2d–4.
22 *Six Town Chronicles*, p.147.
23 TNA, C76/142, m. 24.
24 *The Brut*, i., p.528.

had sailed to Guernsey, waiting for a fair wind to take him to Calais. Doubtless, messengers from both sides had crossed the Channel and Lord Fauconberg was instructed to prepare the town's defences against Somerset's imminent arrival, while those still loyal to the Lancastrian cause pondered their next move. Lord Rivers was paid for raising 1,000 men to accompany Somerset and retake Calais. The Duke, accompanied by Thomas, Lord Roos and John Tuchet, the new Lord Audley, as well as Andrew Trollope, assembled at Sandwich.[25]

Much of our knowledge of events in Calais comes from Jean de Wavrin. The account in his *Recueil des Croniques*, included in the section known as 'Warwick's Apology', does not feature in the work of the so-called Monstrelet Continuator or other European or English chronicles, and Wavrin may have compiled his narrative from information he gathered when he visited Calais in 1470.[26] Jacques du Clercq, however, had some knowledge of events in Calais, naming one of the Lancastrian sailors from Somerset's fleet executed by Warwick, which suggests that newsletters were in circulation in the Low Countries.[27] According to Wavrin, the Lancastrians were delayed at Sandwich by the weather and unable to cross to Calais. Early on 2 November, after eight days' sailing, Warwick, with the Earl of Salisbury, Edward, Earl of March, and John Dynham, landed at Calais. They were received by Fauconberg and conducted to St Peter's Church, where they gave thanks for their arrival. If Wavrin is to be believed, the garrison told Somerset's herald, who arrived in Calais shortly afterwards, that 'no other captain was wanted than the Earl of Warwick', leaving the unfortunate messenger to return to Sandwich to disappoint the Duke. Realising that a landing at Calais was now out of the question – for which Somerset blamed Lord Rivers for delaying at Sandwich – Trollope advised the Duke to cross to Wissant on the southern border of the English Pale and from there to make his way to Guînes. However, part of Somerset's fleet, including Roos and Audley, and ships carrying the Duke's horses and much of his men's equipment, was blown into Calais harbour (although at least one chronicler suggests that Somerset's ships went there 'by their free willes'.)[28] Audley was captured, but Roos managed to escape to Guînes, and from there to Flanders. Warwick distributed the captured horses and harness among the garrison members loyal to him. The captured soldiers and mariners were led to the marketplace, where those who had previously served and sworn oaths to Warwick were imprisoned. The next morning, before the earls of Salisbury and March, they were beheaded for the treason they had committed in breaking their oaths to the Earl of Warwick. A message was sent to Somerset at Guînes thanking him for the horse and harness, and when the Duke learned of the executions, he took an oath to revenge himself against the Yorkist lords.[29]

The scene was now set for several months of raiding, sieges and skirmishes as Somerset attempted to wrest control of Calais and its surrounding fortresses from the Yorkist lords. Both sides continued to draw upon reinforcements from England and from the existing military supplies within the fortresses of the Calais Pale, while the Yorkists received financial support and weapons from the London merchants and from the Burgundians. Somerset, it seems, also 'made alliances across the sea' and received arms, horses and supplies from Charles VII.[30] In England, the Lancastrians

25 *Calendar of Patent Rolls, 1452–1461*, p.555.
26 BNF, MS Français 88, fos. 138v–40.
27 *Mémoires de Jacques du Clercq*, iii., pp.2–4.
28 Kingsford, *Chronicles of London*, p.170.
29 Wavrin, v., p.281; G. Du Fresne de Beaucourt, *Histoire de Charles VII* (7 vols, Paris: Alphonse Picard, 1894), vi., p.271.
30 Wavrin, v., pp.281–2.

attempted to stop the supply of Warwick's men with restrictions on the passage of goods and victuals and on the export of wool to Calais, but they could not prevent the supply of the Yorkist lords entirely. Events in Calais captured the imagination of the London chroniclers, one remarking that 'assone as he [Somerset] was with in the castell he made stronge werre a gaynes Caleys, and they of Calys a gaynes him'.[31] The scale of this 'strong war' can be judged by the meticulous accounts kept by the victualler of Calais, who recorded the munitions spent from the stores by both sides. In October 1459, for example, the victualler had 726 bows in his store; a year later this had dwindled to just 400, while he had expended all the arrows in the Calais armoury. By 1461, as the last Lancastrians continued to resist at Guînes and Hammes, the number of bows stored at Calais was only 461, falling to 233 a year later.[32] In 1460–61 (there are no accounts surviving for 1459–60) the garrison at Calais Castle used 56lbs of gunpowder and 30 gunstones against the 'king's enemies and rebels', while those at Guînes, by then under Yorkist control, used 195lbs of gunpowder and fired 184 gunstones. The victualler also recorded the expenditure by both the Lancastrian defenders and the Yorkist besiegers of Hammes Castle during two attempts to capture the castle in April and in September to December 1461. The Yorkists expended 4,536 crossbow quarrels, 1,030lbs of gunpowder, 122 bows and 998 gunstones in their attacks. The Lancastrian defenders used 131lbs of gunpowder firing 270 gunstones, as well as 370 crossbow quarrels and 25 bows.[33]

By January 1460 Somerset's effective blockade of the Yorkist lords in Calais was beginning to take effect. In October the previous year Rivers had been commissioned to arrest any ships belonging to Warwick and several had been detained in Sandwich. On 10 December he was commissioned to muster men to send to sea under the command of the Lancastrian treasurer of Calais, Sir Gervase Clifton, and resist any attempt by the Yorkist lords to break out of Calais.[34] According to Wavrin, Warwick summoned his men-at-arms to a council of war to determine how to recover his ships laying at anchor in Sandwich. A messenger sent to Somerset by Lord Rivers had been captured and he revealed that the townsmen of Sandwich would not resist an attempt by the Yorkists to recover the vessels. John Dynham volunteered to lead an audacious raid on Sandwich to bring back Warwick's fleet. Wavrin claims Dynham was assisted by Sir John Wenlock, 'a very wise knight' and veteran of the Hundred Years War who had fled to Calais with the Yorkist lords, but no other source corroborates that. A small Yorkist flotilla crossed to Sandwich with between 300 and 800 men in the early hours of 15 January, waiting for the tide to turn before entering Sandwich haven. There, with the active assistance of some local men, they soon overpowered the Lancastrian garrison and carried off all the ships anchored there, complete with their stores and crews, save for the largest, the *Grace Dieu*, which apparently was not then seaworthy.[35]

The stunning success of the raid on Sandwich, in effect scuppering any hopes the Lancastrians had of significantly reinforcing Somerset at Guînes, clearly sent ripples of excitement and shock throughout England. More important to most observers than the recapture of Warwick's ship, however, was the seizure of Lord Rivers and his wife, Jacquetta, dowager Duchess of Bedford, and their son Anthony Woodville, as they slept in their beds. Anthony had apparently only returned to Sandwich the previous evening. William Botoner, writing perhaps less than a week after the

31 *Three Fifteenth Century Chronicles*, p.72.

32 TNA, E364/96, rots. B and C; E364/97, rot. G.

33 TNA, E101/195/14, fos. 11–11v.

34 *Calendar of Patent Rolls, 1452–1461*, p.555

35 Wavrin. v. pp.282–3; Cora Scofield, 'The Capture of Lord Rivers and Sir Anthony Woodville, 19 January 1460', *English Historical Review*, 37 (1922), pp.253–5.

incident with his tongue firmly in his cheek, announced to Sir John Berney that 'the Lord Ryvers, Sir Antonye, hys son, and othyrs hafe wonne Calix by a feeble assault made at Sandwich by Denham, Squyer'.[36] Less than two weeks after the raid, William Paston described to his brother what he had heard of the captured Lancastrians' reception in Calais:

> As for tydyngs, my Lord Ryvers was brougth to Caleys and by-for the lordys wyth viijxx torches, and there my lord of Salesbury reheted hym, callyng hym knaves son that he schuld be so rude to calle hym and these other lordys traytours, for they schull be found the Kyngys treue liege men whan he schuld be found a traytour, &c. And my lord of Warrewyk reheted hym and seyd his fader was but a squyer and broute up wyth Kyng Herry the vte , and sethen hym-self made by maryage and also made lord, and that it was not his parte to have swyche langage of lordys beyng of the Kyngys blood. And my lord of Marche reheted hym in lyke wyse, and Ser Antony was reheted for his langage of all iij lordys in lyke wyse.[37]

There was little that the Lancastrian regime could do to mitigate this disaster in the short term. They had been caught napping, so to speak, undoing all their efforts to reinforce Somerset and take Calais in one fell swoop. A high-powered judicial commission, led by the Earl of Wiltshire, travelled to Kent after Easter to inquire into what had happened and identify those responsible, but the Yorkist horse had bolted. Various commissions attempted to bolster the defences of the English coast and key cities, such as Canterbury and Norwich, while orders were given to imprison anyone supporting the Yorkist lords by word or deed. One enterprising Lancastrian, the Devon knight Sir Baldwin Fulford, offered 'on payne of lesyng his hed, he wolde destroy the Erle of Warrewyk and his nauey, yef the kyng wolde graunte hym his expensis'. Accordingly, he indented in February to take 1,000 men to sea for three months to take on Warwick's ships. Nothing came of his mission and one London chronicler noted laconically 'whanne he had consumed and wasted all that money, his vyage was done and [he] wente home ayene'.[38]

In the aftermath of the raid on Sandwich Warwick decided that, instead of mounting an immediate invasion of England, he would travel to Ireland to meet with the Duke of York. Messengers had been passing between Calais and Ireland since November, but some had been captured, and the Yorkist lords could not risk their plans falling into enemy hands. It was a dangerous and costly journey, and Warwick borrowed heavily to equip and man the ship necessary for the voyage. He departed Calais early in March, accompanied by the Gascon knight and old soldier Gaillard Duras, and met York in Waterford on 16 March.[39] In Calais, Somerset's position at Guînes was gradually weakening amid a shortage of funds, despite the King making grants of offices and revenues there to the Duke's supporters. Shortly after the Woodvilles' capture, Lord Roos had managed to cross to England to make an appeal to the King and council for desperately needed cash.[40] On 23 April Somerset decided to take the initiative and make his attack on Yorkist-held Calais.

The resulting Battle of Newnham Bridge is one of the least known clashes of the Wars of the Roses. Its importance to the outcome of the conflict generally may have been underestimated.

36 *Paston Letters*, ed. Gairdner, iii., p.203.
37 *Paston Letters and Papers*, ed. Davis, i., p.162.
38 *An English Chronicle*, p.82; TNA, C76/142, m. 17; E404/71/4/28.
39 Wavrin, v., pp.286–7.
40 TNA, E404/71/4/33.

Only Abbot Whethamstede and the pseudo-Worcester *Annales* mention the clash of arms. Jean de Wavrin, whose focus throughout his account of events in Calais was the Earl of Warwick, does not mention the engagement at Newnham Bridge. Whethamstede wrote that Lord Audley (who, according to Wavrin, was already a prisoner of the Yorkist lords at Calais) and Humphrey Stafford led a force to relieve Somerset at Guînes, but that the Lancastrians were forced to retreat in the face of bad weather, while the Annalist merely stated that a clash took place on 23 April and that Somerset was heavily defeated. That it took place on St George's Day might be significant, with Somerset making a chivalric statement and desiring to bring the Yorkist lords to battle.[41] The 'battle' may also have been important, as suggested by David Saintiuste, because it afforded the young Edward, Earl of March, his first experience of combat. The Flemish diplomat and historian Philippe de Commynes would later recall that Edward had won eight or nine victories.[42] Northampton, Mortimer's Cross, Ferrybridge and Towton, Empingham, Barnet and Tewkesbury account for six or seven of these battles, and Anthony Goodman suggested that St Albans in 1455 may have provided a first exposure to battle for York's eldest son, but might Newnham Bridge have been the first occasion when the future king participated in the fighting in person? If it was, fighting alongside veterans like Fauconberg, Wenlock and Dynham, the experience would have been priceless preparation for what was to come.

The Earl of Warwick returned to Calais in late May. On the journey back from Ireland he confronted a larger fleet commanded by the Duke of Exeter. Exeter had 14 ships, led by Warwick's former flagship the *Grace Dieu* and 1,500 men, but when Warwick's flotilla sailed towards him in battle formation, the Duke's ships fled and took harbour at Dartmouth. Warwick wisely did not press the attack, not wishing to risk his men and supplies, but also, according to one Yorkist chronicle, out of respect for Exeter's royal blood. He was received with great joy at Calais. Many of the soldiers and townsmen implored him to move immediately against Somerset in Guînes, but clearly the Yorkist lords had decided that an invasion of England was more pressing. Duke Henry had attempted to surrender Guînes to the Burgundians, making the offer to Charles, Count of Charolais, who informed him that his father, Duke Philip, had no interest in the town.[43] In April, Burgundian towns in the Boulonnais were paid compensation by Duke Philip's receiver-general for damage caused by English 'routiers', although it is unclear whether this was Warwick's men or the garrison at Guînes.[44] Warwick certainly maintained sea patrols and preyed on French shipping off the coast of Calais.[45] On 5 June the Lancastrian regime offered a last, desperate pardon to any (except for Fauconberg, Dynham and five others) in Calais who would submit to Somerset. There were no takers.[46] With dwindling supplies and little prospect of relief from England, Somerset was effectively neutralised.

It is unclear whether news from Kent now forced the Yorkist lords' hand or whether their landing at Sandwich on 26 June was long planned. They received intelligence that Osbert Mountford, one of Somerset's oldest-serving captains, had assembled at Sandwich with 400 or 500 men, wearing

41 Whethamstede, pp.369–70; *Letters and Papers*, ii(2)., p.772.

42 Philippe de Commynes, *Memoirs: The Reign of Louis XI*, ed. Michael Jones (London: Penguin Books, 1972), p.358; David Saintuste, *Edward IV and the Wars of the Roses* (Barnsley: Pen and Sword, 2010), p.29.

43 Wavrin, v., pp.287–92.

44 Archives Départementales du Nord, B.2041, *Portefeuille* of the Receiver General of the Duke of Burgundy, 1 Oct. 1460–30 Sept. 1461, unfoliated.

45 C.L. Kingsford, 'The Earl of Warwick at Calais in 1460', *English Historical Review*, 37 (1922), pp.544–6.

46 TNA, C76/142, m. 9.

the Beaufort 'lyvere of portcules', intending to cross the Channel and relieve the Duke in Guînes. Armed with this information, they decided on a pre-emptive attack.[47] The pseudo-Worcester *Annales* and the author of *An English Chronicle* suggested instead that the descent on Sandwich was well planned at Fauconberg's instigation, as he was confident that the Yorkist lords would be well received in Kent and London. On 24 June a Yorkist fleet, led by Fauconberg and Dynham, landed at Sandwich. After a day's hard fighting the port was secured. Dynham was wounded in the arm by gun shot, while Mountford was taken back to Calais and beheaded at Rysbank Tower. It is unclear what Mountford had done to deserve summary execution, although he had served in the Calais garrison himself in the early 1450s, and the raid might have pitched him against his former comrades-in-arms. On 26 June, with a fair wind, the earls of Salisbury, Warwick and March landed in Sandwich with, according to Wavrin, 2,000 men.[48] In all likelihood their force was smaller than this, as they had to leave Calais suitably defended against Somerset, who was still holed up in Guînes. Even so, they must have been encouraged by their reception in Kent and accordingly set off on their march to London.

The Yorkist lords' landing at Sandwich and their subsequent victory at the Battle of Northampton did not end the struggle for the Calais Pale. The London chronicles are silent on the events there in the months following the Yorkist lords' departure, as their attention turned to events in England, but Jean de Wavrin gave a colourful account of what happened next. On hearing news of the Yorkist victory at Northampton, Somerset called a council of war and decided it would be best to reconcile himself to the new Yorkist-controlled government. Warwick returned to Calais in early August. On 5 August the King ordered Somerset to surrender Guînes to Warwick and three days later the two men met in St Peter's Church (or, according to the pseudo-Worcester *Annales*, at Newnham Bridge). Somerset vowed never to take up arms against Warwick again, and he, Lord Roos and Andrew Trollope were given safe conduct to Dieppe before arriving back in England in October. Their passage to England was paid for by Charles VII, who ordered his receiver-general to pay 1,400 *livres tournois* (about £175) towards the Duke's expenses.[49] Somerset's surrender did not, however, secure Calais and its surrounding fortresses completely for the Yorkists. In December Warwick was ordered to inquire why the watch was not maintained in Calais as it should be, presumably amidst increased fears for the town's security.[50] The garrison at Guînes, led by their lieutenant, Nicholas Huse, held out until 9 January 1461 when they received £650 in wages to sweeten their departure and the promise of a royal pardon (which was granted on 26 February). When they surrendered, Warwick installed one of his most steadfast supporters in Calais, Richard Whetehill, as the new commander there.[51]

Elsewhere in the Pale, the garrison at Hammes Castle continued to resist Warwick's control. On 20 April 1461 the Gascon knight Gaillard Duras and Richard Whetehill negotiated a surrender agreement with the Lancastrian garrison. The defenders' representatives were sceptical that Edward IV now reigned in England, despite being shown a newly minted coin, and sent two of their number into England to confirm the change of king.[52] In the meantime, it seems the

47 *Six Town Chronicles*, p.147; *Three Fifteenth Century Chronicles*, p.72.

48 Wavrin, v., p.292; *An English Chronicle*, pp.86–8; *Letters and Papers*, ii (2)., p.772; Whethamstede, p.370; *The Brut*, i., p.529.

49 Wavrin, v., pp.305–7; TNA, C76/143, m. 4; BNF, Français 20683, fo. 51.

50 TNA, C76/143, m. 11.

51 TNA, E101/195/13, fo. 20; 196/2, fo. 31v.

52 Staffordshire History Centre, Stafford Great Cartulary, D.172/1/1, fos. 380v–1.

garrison continued to resist Warwick's command. In May 1461 soldiers from Hammes seized Spanish merchants based in Bruges and the Burgundians appear to have facilitated further negotiations between them and Warwick for their release, and that of English prisoners held in the castle.[53] Their commander, Sir John Marney, was evidently accommodated with the new regime and he and his wife received a pardon from Edward IV on 10 June.[54] As we have seen, twice, in April and in September 1461, men from Calais besieged the castle. The final siege, which lasted from 1 September to 12 December, was overseen by Sir Walter Blount, who had been appointed treasurer of Calais on 2 December the previous year. He had no fewer than 1,500 men under his command during this latter siege and the attackers 'broke' three large guns. On 24 October some of the garrison surrendered and, led by their constable, Thomas Huse, over 100 of the defenders were received into Edward IV's allegiance. However, diehard Lancastrian rebels remained an annoyance to the garrison even after the castle's surrender, mounting raids into the Pale from French-held territory. The following year an extra 33 archers were despatched to Guînes to protect the town from English rebels, aided by the French, who had raided the countryside and attempted to take the castle by force. Seventeen of the English 'thieves' were subsequently captured and hanged in Guînes Castle.[55]

York and Ireland

In returning to Ireland after Ludford Bridge, the Duke of York was also travelling to a place of perceived safety where he might use his own resources, and those of the crown, against his enemies at court. However, as with the Yorkist lords in Calais, his security in the lordship was not guaranteed.[56] York had been appointed the King's lieutenant in Ireland on 30 July 1447. His term was for 10 years, and he was to receive 4,000 marks for the first year and £2,000 annually thereafter. On its expiration, in 1457, his lieutenancy was renewed for another 10 years. Initially York had ruled by deputy, and it was not until July 1449 that he landed at Howth near Dublin. Later Yorkist chroniclers would categorise this time in Ireland as a banishment, that he had been 'exciled from oure soveraigne lords presens', but although York may have been slow to cross the Irish Sea when first appointed, it was a not sentiment he expressed himself. Once in Ireland York set about securing the submission of some of the leading Gaelic chieftains – although the long-term effectiveness of this might be questioned – and building links with the Anglo-Irish aristocracy. In October he summoned a Great Council to meet at Dublin, where concerns about law and order were heard and new arrangements were made for funding of the lieutenant's role. By May 1450 York was already owed £3,200 in arrears of wages and this problem plagued him and his administration throughout the remainder of the decade. York was careful to explain to his allies that any misgovernment was not his fault, but due to the lack of support from England. As his explained to the Earl of Salisbury in June 1450, 'it shall never be chronicled nor remaine in scripture (by the grace of God)

53 Archives Départementales du Nord, B.2041, unfoliated.

54 CPR 1461–67, p.11.

55 TNA, E101/195/14, fo. 10v; E101/196/2, fo. 34; C81/1488/187; DL37/32/67, 68.

56 For York in Ireland generally see Johnson, *Duke Richard of York*, pp.51–77; James L. Gillespie, 'Richard, Duke of York, as King's Lieutenant in Ireland: The White Rose A-Blooming', *The Ricardian*, 5 (1980), pp.194–201; Vincent John Gorman, 'The Public Career of Richard, Duke of York: A Case Study of the Nobility of the Fifteenth Century' (The Catholic University of America, PhD thesis, 1981), pp.119–67.

that Ireland was lost by my negligence'.[57] York returned to England in August 1450, in the wake of Cade's Rebellion, and would not return until forced to after his failure at Ludford Bridge.

One of the biggest problems facing English rule in Ireland in the late Middle Ages was the long-running feud between the great Anglo-Irish families of Butler (earls of Ormond) and Fitzgerald (earls of Desmond and Kildare). These feuds, which involved the principals, cadet branches of the families, and the native Irish to whom they were allied, destabilised political society within the English lordship, but also allowed political rivalries in England to be played out in Ireland. York's arrival in Ireland after Ludford Bridge exacerbated and gave a new dimension to the existing tensions there between the Butlers and the Fitzgeralds.[58] Following his attainder in the Coventry Parliament, York had been removed as lieutenant of Ireland and replaced by James Butler, Earl of Ormond and Wiltshire, on 4 December. Duke Richard ignored this and summoned a Parliament to meet in Drogheda in his own county of Meath instead of the usual venue of Dublin on 7 February 1460. It was soon adjourned and, perhaps with York feeling more secure, it re-assembled at Dublin towards the end of the month. The assembly confirmed his appointment as lieutenant and declared that acts made by the English Parliament had no force in Ireland unless confirmed by the Irish Parliament. It also enacted the minting of a new Irish currency, partly designed to stop the outflow of silver bullion to England and thereby strengthening York's precarious finances. By the end of its first session on 3 March, it had crucially enacted that any plot against the Duke or attempt on his life was to be considered high treason as if against the King himself.

York also renewed his links with the leading Anglo-Irish families, especially the Fitzgerald earls of Kildare and Desmond. Thomas, seventh Earl of Kildare, had served as the Duke's deputy since 1455. For him, alliance with Duke Richard afforded the opportunity to recover the Kildare estates that had been lost to the Butlers by the marriage of the fourth Earl of Ormond to the fifth Earl of Kildare's daughter and heir in 1432. The Lancastrian regime responded to York's arrival in Ireland by sending messengers to Ireland urging the Gaelic chieftains to wage war on his administration. York's reaction was harsh and immediate. Messengers from England bearing the King's letters of privy seal were arrested and executed for actions contrary to 'the liberties of Ireland'. Some Anglo-Irish office holders, such as Richard Bermingham of the Irish Exchequer, were dismissed for plotting against York, but the main threat came from the Gaelic Irish. The Duke secured from Parliament a military levy of one mounted archer from each £20 of land held in the lordship. This offered the potential for men to be used in any invasion of England, but, more importantly, it provided men to resist the Gaelic Irish and, for Kildare, to recover Fitzgerald estates lost to the Irish when the earldom had been in abeyance.

The Earl of Warwick arrived in Waterford on 16 March.[59] He and York remained in the town, missing the final session of the Dublin Parliament, which closed on 5 May, for several weeks. Little is known for certain of his deliberations with York, but they probably agreed on a multi-pronged attack to remove their enemies at court and worked out the details of a manifesto that would be issued from Calais the following month. York may even have considered an offer of support from Scotland made by James II. Their alliance would be sealed by the marriage of one of the Duke's sons, presumably the Earl of March, to one of the King's daughters. If the text of their manifesto

57 *Calendar of the Carew Manuscripts preserved in the Archiepiscopal Library at Lambeth*, ed. J.S. Brewer and William Bullen (6 volumes, London: HMSO, 1867–1873), v., pp.258–9.

58 Peter Crooks, 'Factions, Feuds and Noble Power in the Lordship of Ireland, c.1356–1496', *Irish Historical Studies*, 35 (2007), pp.425–55.

59 Cora L. Scofield, *The Life and Reign of Edward IV* (2 vols, London: Fonthill Media, 2016), i., p.59.

Ireland in the mid-fifteenth century, showing the extent of the English Pale around Dublin.

is to be believed, both the Duke and the earls remained loyal to Henry VI. If York had decided on his bid for the throne by this stage, there is no evidence he shared his intentions with Warwick. In the spring and early summer, prompted by letters from England, the Gaelic Irish had raided into Meath and Louth, defeating the levies sent against them. In early June a raiding party of about 400 men from the Anglo-Irish Power family and the Gaelic O'Driscolls assembled at Ballymacaw in County Waterford to ambush York as he made his way back to Dublin. Unfortunately, they were unaware that they had been spotted and, drunk on whisky as they waited for Duke Richard, they were surprised and routed by a party led by the Mayor of the nearby town of Waterford. In recognition of their support of the Yorkist cause, the townsmen of Waterford were rewarded with a renewed charter in November 1461.[60]

The planned attack at Ballymacaw, however, demonstrated how insecure York and his administration were in Ireland. It may be his desire to ensure the security of the lordship that delayed his return to England after news of the Yorkist victory at Northampton had reached Ireland in early July. In September another Gaelic army led by Sean O'Reilly, comprising perhaps 2,500 men and including both gallowglass, armed with battleaxes, and 'naked' – that is unarmoured – bowmen and spearmen, entered County Louth to despoil the 'lands of peace' between Dundalk and Drogheda. It was met by an Anglo-Irish army led by the Mayor of Drogehda which numbered fewer than 1,000 men. The force included the town militia and local levies and comprised 500 'chosen' archers, 200 men armed with poleaxes and bills and perhaps 70 horsemen. On 3 September, the Anglo-Irish army held a solemn mass at St Mary's Church, Drogheda, before marching out and meeting the enemy at Corbollis by Mapastown Bridge. The Irish were crushed, losing 300 or 400 men and all their leaders killed.[61]

This victory secured the lordship of Ireland for the Yorkists and put an end to the Gaelic raids encouraged by Wiltshire's men. More importantly, the Battle of Corbollis by Mapastown allowed Duke Richard to return to England. York sailed to England aboard the *Juilan* of Fowey, a ship left for him by Warwick back in May, suggesting perhaps that the Duke's departure was then expected imminently. It was not until 9 September 1460, however, accompanied by a small retinue dressed in his livery of blue and white and wearing the badge of the falcon and fetterlock, that York made landfall in the Wirral, arriving in Chester four days later. From there he made his way to London, via his estates in the Welsh marches, Gloucester and Abingdon, to the fateful Parliament that had assembled at Westminster on 7 October.

* * *

There can be little doubt that control of Calais in the autumn of 1459 saved the Yorkist cause. It is difficult to see how York could have led a successful invasion of England from Ireland, whereas Warwick had the military, naval and, through the close connections to London's mercantile community, economic resources in Calais to reestablish the Yorkist cause and lead a return to England in the summer of 1460. The Calais lords' dominance of the Channel prevented the Lancastrians from supplying and reinforcing Somerset's attempts to regain the English Pale. Once

60 Randolph Jones, 'The Battle of Ballymacaw and its Aftermath: Fresh Perspectives on Waterford's role during the Lancaster–York Struggle in Ireland, 1460–62', *Decies*, 72 (2016), pp.1–23.

61 Randolph Jones, 'How Drogheda Won its Civic Sword in the 1460s: the Battle of Corbollis by Mapastown Bridge and its Aftermath', *Journal of the Old Drogheda Society*, 23 (2017), pp.120–55.

established in Kent, it was a just a few days' march through friendly territory to London. Calais was also a barometer of how neighbouring European princes would react to events in England. Warwick worked hard to maintain good relations with both the French and Burgundians, and he was able to deny foreign assistance to Somerset's efforts to retake Calais through both careful diplomacy and military means.

Sources and Further Reading

The London chronicles showed a keen interest in events in Calais, but it was Jean de Wavrin who provided much of the detail of what happened there. Wavrin's account of these months was written a decade or so later, after Warwick's death in 1471, and formed a separate section in his *Receuil des croniques*. Although it is biased towards the Earl, Wavrin had 'some special knowledge about Warwick's doings' and is our best source for this episode.[62] Our knowledge of the Yorkist earls' military activities can be supplemented from the accounts of the treasurer and victualler of Calais, preserved in The National Archives. For Warwick's activities in the Channel and the nature of his 'piracy', see now the important article in *Southern History* (2022) by Penny Tucker. English and continental sources seem to have little idea of what happened in Ireland during 1459–60. The remarkable labours of Randolph Jones among the scattered records of the lordship, however, allow a reconsideration of events in Ireland in these months and its importance in securing the eventual Yorkist victory.

62 Visser-Fuchs, *History as Pastime*, p.406.

5

The Battle of Northampton

The Yorkist lords' platform in the summer of 1460 was based upon an unambiguous appeal to the commons, precisely what the author of the *Somnium Vigilantis* had accused them of the previous year. Days before their landing at Sandwich the manifesto, which York and Warwick had drafted in Ireland, was distributed in Kent. It was addressed to Archbishop Bourchier 'and at large to the Communes of Engelond'. It rehearsed the familiar grievances of unjust taxation, maladministration of justice and the poverty of the King, echoing the articles issued by Warwick in 1459. It blamed the ills of the realm on evil counsellors – named as the earls of Shrewsbury and Wiltshire and Viscount Beaumont – who were the Yorkists' sworn enemies, determined to enrich themselves at the King's expense and working 'to thentent of oure destruccion and of our yssew'. The manifesto, however, was no mere recital of the familiar cliches of noble opposition to royal government. Specific clauses accused their enemies of impressing men 'for the kyngis garde', of conspiring with the French to betray Calais, and of sending privy seal letters to Gaelic Irish enemies of the crown inviting them to attack the English lands there, 'whyche neuer kyng of Englond dyd heretofore'. The evil counsellors, if allowed to remain at the King's side, would deliver the realm 'into the hands and gouernaunce of the seyde enemyes'. The Yorkist lords pledged the 'trew hert that God knoweth we euer haue borne, and bere, to the profyte of the kyngis estate, to the commone wele of the same reame, and defens therof'. This propaganda campaign was coordinated and widespread. As the Yorkist lords swept up through Kent an elaborate verse ballad, praising Salisbury, March and, above all, Warwick ('that noble knyght and floure of manhode … sheelde of our defence'), appeared on the gates of Canterbury.[1] To reinforce their appeal to the ordinary men and women of the county, the Yorkist lords also reissued in the name 'of the commones of Kent' one of the manifestoes circulated by Jack Cade 10 years earlier.[2]

In contrast, the Lancastrians singularly failed in the propaganda war. The Earl of Wiltshire had equipped five ships in Southampton to prevent a Yorkist landing, but this was presented by the pro-Yorkist London chroniclers as a cynical attempt to escape to the Low Countries with his treasure. More dangerously for the Lancastrians, news spread that they had arrested and executed for treason several of York's tenants in his town of Newbury. This, it was claimed, led the commons of Kent, 'dredyng the malice and the tyranny of the forseyde Erll of Wylshyre', to appeal to the rebel lords to come from Calais. When the Yorkist lords knew the 'trew hartes of the peple', they

1 *An English Chronicle*, pp.82–8.
2 *John Vale's Book*, pp.210–12.

crossed the Channel.[3] Salisbury, Warwick and March arrived outside Canterbury on the evening of 26 June. The county had mustered under three 'famous men of Kent', John Fogge, John Scott and Robert Horne, to defend the city against the Yorkist lords. Scott was the stepson of the Lancastrian treasurer of Calais and treasurer of the king's household, Sir Gervase Clifton, while Horne was an old soldier who had served the Earl of Shrewsbury's father in France. Nevertheless, the three men met with the Yorkist lords and after some negotiation 'they discussed peace and reached a conditional agreement'.[4] The way was open for the earls to march on London.

On 28 June the Mayor of London sent a delegation of aldermen asking the earls to avoid the city and, at first, it looked as if the citizens might resist them, placing cannon on London Bridge. The aldermen returned on 1 July with news that the Yorkist lords were determined to enter the city, which they duly did the next day. Many in the city were sympathetic to the Yorkist cause, while others had already invested in the earls' success by making loans to support Warwick in Calais. Over the subsequent months the Londoners lent over £11,000 to the Yorkist lords. The earls were met in Southwark by the bishops of Ely and Exeter and escorted across London Bridge, before making their way to St Paul's to give thanks for their safe arrival. The following day, while their army camped near Smithfield, the earls returned to the cathedral to address the assembled bishops and clergy of the southern convocation. In an elaborate ritual, they swore on the cross of St Thomas not to take up arms against Henry VI. Most importantly, Archbishop Bourchier and the bishops of Ely, Exeter, Lincoln, London and Salisbury agreed to intercede with the King on the earls' behalf.[5] They must have hoped that they could sway the bishops who were present at the royal court, led by the chancellor, Bishop Waynflete of Winchester, to counsel King Henry and avoid further bloodshed.

The meeting with the southern clergy was also notable because of the intervention of the papal legate, Francesco Coppini, who recited the letter he had written to the King admonishing him for not negotiating with the Yorkist lords. Coppini, Bishop of Terni, had been sent by Pope Pius II to England in June 1459 with instructions to persuade the English to join – and contribute money towards – a crusade against the Ottomans. He was also to offer to mediate between the rival noble factions. Coppini met the King at Coventry but appears to have made no headway with either of his missions. In December he persuaded the Pope to make him a papal legate, giving him wider powers especially with regard to the special papal taxation which he was authorised to levy in February 1460. His entreaties, it seems, were further rebuffed by Queen Margaret, and in March he left England for Calais, where he met Warwick. Coppini was impressed by the Earl and persuaded, it seems, by the Yorkist lords' arguments. The legate left for Bruges, where he remained until the earls crossed the Channel to Sandwich. On 25 June they wrote to Coppini, asking him to return and intervene with the King on their behalf. He wrote at least two, probably three, letters to Henry VI demanding that he gave the Yorkist lords a chance to protest their loyalty to him. A final letter, agreed by the convocation of the southern clergy at St Paul's, was dispatched to the King on 4 July as the legate travelled towards Northampton.[6]

---

3 *An English Chronicle*, pp.85–6; *John Benet's Chronicle*, p.46.

4 *John Stone's Chronicle: Christ Church Priory, 1417–1472*, ed. Meriel Connor (Kalamazoo, MI: Medieval Institute Publications, 2010), p.104. For Horne see *The House of Commons, 1422–1461*, iv., pp.995–8. For Fogge and Scott see Josiah C. Wedgwood, *History of Parliament: Biographies of the Members of the Commons House 1439–1509* (London: HMSO, 1936), pp.339–42, 750–2.

5 *An English Chronicle*, pp. ; *Three Fifteenth Century Chronicles*, pp.73–4; *Letters and Papers*, ii(2)., pp.772–3.

6 A. Gottlob, 'Des Nuntius Franz Coppini Antheil an der Entthronung des Königs Heinrich VI. und seine Verurtheilung bei der Römischen Curie', *Deutsche Zeitschrift für Geschichtswissenschaft*, 4 (1890), pp.75–111

The Battle of Northampton

The Lancastrians seem to have been rather desultory in their preparations for the expected invasion from Calais and the inevitable confrontation with the Yorkist lords. Exeter's promise to keep the seas had come to nothing, and the Earl of Northumberland and other northern lords loyal to the court seem to have been slow to mobilise their resources. On 28 April, the crown issued commissions throughout the country to various nobles, led by the dukes of Buckingham, Exeter and Norfolk, the earls of Northumberland, Shrewsbury and Wiltshire, and Viscount Beaumont, to muster men and resist the rebels. The mayors of Winchelsea and Southampton were specifically instructed to resist an expected invasion. Watches and beacons had been established in the south-west as early as February in expectation of a landing, and numerous commissions of enquiry throughout the realm attempted to assess the extent of pro-Yorkist plots. In February and March Prince Edward headed commissions to assemble the King's loyal subjects in Wales and the marcher counties and to arrest and punish Yorkist supporters who were 'wandering through Wales' and those who abetted them. Commissioners were also instructed to seize the Duke of York's castles and lands in the principality, Gloucestershire and Herefordshire. At the end of May a Yorkist landing was expected in Norfolk and royal commissioners were instructed to compel those who refused to mount watches to do so. Similarly, in early June commissions in Northumberland, Devon, Cornwall and Hampshire were appointed to arrest named individuals, presumably for their involvement in Yorkist plots.[7]

Despite this evident concern – even panic – over the imminent Yorkist invasion, there seems to have been little overt military preparation to resist them. On 2 March the Breton-turned-London merchant John Judde was commissioned to impress workmen for the King's ordnance.[8] Judde had been involved in supplying arms to the crown since 1449 and in 1459 he had taken custody of the artillery of the attainted Yorkist lords. On 22 June, while carrying guns and other equipment between St Albans and Dunstable, Judde was ambushed and killed. He had been one of the targets of Cade's rebels a decade previously, and his notoriety attracted the attention of several contemporary chroniclers. One remarked that he 'hadde maliciously ymagined and laboured to ordeyn and make all things for werr to the distruccion of the seid duke of yorke and all the other lordes and reported them for traitors, in greet violence was slayn after his demerit be yond seint albons and so wrechedly as a caitif ended his life'.[9] It is impossible to say how important Judde was to the military preparations of the Lancastrian court in the early summer of 1460, but, as we shall see, the failure of the Lancastrian artillery at Northampton may have had an impact on the outcome of the battle.

It is possible that the speed of the Yorkist lords' landing at Sandwich, their march on and subsequent capture of London, and their departure from the capital to confront the King, simply caught the Lancastrians by surprise. The Lancastrian garrison of the Tower of London, led by Thomas, Lord Scales, and Robert, Lord Hungerford, had attempted to take command of the city in anticipation of the earls' arrival. Their demand to have 'the rewle and gouvernaunce' of London was refused by the Mayor and aldermen and they retreated to the Tower. On 4 July the advance guard of the Yorkist army, led by Lord Fauconberg, left London. A day later the main Yorkist army, led by Warwick and accompanied by the Duke of Norfolk, the Earl of March and lords Abergavenny,

7 *Calendar of Patent Rolls, 1452–1461*, pp.602–6.
8 *Calendar of Patent Rolls, 1452–1461*, p.605.
9 *Six Town Chronicles*, p.149.

Audley, Saye and Sele, and Scrope of Bolton, marched north accompanied by their artillery. We cannot be certain of the size of the Yorkist host. As well as the core of soldiers brought from Calais, it must have principally consisted of men assembled through the commissions of array in the southern counties, with perhaps smaller contingents from East Anglia. According to Robert Bale, the Yorkist lords had been accompanied by only 500 horsemen when they arrived in London, but 60,000 footmen from Kent, Sussex and Surrey. The author of the 'Short English Chronicle' says they had with them 40,000. Both numbers are almost certainly exaggerations, but the Yorkists left London with a sizeable force.[10] At this point, they divided their forces: Fauconberg first marched to Ware in anticipation of a Lancastrian plan to spirit the King away to the Isle of Ely, while Warwick and the main army went on to St Albans. The two forces then met at Dunstable to carry along Watling Street into the Midlands. According to one London chronicle, Fauconberg arrived first in Northampton on 2 July, followed by Coppini the following day, and the earls of Warwick and March and Archbishop Bourchier on the 5th. Immediately, Warwick, March and a party of bishops then sent word to the King. They showed Henry and his lords the papal bulls demanding the reversal of the attainders made in the Coventry Parliament and threatening excommunication if these were not obeyed.[11]

Henry VI and his council were at Kenilworth when they learned of the landing of the Yorkist lords at Sandwich. From there the Lancastrians moved to Northampton, where they were already encamped when Fauconberg arrived on 2 July. The route from London to St Albans and on to Nottingham via Northampton was one of the main routes north in the fifteenth century, and it was outside Northampton that Henry and his lords decided to confront the rebel earls. Northampton may have been considered a Lancastrian stronghold, as in March the King had granted the town a new charter, partly 'for good services rendered ... in resisting certain rebels against the king'.[12] It is unclear precisely when the royal army arrived in Northampton, but it was some time before the Yorkists as they had time to pass through the town and establish their camp near the house of Cluniac nuns of St Mary-in-the-Meadow, now known as Delapré Abbey. There are no reliable estimates for the size of the Lancastrian force. Contemporaries estimated their host at between 50,000 and 20,000, but modern estimates of between 6,000 and 8,000 seem much more likely. All the chroniclers agree that they were outnumbered by the Yorkists, who likely numbered between 12,000 and 15,000 men. To mitigate the disadvantage of their smaller army, the Lancastrians made a fortified camp. The use of such fortified positions was not unknown – or even unusual – at this time. Cade's rebels had fortified their camp in 1450, as had the Duke of York at Dartford two years later, while in 1453 the Earl of Shrewsbury had been killed assaulting a fortified field position, protected by guns, at Castillon. The previous year, the Yorkists had made a fortified camp of their position at Ludlow. The Battle of Northampton, however, is the only clash of the Wars of the Roses where the decisive action took place around a field fortification.

Unusually for the battles of the Wars of the Roses, the location of the Battle of Northampton was recorded with some precision in the contemporary sources. The author of *An English Chronicle* placed the battle 'in the medowys beside the Nonry' with the King 'havyng the ryver at his back'. The Canterbury monk John Stone was even more precise, locating the battle between 'Cowemedowe', 'Menthynfeld', 'Sandyngford bregge' and a water mill called 'Sandford melle'. Writing shortly after

---

10 *Six Town Chronicles*, p.149; *Three Fifteenth Century Chronicles*, p.73.

11 G. Baskerville, 'A London Chronicle of 1460', *English Historical Review*, 28 (1913), pp.124–7.

12 *Calendar of Charter Rolls*, vi. 135–6; *Calendar of Patent Rolls, 1452–1461*, p.601.

1471, the author of 'A Short English Chronicle' stated that the battle took place 'in the Newfelde be twene Harsyngton [Hardingstone] and Sandyfforde', a location roughly that identified by John Benet a few years earlier. Jean Wavrin, who wrote two at times contradictory accounts of the battle, described how Henry's army was drawn up 'in a park outside the town by a little river'.[13] This was unlikely to have been the River Nene, still in the fifteenth century a substantial waterway navigable to the sea, and was more likely to have been the stream stemming from a natural spring which ran in front of the abbey and which in July 1460 was swollen by unseasonable rain. Nevertheless, modern historians have struggled to locate the battlefield precisely. It has usually been placed between the northern boundary of the abbey and the River Nene, a mile or two north-east of the abbey on the banks of the river, or south of the abbey in the area now covered by a golf course. It seems likely, however, that the Lancastrian fortified camp was to the south of the abbey, along the edge of the current golf course and parallel to the main London Road, rather than parallel with the abbey buildings across the ridge-and-furrow field system still visible today. Here the camp would have effectively blocked the Yorkists' advance and the Lancastrian artillery's field of fire would have been unobstructed by the abbey or any other buildings. The Yorkists took up position on the high ground facing and looking down upon the royal army, their right flank close to the Eleanor Cross (from where, John Stone tells us, Archbishop Bourchier observed the battle).[14]

The fullest account of the Battle of Northampton can be found in a section of Wavrin's *Recueil des chroniques* known as 'Warwick's Apology'. It stresses the Earl's leadership of the Yorkist cause, but some of its details are corroborated by other sources and it seems our best account of the events of 10 July. His second account, the so-called 'Short Account', seems less reliable, but again probably contains elements of truth. It is unclear what Wavrin's sources were for these accounts.[15] Neither features in other Franco-Burgundian chronicles of the period, although the French lawyer Jean de Roye included a very garbled account of Northampton in his chronicle of the reign of Louis XI, perhaps written in the mid-1460s.[16] As the Bishop of Bayeux complained to the Seneschal of Normandy, Pierre de Brezé, there was little news out of England in the summer of 1460 that did not come via Calais and Warwick's men. De Brezé had sent his own servant to monitor events in England, but he had been captured at Northampton and was not released until the autumn.[17] Both Wavrin and Whethamstede tell us that the Yorkist vanguard was commanded by Lord Fauconberg, with March and Warwick having command of the two other battles. They may have been accompanied by as many as eight other lords, including the Duke of Norfolk, the Earl of Arundel, Henry, Viscount Bourchier and lords Abergavenny, Audley, Clinton, Scrope of Bolton, and Saye and Sele.[18] Wavrin stated that the Yorkist earls met 'le seigneur de Scaulay' with 400 archers from Lancaster at St Albans. This may have been Warwick's brother-in-law, Thomas Stanley, who was knighted after the battle and first summoned to Parliament as Lord Stanley at the end of month, or his younger brother, William, who had been with Salisbury at Blore

13 *An English Chronicle*, p.90; John Stone's Chronicle, ed. Meriel Connor (Kalamazoo, MI: Medieval Institute Publications, 2010), p.105; *Three Fifteenth Century Chronicles*, p.74; *John Benet's Chronicle*, p.46; Wavrin, v., p.323.

14 Mike Ingram, 'The Battle of Northampton, 1460: a Re-Appraisal', *The Hobilar*, 82 (2010), pp.3–8.

15 'Warwick's Apology' runs from chapter 12 to chapter 34 of Book 3 of Volume 6 of the *Receuil*, with the account of Northampton at chapters 23–25: Wavrin, v., pp.271–317. The 'Short Account' is chapter 38 of the same book: Wavrin, v., pp.322–4.

16 BNF, MS Français 5062, fos. 1–1v.

17 BNF, MS Français 20428, fo. 64; *Œuvres Complètes de Duclos* (3 vols, Paris: A. Belin, 1820–1), ii., pp.509–10.

18 See appendix.

A view of the battlefield of Northampton, looking from the Eleanor Cross, across the modern golf course, down towards Delapré Abbey. (Graham Evans)

Heath.[19] As well as Archbishop Bourchier and the papal legate, four bishops and the prior of St John were also among the Yorkist party. The Lancastrians were led, of course, by King Henry VI, but effective command was in the hands of Humphrey Stafford, Duke of Buckingham. They were accompanied by the Earl of Shrewsbury, Viscount Beaumont and lords Egremont and Grey de Ruthin, as well as the bishops of Durham and Hereford. There were some notable Lancastrian absentees: the Earl of Wiltshire had contrived not to be present, while Somerset and Lord Roos were still holed up in Guînes and the Earl of Northumberland remained in the north. Only Wavrin in his 'Short Account' stated the Duke of Exeter was present, but it seems more likely that the feckless Holland was still licking his wounds after his embarrassment at sea the previous May or had been tasked with guarding the Queen in Coventry.[20]

Our sources for what happened next are fuller than for almost any other clash of arms of the Wars of the Roses, yet we are still largely reliant on Wavrin, and to a lesser extent *An English Chronicle* and Abbot Whethamstede, for the course of the battle. Wavrin and *An English Chronicle* agree that the Yorkist lords first sent a delegation led by John Lowe, Bishop of Rochester. He was to

19 Stanley had succeeded to this father's estates the previous year but had not been summoned to the Coventry Parliament in November 1459. Indeed, he narrowly escaped attainder for his role at Blore Heath, see above p.41.

20 Wavrin, v., p.323. See appendix.

tell the King that the rebel lords had come to 'deliver him from the hands of his enemies' and warn the Duke of Buckingham to leave the King's camp. Unsurprisingly, this met with a cold reception from Buckingham, who would not allow the Yorkist delegation to address Henry directly. According to *An English Chronicle*, Buckingham told them, '"Ye come nat as byshoppes forto trete for pease but as men of armes", because they brought with thaym a notable company of men of armes. They answered and sayde, "We come thus for our suerte of our persones for they that beth about the kyng byth nat our frendes."' Buckingham responded that Warwick would not be allowed to come into the King's presence, 'and yef he come he shall dye'.[21] One London chronicler claimed that the Yorkist lords were granted an audience 'and boldy entered the tent of the king, and were graciously received by him', but this seems unlikely.[22] The Lancastrian response was predictable and spoke to the deep animosity and lack of trust that characterised both sides. Yet it is also clear that the delegation had the opportunity to inspect the royal camp, noting 'the great preparation of men at arms and artillery and the great ditches they made around the camp in which the water of the river flowed, which [water] encircled the whole camp'.[23]

Warwick, who both *An English Chronicle* and Wavrin present as the leader of the Yorkist party, then sent his herald to the Lancastrian camp. Earl Richard offered to come unarmed into the King's presence to plead his cause but this entreaty was again rebuffed by Buckingham. According to *An English Chronicle*, Warwick then sent a third message, saying that he would speak to the King at two in the afternoon 'or ells dye in the feeld'.[24] *An English Chronicle* is clear that the Yorkist assault on the Lancastrian camp began promptly after the expiration of Warwick's ultimatum at two in the afternoon. In 'Warwick's Apology', Wavrin related how Warwick ordered two Yorkist captains, John Stafford and Lord Scrope of Bolton, to begin the attack, but in his later 'Short Account' he stated that there was an earlier encounter between the Yorkist forces and some 1,300–1,400 Lancastrians led by 'le seigneur de Greriffin' outside the gates of Northampton. Wavrin listed 'le seigneur de Greriffin' among the Lancastrian dead, suggesting he may have meant Lord Egremont, who was not mentioned otherwise. His second account is very garbled, however, as it also placed the dukes of Exeter and Somerset and the Earl of Northumberland at Northampton.[25] A newsletter written in Bruges also suggested that there was a skirmish outside the Lancastrian camp, which was flooded because of the recent heavy rainfall.[26] No other contemporary sources mentioned this prelude to the main Yorkist attack on the King's camp, but Edward Hall, writing in the 1540s, stated the battle began with a clash between the Yorkist vanguard and Viscount Beaumont on the evening of 9 July. It has been suggested that these accounts describe the Yorkist vanguard, led by Lord Scrope of Bolton and Sir John Stafford, skirmishing ahead of the main force up to the gates of Northampton and burning part of the town. Although the town would later plead poverty and gain a 20-year remission from its fee farm from Edward IV, there is no contemporary documentary evidence to confirm this interpretation. Indeed, it seems more likely that the poverty was caused by Lancastrian depredations in 1461.[27]

21 *An English Chronicle*, p.90.
22 Baskerville, 'A London Chronicle', p.125.
23 Wavrin, v., p.297.
24 *An English Chronicle*, p.90.
25 Wavrin, v., pp.323–4.
26 *Calendar of State Papers, Milan*, p.27.
27 Mike Ingram, *The Battle of Northampton* (Northampton: Northampton Battlefields Society, 2015), pp.85–6; *Hall's Chronicle*, p.244. See below pp.116-17.

The Battle of Northampton, in fact, was probably a short and decidedly one-sided affair. At two in the afternoon, true to his word, Warwick gave the order to attack the royal camp. A cry went through the Yorkist host to spare the King and commons and only harm the lords, knights and esquires in the royal army. It is likely that the recent rain had indeed weakened the Lancastrian defences. As *An English Chronicle* related, 'The ordenaunce of the kyngis gonnes avayled nat, for that day was so grete rayn that the gonnes lay depe in water, and so were queynt and might nat be shott.'[28] Treachery, however, determined the victor at Northampton. According to Wavrin's longer account, orders had been given in advance that those wearing the black ragged staff, the livery of Edmund, Lord Grey de Ruthin, were to be spared 'for they were men who were to give them entry into the camp'. Several sources agree that Lord Grey, instead of resisting the Yorkist attackers, helped them over the ramparts. Writing from St Albans, Abbot Whethamstede described how 'when the [Yorkist] troops came to the ditch before the rampart and wanted to climb over it, which they could not do quickly because of the height, Lord Grey himself met them with his men and, extending his right hand, hauled them into the embattled field'.[29] In his second 'Short Account', Wavrin added that some of the King's gunners loaded charges but no shot in their guns. Whatever the extent of the treachery, the Lancastrian position appears to have soon collapsed. Wavrin stated the fighting lasted three hours, but other sources claimed it lasted only 30 minutes. An *English Chronicle* recounted how in the immediate aftermath 'many were slayne, and many were fled, and were drouned in the ryuer', while Wavrin wrote that Grey's defection led to 'great slaughter' with some 12,000 killed. The author of 'A Short English Chronicle' repeated the story that 'many comyners were drowned', while 'Gregory's Chronicle' also stated that many were drowned 'bysyde the fylde in the reuyr at a mylle'. Drowning while attempting to flee a battle was a common fate for chroniclers to ascribe to defeated combatants in medieval battles.[30] Another London chronicler, Robert Bale, may have been closer to the mark, however, when he reported that the Lancastrians had lost only 50 men killed, while a mere eight Yorkists had fallen. The small number of casualties is also suggested by a newsletter composed in Bruges shortly after the battle, which reported that 'without a serious fight, or much slaughter, Warwick very soon had the king in his power'. A contemporary English poem also expressed surprise at 'so few men slain in so great a fight'.[31]

Nevertheless, and in accordance with Warwick's pre-battle instructions, the Lancastrian leadership paid a heavy toll for its opposition to the Yorkist lords. Buckingham, Shrewsbury, Beaumont and Egremont were all killed 'besyde the kyngis tent'. Wavrin adds the Cambridgeshire knight Sir Thomas Fynderne, the erstwhile captain of Guînes Castle, to the list of prominent Lancastrian dead. In fact, Fynderne, a retainer of the Duke of Buckingham, survived the battle and went on to fight at Towton, going into exile with the Lancastrians before being captured and executed after the Battle of Hedgeley Moor in 1464.[32] One prominent Lancastrian who was captured at Northampton, however, was the lawyer Thomas Thorpe. Thorpe had been identified in the 1455 Parliament as one of the three men responsible for preventing the Yorkist lords' declaration of loyalty from reaching the King; four years later he was one of the architects of the Act of Attainder against York and his followers. According to a petition presented later by his son, he was imprisoned

28 *An English Chronicle*, p.91.

29 Wavrin, v., p.299; Whethamstede, p.374.

30 Wavrin, v., p.323; *An English Chronicle*, p.91; *Three Fifteenth Century Chronicles*, p.74; *Contemporary English Chronicles*, p.67.

31 *Six Town Chronicles*, p.151; *Calendar of State Papers, Milan*, p.27; *Historical Poems*, ed. Robbins, pp.210–15.

32 Wavrin, v. 300; *The House of Commons, 1422–1461*, iv., pp.498–501.

in London, but on 17 February the following year he escaped, only to be captured and murdered by a group of Kentishmen near Highgate.[33] The story of a more unfortunate casualty of the Battle of Northampton is related in 'Gregory's Chronicle'. Sir William Lucy of nearby Dallington had donned his armour and made for the King's camp when he had heard 'the gonneschotte', probably the opening salvoes of the Yorkist artillery. By the time he arrived at the field, however, the fighting was over. The chronicler continues 'one of the Staffordys was ware of hys comynge, and louyd that knyghtys wyffe and hatyd hym, and anon causyd hys dethe'.[34] Three years earlier, Lucy had married Margaret, the granddaughter of John Montagu, Earl of Salisbury, and a kinswoman by marriage of both the Earl of Wiltshire and Duke of Somerset. His bride, at just 17, was some 40 years his junior and offered the childless Lucy the possibility of a male heir after two previous barren marriages. Quite how John Stafford, an obscure Worcestershire esquire, knew Margaret and whether this was a crime of passion or one motivated by the generous jointure of 12 manors, including Dallington, that Lucy had settled on his wife, we cannot tell, but the incident was notable enough to attract the notice of two contemporary chroniclers. Stafford went on to be elected as one of the MPs for Northamptonshire later that month and fought for the Yorkists at the Second Battle of St Albans and at Towton, where he lost his life, leaving poor Margaret a widow whose hand was eagerly sought by other ambitious suitors.[35]

Once the fighting had stopped the victorious Yorkist lords made their way to the King's tent. *An English Chronicle* provided an account of the speech they delivered to the King:

> Most noble prince, dysplease yow nat, though it haue pleased God of His grace to graunt vs the vyctory of oure mortall enemyes, the whyche by theyre venymous malice haue vntrewly stered and moued youre hyghnesse to exyle vs oute of youre londe, and wolde vs haue out to fynall shame and confusyone. We come nat to that entent forto inquyete ne greue your sayde hyhgnesse, but forto please your moste noble personne, desiring moste tenderly the hygh welfare and prosperyte thereof, and all your reame, and forto be youre trew lyegemen, whyle oure lyfes shall endure.[36]

According to the pro-Yorkist author of this chronicle, the King was 'gretely recomforted' by the earls' approach, although even this most forgiving of monarchs could not fail to appreciate the significance of the death of his leading counsellor, Buckingham, and other Lancastrians. Henry was taken to Northampton, where he remained for three days before returning to London with the victorious Yorkists, arriving in the capital on 16 July.

The Duke of York's Return

When Warwick, March and Fauconberg had left London on 4 and 5 July, they had done so in the knowledge that the Tower of London was still held by its Lancastrian garrison. The Earl of Salisbury, who was appointed 'ruler and governor' of the city by its inhabitants, John, Lord Cobham

33 *The House of Commons, 1422–1461*, vii., pp.58–72.
34 *Contemporary English Chronicles*, p.67.
35 *The House of Commons, 1422–1461*, v., pp.323–31; vi., pp.692–3.
36 *An English Chronicle*, p.91.

and Sir John Wenlock remained behind to defend London against the Lancastrians in the Tower. The Tower's garrison contained men with extensive experience of the wars in France, including Thomas, Lord Scales, Henry Brounflete, Lord Vessy, the Gascon John de Foix, styled Earl of Kendal, and the former treasurer of Calais and now treasurer of the King's household, Sir Gervase Clifton. They were joined by the new Lord Hungerford, Robert (first summoned to Parliament the previous year), the young John, Lord Lovell and, according to one source, Richard, Lord de la Warre.[37] More importantly, many of the leading defenders were individuals who had spent almost their entire careers in the personal service of Henry VI or his father. The Tower was a formidable fortress and there was little realistic prospect of taking it by assault. The Yorkists and the Londoners established a blockade by land and the river. Attempts to negotiate the garrison's surrender proved fruitless and from 4 July the defenders began to shoot guns into the city. The author of *An English Chronicle* described how they 'caste wylde fyre into the cyte, and shot in smale gonnes, and brend and hurte men and wymmen and children in the stretes'.[38] While the author's Yorkist bias cannot be underestimated, his account probably reflects the Londoners' attitude towards the Tower's defenders, and their actions can hardly have endeared the citizens to the Lancastrian cause.

Now the besiegers divided their forces into two to attack the Tower. Lord Cobham and the city militia, led by the sheriffs, attacked from the west, while Wenlock and a force led by the merchant John Harow came from St Katherine's by the Tower to the east of the fortress. Heavy bombards were set up on the southern bank of the Thames and on the city side, and these pounded the Tower's walls. The defenders did not sit idly by, however, and launched several raids, on one occasion seizing a boat laden with wine and fish near St Katherine's Wharf. The Lancastrians also had their friends in the city. On 10 July a group of Londoners, led by one William Barton, entered the Tower to assist the garrison. Negotiations between the city's leaders and the garrison continued, but news of the Yorkist victory at Northampton rendered the defenders' position untenable. According to Wavrin, the ladies present in the Tower pleaded with Scales to come to terms and negotiations began between the defenders and Salisbury, mediated by the Mayor of London. On 16 July articles of surrender were agreed and three days later Wenlock took custody of the Tower. Most of the defenders were taken into captivity, but Lord Scales, according to the author of 'A Short English Chronicle', was allowed to leave by Sir John Wenlock, perhaps out of respect for his service in France. Scales headed for sanctuary in Westminster Abbey, but he was recognised by a woman as he attempted to escape and was captured and killed by boatmen who left his corpse, 'nakyd as a worme', on the banks of the river by St Mary's Overy. *An English Chronicle* captured the sense of tragedy: 'And gret pyte it was that so noble and so worshypfull a knight, and well so approued in the warrys of Normandy and Fraunce, should dye so myscheuously.'[39] Others faced retribution. Sir Thomas Brown, the Lancastrian sheriff of Kent, and five others were convicted of high treason before the earls of Salisbury and Warwick and were hanged, drawn and quartered for their part in the defence of the Tower. Several others successfully pleaded pardons, while the sheriffs of London returned the names of 81 other named defenders, almost all Londoners, who could not be found to answer the charges against them.[40]

37 See appendix.

38 *Three Fifteenth Century Chronicles*, p.73; *An English Chronicle*, p.91.

39 *Contemporary English Chronicles*, p.70; *An English Chronicle*, pp.91–2; *Three Fifteenth Century Chronicles*, p.75; Wavrin, v., p.304; *Letters and Papers*, ii(2), pp.773–4.

40 Sean Cunningham, 'Narratives of the Siege of the Tower of London in July 1461', in *Loyalty Binds Me*, ed. Richard Asquith and Christian Steer (Donington: Yorkist History Trust, 2025), pp.174–182.

The Yorkist lords now found themselves in a similar situation to the one they faced in the aftermath of the First Battle of St Albans. They were in control of the King and government by force of arms. Their response was similar: George Neville, Bishop of Exeter, replaced Archbishop Bourchier as chancellor, while Viscount Bourchier was appointed treasurer in place of the dead Earl of Shrewsbury. On this occasion, however, the King's household was also purged and Salisbury's younger son, John Neville, was appointed chamberlain. On 30 July the chancellor despatched writs summoning a new Parliament to assemble at Westminster on 7 October. The realm now awaited the return of the Duke of York from Ireland. In the meantime, there was an uneasy peace between the Yorkist-controlled government and the Lancastrians loyalists, especially in Wales and the north of England. In Wales, the commanders of important castles, such as Roger Puleston at Denbigh, were instructed by the new government to keep their fortresses secure and deliver them only to such men as they were commanded to do so by the King. The Yorkist partisans William Herbert, Walter Devereux and Roger Vaughan were ordered to move against certain persons who had seized castles in the principality. In the north of England a powerful commission headed by the Duke of York and the earls of March, Salisbury and Warwick, and including Salisbury's younger sons and several of his retainers, was appointed on 26 August to arrest 'oppressors, plunderers and slayers of the king's people' in York, while two days earlier the Earl of Northumberland and his servants had been ordered to deliver the castles of Pontefract and Wressle to Salisbury. Similar commissions were issued throughout the realm. In Rutland, for example, the JPs were instructed to arrest certain named individuals 'who, with other evildoers go about Rutland, spoiling, lying in wait and accusing others of treason.' The government's orders probably met widespread resistance. Salisbury's messenger, for instance, was murdered when he delivered the writ ordering the Earl of Northumberland to surrender Wressle Castle. Both sides spent the summer preparing themselves for further conflict, and on 14 August the new master of the ordnance, Thomas Vaughan, was commissioned to make search for royal artillery remaining in private hands and take custody of it.[41]

Writs for a new Parliament had been issued on 30 July. The lords temporal and spiritual and the Commons took their seats at Westminster on 7 October and Parliament was opened by the new chancellor in the presence of the King. The dukes of Somerset and Exeter, although summoned, did not attend; nor did the Earl of Northumberland and several other northern lords. The principal task of the new assembly was to annul the acts of the Coventry Parliament, which had attempted 'to distroy certayne of the grete, noble and faithfull true lordes and estates of youre blode'.[42] In fact, the King's council had already begun to overturn the forfeitures imposed upon the Yorkist lords and their followers in the summer, and it is likely that royal proclamations had already been made throughout the realm declaring that the Yorkist lords were not traitors. The usual business of Parliament was, however, soon superseded by the arrival of Richard, Duke of York. York had landed in Cheshire on 9 September. His journey across England had been leisurely but, according to one of John Paston's correspondents, the Duke had been issued 'dyuers straunge commyssions fro the kyng to sitte in dyuers townys' on the way, punishing them for their loyalty to the Lancastrians.[43] The pace of York's progress from Cheshire to London can only have fuelled speculation as to his intentions. As Abbot Whethamstede observed, 'Some said that

41 *Calendar of Patent Rolls, 1452–61*, pp.610–12; TNA, C49/32/8.

42 *Parliament Rolls of Medieval England*, Parliament of October 1460, item 8.

43 *Paston Letters and Papers*, ed. Davis, ii., p.216.

his arrival was peaceful … yet others, including those who were older and wiser, suspected that he meant to act litigiously against the king for the royal crown and claim it for himself by title of hereditary right.'[44]

York arrived at Westminster at ten in the morning on Friday, 10 October. In the presence of the lords, the Duke laid his hand on the throne and announced, 'that he purposed nat to ley daune his swerde but to challenge his right … and purposed that no man shuld haue denyed the croune fro his hed'.[45] But instead of popular acclamation Duke Richard met with general consternation. Archbishop Bourchier asked if he wished to see the King, to which York replied that he could think of no one who ought not rather come to see him. The Duke's bold, even brash, move had backfired; it did not meet with the public support of even his closest friends, never mind those lords hostile to York assembled in Parliament. On 16 October Duke Richard was forced to submit a formal, written case. This was based entirely on his descent from Lionel of Clarence and a rejection of any legitimacy in the Lancastrian claim. The lords hesitated and passed the matter to the King. Henry prevaricated further: 'in so moche as his seid highnes had seen and understouden many dyvers writyngs and cronicles', he asked York to do the same and present more evidence in support of his claim.[46] Two days later the lords passed the matter to the judges, who claimed that matters touching the King's estate were for the lords not them. The lords turned next to the sergeants of law who, unsurprisingly, said that matters outside the competence of the judges were also too high for them. Finally, on 25 October the lords came up with a compromise. Henry was to remain King, but on his death the throne was to be settled on York and his heirs. The duchy of Lancaster, it seems, was to remain with Henry and pass to his son.

The dispassionate recording on the Act of Accord on the Parliament Roll obscures what was a probably a bitter row between York and his allies. His desire to be crowned king was probably in the first instance undone by the refusal of Archbishop Bourchier to participate in any coronation, but Duke Richard almost certainly also faced opposition from Warwick. It seems inconceivable that the two men had not discussed York's claim to the throne in their meeting the previous March, and Warwick may initially have backed the Duke's action. Indeed, Warwick and March acquiesced in Duke Richard's brazen rejection of Henry VI's authority and royal title once he had landed in England.[47] Nevertheless, when faced with overwhelming opposition from the bishops and the rest of the Parliamentary peerage, it seems that that both earls may have wavered in their support for York. Indeed, up to the Battle of Northampton and throughout the summer of 1460, the whole platform upon which the Yorkist lords had campaigned was one of loyalty to the King and a determination to work for the commonweal. This was at once undone by York's actions; his opponents were now confirmed in their opinion that the entire decade of resistance had been driven by the Duke's ambition and pride. His own defence of his position was feeble: York was absolved from breaking the oaths of allegiance and promises to eschew 'the wey of fayt' he had made throughout the 1450s because they were against God's law. He had, in fact, been rightfully king all along. It was a sentiment that few appear to have shared.

* * *

44 Whethamstede, p.376.
45 Johnson, *Duke Richard of York*, pp.213–14.
46 *Parliament Rolls of Medieval England*, Parliament of October 1460, item 12.
47 Michael K. Jones, 'Edward IV, the Earl of Warwick and the Yorkist Claim to the Throne', *Historical Research*, 70 (1997), pp.342–52.

The Battle of Northampton was the culmination of a remarkable journey and recovery by the Yorkist lords based in Calais. Their campaign from the landing at Sandwich on 26 June to the outskirts of Northampton just two weeks later demonstrated the same dynamic leadership that the Earl of Warwick, Lord Fauconberg, and Edward, Earl of March, had shown in defeating the Lancastrian attempts to wrest Calais from their control in the previous months. While the relatively bloodless victory was won as much through the treachery of Lord Grey of Ruthin as it was by the prowess of the Calais lords, it nevertheless catapulted Warwick to the forefront of national events. Crucially, while the murder of Beaumont and Egremont removed two implacable enemies of the Yorkist lords, the death of Buckingham lost the principal voice of moderation on the Lancastrian side. In the summer of 1460, the fame of Warwick and March threatened to eclipse Richard, Duke of York. The relatively stable government they ran throughout the summer of 1460, with the King effectively under Warwick's control, was shattered by York's return from Ireland. The Yorkist lords surely cannot have planned for Duke Richard to lay claim to the throne when they landed in June, and there seems to have been genuine shock and surprise among his allies at his actions. Yet there was a grim inevitability to it all: York claiming the throne, the rest of the lords being unable to depose an anointed king who they had publicly sworn loyalty to less than a year before, and another compromise that could not reconcile the Yorkist and Lancastrian positions. Indeed, events in the north would soon lay bare the lie that there could be a peaceful settlement of the question of who should rule England.

Sources and Further Reading

The fullest account of the Battle of Northampton, not least because it collects and translates the main primary sources (particularly both accounts of the battle by Jean de Wavrin), is Mike Ingram's *Battle of Northampton*. It was published in 2015 by the Northamptonshire Battlefield Society, who have done so much to preserve and protect the battlefield. An excellent account of the Yorkist siege of the Tower of London can be found in Dan Spencer, *The Castle in the Wars of the Roses* (Barnsley: Pen & Sword 2020). The debate over the Duke of York's intentions and his claim to the throne in 1460 is best surveyed in Paul Johnson's seminal 1988 study of his life and career.

6

The 'Battle' of Wakefield

Queen Margaret, accompanied by her son and a small household, had waited at Coventry while the King and the Lancastrian army had confronted the Yorkist lords at Northampton. On receiving news of the battle's outcome, she immediately made her way towards Wales, via Eccleshall in Staffordshire, where she probably lodged with John Hales, Bishop of Coventry and Lichfield. In Wales, she sought refuge with Jasper Tudor, Earl of Pembroke. The journey was not without incident. Near Malpas in Cheshire, the Queen was robbed of her jewels and goods worth some 10,000 marks (£6,666 13*s.* 4*d.*), either by retainers of the Stanleys or by one of her own servants. Soon afterwards, Margaret arrived at Harlech, where she was greeted warmly, before travelling on to Denbigh and Pembroke's protection.[1] There is no doubt that as summer wore on the Yorkist lords became more concerned about the Queen's plans. On 9 August they instructed, in the King's name, 'our right trusty and entirely welbeloved brother Therl of Pembroke' to deliver Denbigh Castle to his deputy and 'accept our right trusty and entirely welbeloved cousyn the Duc of York our approved and true liege man and noo traytour, our true subget and noo rebell, our right faithful frende and no one ennemye'. The reception of this command in Wales was predictable enough, and eight days later William Herbert, Walter Devereux and Roger Vaughan were dispatched to Wales to subdue the rebels.[2]

Just as concerning as events in Wales was the news that the Scottish king, James II, had crossed the border and was laying siege to Roxburgh Castle. Plans were made for the Earl of Salisbury to go north, and northern lords were commissioned to raise men to resist the invaders. Fortune intervened, however, on 3 August, when James was killed by one of his own cannons exploding, leaving the Scottish throne to his nine-year-old son, James III. James's death precipitated a Scottish withdrawal from the borders and alleviated the immediate need for Salisbury to go north with a relieving army. Queen Margaret's precise movements in the autumn of 1460 are unclear, but by October she had been joined by the Duke of Exeter (although he may well have accompanied her to Wales immediately after Northampton).[3] Margaret sought a safe conduct from Charles VII of France, who reluctantly granted one on 20 October while urging her to stay put for as long as she could. However, when the French ambassadors reached Wales, they learned the Queen had already left, and in early December Margaret arrived in Dumfries before making her way to

1 *Contemporary English Chronicles*, pp.68–9.
2 *Proceedings and Ordinances of the Privy Council*, vi., pp.302–5.
3 *Paston Letters and Papers*, ed. Davis, ii., pp.216–7; G. du Fresne de Beaucourt, vi., pp.291–2.

nearby Lincluden Priory to meet the Scottish regent, Mary of Guelders.[4] Despite her representations, Margaret received nothing concrete in support from the Scots, who were beset by their own internal problems and caught up in the diplomatic wrangling between the French king and the Duke of Burgundy, save a vague promise to cease their attacks on the border.[5] Indeed, it must soon have become clear to Margaret that the only way to restore her son's rights was to rely on her Lancastrian supporters in England and especially those lords who had sworn to defend her son and husband in the Coventry Parliament.

Around the end of October, the Duke of Somerset had returned to England, probably first establishing himself at his castle at Corfe in Dorset. By 10 November, Somerset was with the Earl of Devon raising troops in Exeter, before moving to Bridgwater and travelling north.[6] The French king had made encouraging noises about aiding the Lancastrian cause, but, as was the case with the Scots, no real aid was forthcoming. Earlier in the year, according to a letter written by Gaston IV, Comte de Foix, to Charles, Duc de Berry, the French king had rebuffed overtures from the Duke of York. Charles and his advisors were clearly content to let matters in England take their course.[7] Nevertheless, Queen Margaret could count on considerable support from within England. As well as Somerset and Devon, the Earl of Northumberland and lords Clifford and Roos could be counted upon to resist the Duke of York and his allies. These lords and the Queen now set about organising themselves to overturn the Act of Accord and reinstate Prince Edward as heir to the throne. Other northern lords initially wavered in their support for the Queen. Although later pro-Yorkist lords identified them as partisans of the Queen as early as the autumn of 1460, lords Dacre of Gilsland, Greystoke, Latimer, Neville of Raby and Welles were still being named to commissions in the north by the council in Westminster in November and December.[8] Margaret's efforts were principally focused on countering Yorkist claims and propaganda. In November she wrote to the Mayor, aldermen and common council of London. Her letter decried the 'verray pure malice' of York in seeking to destroy the King, herself and their son and explained how the Duke had through 'untrewe pretense feyned a tytle to my lordis coronne and roiall estate'. She denied Yorkist propaganda that an 'unsen power of straungeres' had been assembled to rob the citizens of their goods, promising that should the Lancastrians come to London, 'ye nor noon of you shalbe robbed, dispoiled nor wronged by any personne' in her company. The appeal, and a similar one in the name of the Prince of Wales, fell on deaf ears and does not appear to have been answered.[9]

The responsibility for military preparations to overturn the Act of Accord fell upon a small coterie of Lancastrian lords. There is nothing to suggest that their assembling of men predated the end of October, and while Yorkist chroniclers would later present the Queen as the mastermind behind the Lancastrian mobilisation, the reality was probably more a piecemeal and ad hoc reaction to events. According to 'Gregory's Chronicle', Clifford, Greystoke, Neville, Roos and Latimer waited at Hull for the Duke of Exeter, while the pseudo-Worcestre *Annales* adds that Northumberland, Clifford, Dacre and Neville met at York and ordered their men to despoil the Yorkshire estates of York and Salisbury. Somerset and Devon marched north with 800 men, travelling via Bath, Cirencester, Evesham and Coventry, before arriving in York in early December where they joined

4 Beaucourt, vi., pp.296–7.
5 See below pp. xx.
6 Devon Archives, Exeter Receivers' Accounts, 39 Hen VI – 1 Edw.
7 Duclos, *Oeuvres Complètes*, iii., pp.508–13.
8 *Calendar of Patent Rolls, 1452–1461*, pp.651–3.
9 *Letters of Margaret of Anjou*, pp.225–6; *John Vale's Book*, pp.142–3.

forces with Northumberland.[10] However, far from immediately assembling a vast northern army, the lords first had to secure their position locally. Securing the port of Kingston-upon-Hull was crucial to Lancastrian ambitions. Its mercantile community, alongside those of York and Beverley, provided the Lancastrians with the only realistic prospect of keeping any sort of army in the field in the middle of winter. Hull's loyalties were less than assured though. Throughout the 1450s they had been embroiled in a violent dispute with Henry Percy, Lord Egremont, whom the Duke of Exeter had appointed as his deputy admiral, over the right to hold the admiralty court in the town. Egremont's death at Northampton had strengthened the townsmen's position and the election of Richard Anson, a servant of the Earl of Warwick who had been one of the few named individuals excluded from pardon offered to the rebels in Calais in June, probably pointed to wider Yorkist sympathies in the town.[11] Hull's magistrates took measures to protect themselves from any Lancastrian attack. A chain was put across the haven, barring its entrance but also preventing wheat and other foodstuff from being exported. On 12 November, while their Yorkist-supporting mayor was attending Parliament, the magistrates agreed that no victuals should leave the town, but whether this was due to pressure by the Lancastrian lords is unclear.[12] Probably due to a lack of widespread support, the Lancastrians resorted to coercion to gather men. In Beverley, Northumberland and Lord Neville, allegedly in the name of the King, ordered every man between the ages of 16 and 60 to attend upon them defensibly arrayed upon pain of 'lyffe and lyme' and march to rescue Henry VI from his captors.[13]

News of the Lancastrian preparations reached Westminster early in December. Throughout the autumn, the Yorkists had made efforts to assert their control in the north of England. At the beginning of October writs to the Earl of Northumberland, Lord Clifford and Lord Roos had ordered them to deliver Penrith, Wressle and Pontefract castles to the Earl of Salisbury and not make any gatherings, except for the purposes of resisting the Scots. They had clearly refused, and Salisbury had remained in London. Around the same time the Mayor and aldermen of York were ordered to accept only the King's commandments. A week later a powerful commission, headed by Salisbury's retainers and kinsmen lords Fitzhugh, Greystoke and Scrope of Masham, was empowered to raise men and take the castles by force. Again, no action seems to have been taken.[14] As the Lancastrian threat grew, York approached the Londoners for loans, but only half of the requested amount of a thousand marks was received as Duke Richard refused to guarantee repayment of previous loans made to the Lancastrian Earl of Wiltshire.[15] Margaret's letter to the corporation of London, received and read on 2 December, could have left no doubt over her and her followers' intentions. Six days later the chamberlains of the Exchequer were instructed to deliver £118 13*s.* 4*d.* to the Duke of York and Edward, Earl of March, 'for Artillerye, gounepoudre and other habilmentes of were'.[16] The following day, 9 December, York, accompanied by his eldest son, the Earl of Rutland, and the Earl of Salisbury left London to confront the Lancastrians with as few as 500 men.[17] Although some sources give 2 December as his date of departure, the evidence of military

10 *Contemporary English Chronicles*, p.69; *Letters and Papers*, ii (2), pp.774–5. See appendix.
11 TNA, C76/142, m. 9.
12 Hull City Archives, Bench Book 3A, 1449–1552, BRB1, fos. 72–4; *House of Commons 1422–1461*, ii., pp.664–7.
13 TNA, C1/27/435.
14 *Calendar of Patent Rolls 1452–1461*, pp.649–51.
15 TNA, E404/72/1/23; Scofield, *Edward IV*, i., p.118.
16 TNA, E404/71/5/38.
17 *Six Town Chronicles*, p.152.

and financial preparations militate against the earlier date. The urgency of York's commission was underscored by the decree made in Parliament before it was prorogued at the end of November. Parliament made arraying for war against York the equivalent of treason:

> Any rebellion, insurrection, disobedience or offence done to or against his said cousin, in executing the said charge under the king's authority or doing anything associated with it, by any person or persons of whatever estate or condition he or they may be, shall be taken, deemed, considered, held and accepted, as if it had been done to or against the king's person and command.[18]

York and Salisbury were accompanied – or later joined – by many of their leading retainers and relatives: Salisbury's son, Sir Thomas Neville, was present, along with the Earl's son-in-law, Sir William Bonville, Lord Harington, and the Yorkist retainers Sir Thomas Harrington, Sir James Pickering, Sir Thomas Parr, Sir Henry Radford, Sir James Strangeways, Edward Bourchier and Thomas Colt.[19] Towns sympathetic to York also contributed men – Shrewsbury sent 40 men to join the Duke in the north – while men doubtless joined his army as he made his way north through Nottinghamshire.[20]

As his father left for the north, the Earl of March prepared to travel to the Welsh marches to raise men from the Yorkist estates in Herefordshire. He was also probably instructed to keep a watchful eye on the activities of the Earl of Pembroke. The Earl of Warwick was initially tasked to remain in London and guard the capital, but evidently the Yorkists feared attack by sea or by the French for on 17 December he was appointed to take a fleet to sea.[21] He remained in the capital, however, a fortuitous decision as it would turn out.

The Battle of Wakefield: Alternative Explanations

The Battle of Wakefield is probably the most controversial battle of the first stage of the Wars of the Roses. Contemporaries offered conflicting explanations for York's defeat. This is not surprising. For the Earl of Warwick, it was a potentially disastrous setback, one that needed to be explained and for which allies needed to be reassured. To the pro-Yorkist London chroniclers, it was a piece of bad news that happened a long way away, and an event which was soon eclipsed by events closer to hand. Later Tudor chroniclers embroidered their accounts with invented scenes, speeches and personalities, and their inventions have formed the basis of most modern historians' accounts. Yet even the most basic details of Wakefield – when it was fought, where it was fought and by whom – remain obscure and contested. We cannot be sure of the size of York's army as it marched north. It likely numbered only a few hundred at the outset, and as the Yorkist lords marched north, they presumably gathered more men through commissions of array in the King's name. Some indication of the size of York's army is suggested by the quantities of weapons allegedly stolen by the Lancastrians in the aftermath of Wakefield: 24 guns, 200 lances, 600 bows and 500 sheaves of

18 *Parliament Rolls of Medieval England*, Parliament of October 1460, item 32.

19 Johnson, *Duke Richard of York*, p.222.

20 D.R. Walker, 'An Urban Community in the Welsh Borderland: Shrewsbury in the Fifteenth Century' (University of Wales, PhD, 1981), pp.391–2; TNA, E159/238, *brevia directa baronibus*, Mich 1 Edw IV, rot. 43d.

21 *Calendar of Patent Rolls 1452–61*, pp.642–3.

arrows.[22] We can be sure that the journey north was not easy. As several contemporaries observed, the weather had been terrible throughout 1460, and heavy rain had flooded the countryside, destroyed crops and turned the roads into quagmires. According to the chronicler Robert Bale, 'oon called Lovelac', a Kentishman, accompanied the Duke 'with greet ordnennance of Gounnes and other stuffs of werre', although the bad weather may have forced him to turn back.[23] The shortage of victuals and billets meant the Yorkists likely split their forces.

Near Worksop, perhaps in preparation for crossing the River Ryton or to visit the town's fair, held annually on 17 December, a party of York's scouts were surprised and routed by Somerset's men. In some modern accounts the Yorkist force is described as the vanguard, but the Latin manuscript of the pseudo-Worcestre *Annales*, the origin of the tale, describes them as 'praeeuntes' (goers before), while the part of the manuscript that enumerates them is damaged. Worksop seems to have been a minor skirmish at most, and it did not materially affect the Yorkist march north.[24] Nevertheless if York's men were attacked it was, as Parliament had made clear, an act of treason which can only have stiffened the Duke's resolve. Richard now made his way to his castle at Conisbrough, held by his retainer Edmund Fitzwilliam and well stocked with artillery taken from the Lancastrian Earl of Shrewsbury's castle at Sheffield after Northampton.[25]

Most historians have assumed that the Duke's party then headed to Sandal Castle, where York took up residence on 21 December. Sandal Castle itself, however, would not have offered much protection to York. It was a relatively small castle – much smaller than Pontefract or Middleham – and ill-suited for accommodating anything more than a small riding household.[26] It may have been in disrepair even before the events of December 1460. York more likely headed to the town of Wakefield itself, as his tenants there and in the surrounding lordship were already being harried by the Lancastrians operating from nearly Pontefract, driving away livestock and destroying the fulling mills along the River Calder.[27] Even if Duke Richard and his leading captains did take lodgings in the castle, the bulk of the Yorkist army must have been billeted in the surrounding countryside. During the siege of 1645 the castle was garrisoned by 100 men who lived in cramped and uncomfortable conditions, so there could be no more than a couple of hundred men lodged in the castle itself in 1460.[28] Indeed, Abbot Whethamstede states that when the Yorkists arrived they erected their tents not far from the town of Wakefield, which itself was some two miles from the castle which dominated the high ground to the south on the opposite bank of the River Calder.[29] Although there was an enpaled deer park of some 40 acres adjacent to the castle, two further parks on the north bank of the Calder, and a relatively large wood a little over a mile away to the south at Thurstonhaugh, most of the land between Wakefield and Sandal Castle was hedged, and probably ditched, ridge-and-furrow fields. In December 1460 the ground would probably have been waterlogged and not easily traversable by large bodies of men.[30]

22 TNA, KB27/803, rot. 16d.
23 *Six Town Chronicles*, p.152.
24 *Letters and Papers*, ii. (2), p.775; Helen Cox, *The Battle of Wakefield Revisited* (York, 2010), pp.48–52.
25 TNA, DL29/560/8899, m. 11.
26 Lawrence Butler, *Sandal Castle, Wakefield: The History and Archaeology of a Medieval Castle* (Wakefield, 1991), pp.49–57.
27 TNA, DL29/560/8899, mm. 1–1d.
28 Butler, *Sandal Castle*, pp.86–94.
29 Whethamstede, p.381.
30 Richard Knowles, 'The Battle of Wakefield: The Topography', *The Ricardian*, 9 (1992), pp.259–65.

Plate A. Yeoman archer of the king's household, First Battle of St. Albans, May 1455.
(Illustration by Bruno Mugnai © Helion & Company)
See Colour Plate Commentaries for further information.

Plate B. Man-at-arms of the Earl of Salisbury's retinue, Battle of Blore Heath, September 1459.
(Illustration by Bruno Mugnai © Helion & Company)
See Colour Plate Commentaries for further information.

Plate C. Edmund, Lord Grey de Ruthin, Battle of Northampton, July 1460.
(Illustration by Bruno Mugnai © Helion & Company)
See Colour Plate Commentaries for further information.

Plate D. Sir Ralph Percy, Wakefield, December 1460.
(Illustration by Bruno Mugnai © Helion & Company)
See Colour Plate Commentaries for further information.

Plate E. Billman, Yorkist army, Battle of Mortimer's Cross, February 1461.
(Illustration by Bruno Mugnai © Helion & Company)
See Colour Plate Commentaries for further information.

Plate F. Lancastrian man-at-arms, Second Battle of St. Albans, February 1461.
(Illustration by Bruno Mugnai © Helion & Company)
See Colour Plate Commentaries for further information.

Plate G. King Edward IV, London, March 1461.
(Illustration by Bruno Mugnai © Helion & Company)
See Colour Plate Commentaries for further information.

Plate H. John Radcliffe, Lord Fitzwalter, The Battle of Ferrybridge, March 1461.
(Illustration by Bruno Mugnai © Helion & Company)
See Colour Plate Commentaries for further information.

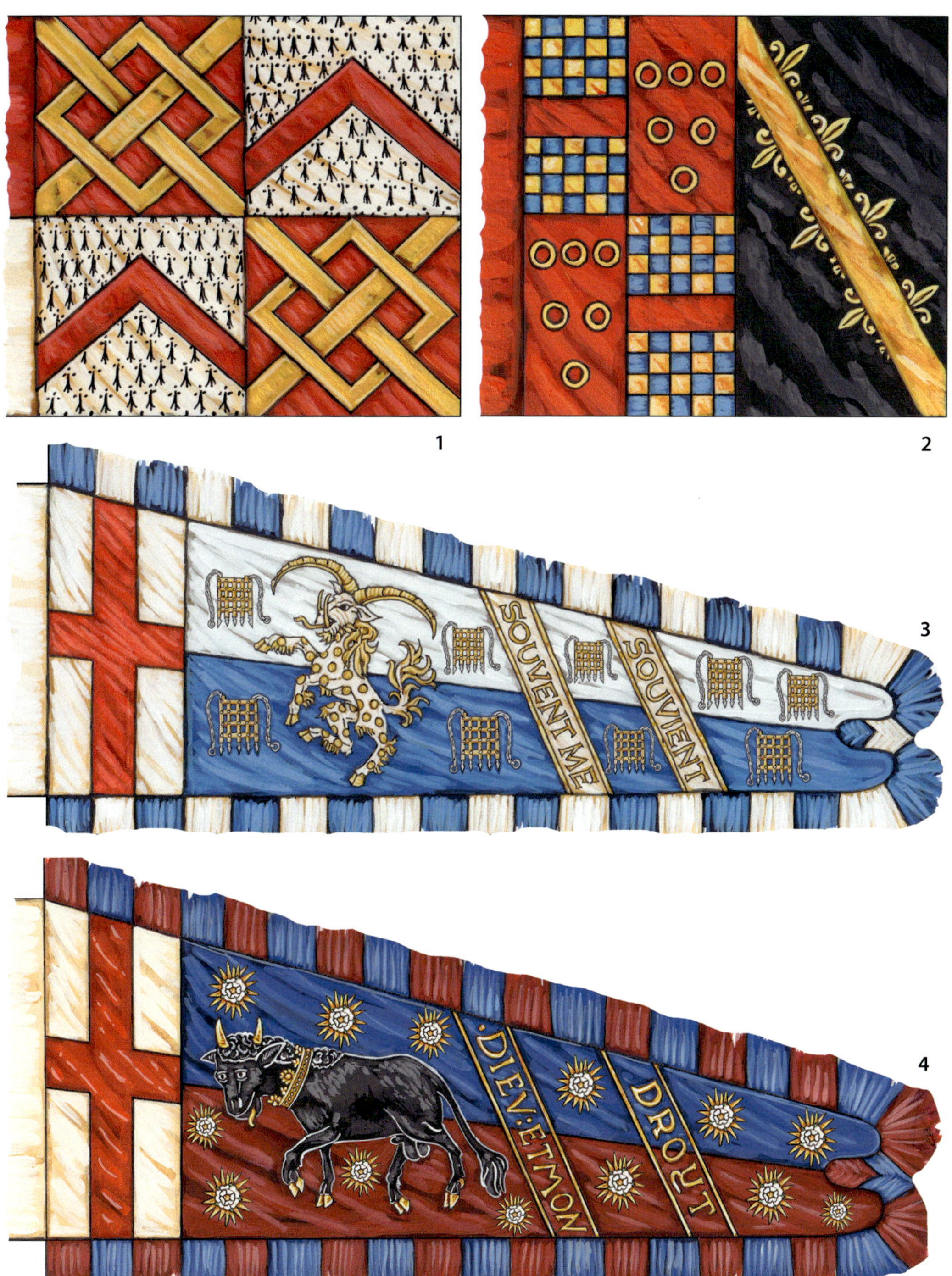

Plate I. Banners and Standards

(Illustration by Peter Smith © Helion & Company)

See Colour Plate Commentaries for further information.

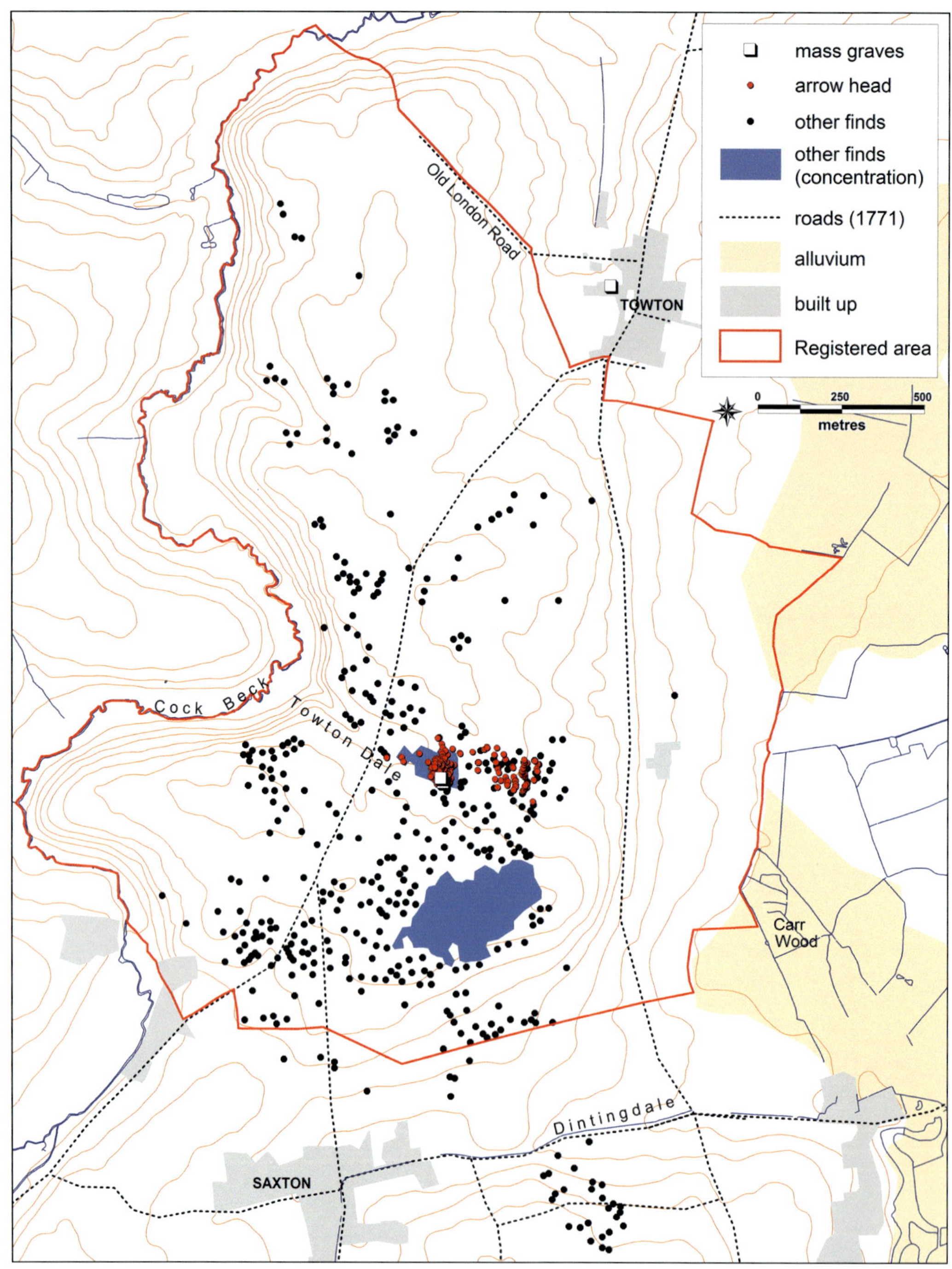

Plate J. A scatter diagram showing the archaeological finds on the Registered Battlefield area between Towton and Saxton.

(Illustration by Glenn Foard © Glenn Foard)

See Colour Plate Commentaries for further information.

By the time the Yorkists arrived in Wakefield, the Lancastrians were well established at Pontefract Castle, some nine miles to the east. Some chroniclers, writing in the 1460s and influenced by Yorkist propaganda, presented the Lancastrian army as predominantly northern in character. *An English Chronicle* and Robert Bale identified Somerset, Northumberland and Clifford, the children of the Lancastrian lords killed at St Albans in 1455, as the main protagonists alongside John, Lord Neville, and Thomas, Lord Roos.[31] John Benet named the Duke of Somerset and the earls of Devon and Northumberland alongside the northern lords Clifford, Neville and Roos. His account was unique in stating the lords Fitzhugh, Greystoke and de la Warre also fought for the Lancastrians.[32] Abbot Whethamstede was, as usual, forthright in his characterisation of the Yorkists' enemies as northerners.[33] Yet other contemporary writers gave the Yorkists' opponents a distinctly Lancastrian, rather than northern, identity. 'Gregory' stresses the Lancastrian character of the army by adding the Duke of Exeter to the list of Lancastrian lords who faced York and Salisbury, while the author of the 'Short English Chronicle' was alone in identifying the Earl of Wiltshire as one of the Lancastrian commanders at Wakefield.[34] In October Wiltshire was in Utrecht. He had been tasked with raising men and money on the continent and in Ireland rather than joining the other Lancastrian lords in Yorkshire. At the end of December, he landed in Wales in support of Jasper Tudor, Earl of Pembroke. He was certainly not at Wakefield, despite the prominence given to him by some recent historians.[35] Later chroniclers writing in the early sixteenth century assigned the command of the Lancastrian army directly to Queen Margaret, but she was still in Scotland when the battle was fought.[36]

The Parliamentary and legal records reinforce the picture of a broadly Lancastrian, rather than narrowly northern, force that had assembled to face York at Wakefield. According to the November 1461 Act of Attainder, the army was commanded by the Duke of Somerset and the earls of Devon and Northumberland, accompanied by lords Neville and Roos. No other lords are mentioned. A substantial number of prominent Lancastrians had joined it, however, representing the various noble affinities that now lent their weight in opposition to York: from the south-west, servants of Exeter and Devon such as Sir Baldwin Fulford, Alexander Hody, Nicholas Latimer and James Luttrell; Somerset's men Sir Thomas Fyndern and Sir Andrew Trollope; Northumberland's retainers Sir John Heron of Ford, Henry Bellingham and Sir Richard Tunstall; and men associated with the royal household such as Sir Edmund Mountfort, Robert Whittingham and William Grimsby.[37] A private lawsuit brought by Alice, the widowed Countess of Salisbury, in 1462 appealed ten men for the murder of her husband and named more prominent Lancastrians as accessories, adding their names to the roll-call of those present at Wakefield: Sir Gervase Clifton, the former Lancastrian treasurer of Calais; Northumberland's younger brother Sir Ralph Percy; the Yorkshire knights Sir William Plumpton, Sir John Pudsey, Sir William Everingham, Sir Roger Clifford (Lord Clifford's brother) and Sir Thomas Tunstall; as well as Devon's younger brother, Sir John Courtenay (whom the Earl knighted on the field at Wakefield). Most of the non-armigerous men attainted or appealed

31 *Six Town Chronicles*, p.152; *An English Chronicle*, p.96. See appendix.

32 *John Benet's Chronicle*, p.49.

33 Whethamstede, p.381.

34 *Contemporary English Chronicles*, p.70; *Three Fifteenth Century Chronicles*, p.76.

35 Cox, *Wakefield*, pp.83–94.

36 Robert Fabyan, *The New Chronicles of England and France*, ed. Henry Ellis (London: Longman, 1811), pp.637–8; *Polydore Vergil*, pp.108–9; *Hall's Chronicle*, pp.250–1.

37 *Parliament Rolls of Medieval England*, Parliament of November 1461, items 13 and 19.

The ruins of the once impressive Pontefract Castle. This was a Lancastrian stronghold in December 1460, and it was here that the Earl of Salisbury and probably the Duke of York were murdered after their capture at Wakefield. (Dan Moorhouse)

for Salisbury's murder were indeed from Yorkshire, with many from the area around Pontefract, but in terms of its leadership, those named were not solely an array of northern lords and their retinues.[38] Benet claims the Lancastrian army was 20,000 strong, a figure repeated in legal cases in the early 1460s, but no other contemporaries ventured an estimate of its size. The topography around Wakefield and Sandal Castle would not have permitted the manoeuvre of armies of anywhere near this size and the forces involved were probably significantly smaller. From the manorial accounts of Wakefield, the only Lancastrian lords that can placed in the vicinity in the immediate aftermath of York's death were the Earl of Northumberland and Lord Clifford.[39]

What happened when York met his enemies is not clear. The elaborate account of the battle and its aftermath devised by Edward Hall in the 1540s is largely imagined, although it took some of its inspiration from Polydore Vergil's earlier narrative. Hall has been given credibility by his claim that his relative, Sir Davey Hall, was one of York's councillors and his account forms the basis of many modern analyses of the battle.[40] However, as Paul Johnson has shown, there was no such individual among the Duke's annuitants or known servants, and no contemporary account

38 TNA, KB27/804, rot. 65.
39 TNA, DL29/560/8899, rot. 5d; *John Benet's Chronicle*, p.49.
40 *Hall's Chronicle*, pp.250–1; *Polydore Vergil*, pp.108–9.

An annotated aerial photograph showing Sandal Castle and other landscape features associated with the traditional interpretations of the Battle of Wakefield. (Roger Keech courtesy of Helen Cox)

mentions him. Equally, the accounts of nineteenth-century historians like Richard Brooke, Alex Leadman and Clements Markham, who relied heavily on Hall's account, contain much that is pure fiction.[41] No contemporary described the composition of the opposing armies, how command was apportioned between the lords present, or the course of the battle itself in any detail. All that can be said with certainty is that at end of December 1460, York and Salisbury met their Lancastrian opponents somewhere near Wakefield, and in the ensuing encounter the Yorkists were routed and their leaders either killed on the field or taken captive and shortly afterwards executed.

Four main explanations have been advanced for the Yorkist defeat. First, both fifteenth-century chroniclers and recent historians have argued that the Lancastrians achieved victory through deception.[42] *An English Chronicle* claimed that Lord Neville asked York for a commission to raise men, which the Duke granted, 'demyng that he had to be trew and on hys parte'. Thus granted, Neville used the commission to raise 8,000 men which he duly employed to attack and defeat the Yorkists.[43] This seems unlikely. As the brother of the feeble-minded Earl of Westmorland, head of the senior branch of the Neville family, he was an implacable enemy of Salisbury, head of the younger branch. He had been first summoned to Parliament as Lord Neville in November 1459,

41 Clements Markham, 'The Battle of Wakefield', *Yorkshire Archaeological and Topographical Journal*, 9 (1886), pp.105–23; A.D.H. Leadman, 'The Battle of Wakefield', *Yorkshire Archaeological and Topographical Journal*, 11 (1890), pp.348–60; Brooke, *Visits to Fields of Battle in England*, pp.53–66.

42 Cox, *Wakefield*, pp 77–93.

43 *An English Chronicle*, p.97.

and he had received numerous rewards from Salisbury's forfeited estates. He was again rewarded by Henry VI in March 1460 for his efforts against Yorkist rebels in the north and raised men for the Lancastrians at Northampton. He did not attend the October 1460 Parliament, although he was named to the broad commissions to arrest rebels issued by the Yorkist government in November and December alongside other northern nobles.[44] Despite being included in these commissions, it seems incredible that York would have trusted him to raise men on his behalf in December. In fact, he was openly using these commissions to raise men for the Lancastrian cause around Beverley.[45] Yet it seems highly unlikely that Neville was anywhere near Wakefield at the end of December 1460. The Duke of Exeter, still nominally admiral of England, had appointed him as his deputy in Yorkshire following Egremont's death. On 28 December, Neville wrote from his castle at Raby in the palatinate of Durham to the town council of Hull informing them of Exeter's grant and asking them to 'certifie to me of what that I can doo to your hertes ease & wele of your towne & the cominaltie of the same'.[46]

A more elaborate tale of deception involved Somerset's leading captain, Andrew Trollope. Jean de Wavrin claimed that Trollope, whom he described as a 'very subtle man of war', dressed 400 of his best men in the ragged staff livery of the Earl of Warwick and posed as a relief force. The next day York, emboldened by these apparent reinforcements, left his stronghold and was immediately set upon by Somerset and Trollope's turncoats and killed.[47] Trollope would have been no stranger to York or Salisbury from his recent exploits at Ludford Bridge and in Calais. Although he may have stressed his loyalty to the King or successfully hidden his identity at first, it seems unlikely that York or his captains could have been so easily deceived by a man whose association with Somerset was well known. Although Somerset had promised not to take up arms against Warwick the previous August, if York's men had been attacked at Worksop, then his intentions towards the Yorkist lords would have been clear. Equally, would York and Salisbury have trusted a detachment of men wearing Warwick's livery without letters of credence from the Earl himself? The story appears to have originated in one or more now lost newsletters distributed from Calais in the early months of 1461 and designed to explain the Earl of Warwick's part in recent events in England. The essence of the account was contained in the manuscript from which Jean de Wavrin seems to have copied. Writing around 1471, it described how Trollope plotted with Somerset to bring 400 men to York, claiming they had come from Lancashire 'to rescue him'.[48] Trollope was something of a Black Legend in Yorkist propaganda and his inclusion in the narrative of what happened at Wakefield may simply have been designed to obscure York's fatal blunders.

Second, some sources suggest that York may have been overwhelmed when coming to the rescue of a foraging party that had been attacked by the Lancastrians. This theory has been backed by historians from Clements Markham to John Gillingham, and it seems to have had some contemporary support.[49] Writing on 9 January 1461, Antonio de la Torre, a Milanese servant of Warwick and member of the Calais garrison, informed Francisco Sforza, Duke of Milan, of events in

44 James Petre, 'The Nevills of Brancepath and Raby 1425–1499. Part 1 1425–1469: Nevill vs Nevill', *The Ricardian*, 5 (1981), pp.418–35.

45 TNA, C1/27/435.

46 Hull City Archives, BRL 4, BRB 1, fos. 73–4; Poulson, *Beverlac*, pp.227–30, 232–4.

47 Wavrin, v., pp.325–6.

48 BNF, MS Français 88, fo. 141.

49 Markham, 'Battle of Wakefield', p.113; Gillingham, *Wars of the Roses*, p.119; Haigh, *Military Campaigns*, pp.34–37.

England and the setback the Yorkists had recently suffered at Wakefield. He observed that the York's men had been defeated 'from lack of discipline, because they allowed a large part of the force to go pillaging and searching for victuals, [while] their adversaries, who are desperate, attacked the duke and his followers'. De la Torre's account is problematic: he did not know the distance between Wakefield and London (which he gave as 80 miles) and he was alone among contemporaries in stating the Yorkists *outnumbered* the Lancastrians.[50] The author of the pseudo-Worcestre *Annales* also suggested that battle was joined while the Yorkists were 'wandering through the country seeking provisions', while Abbot Whethamstede referred, albeit somewhat cryptically, to York men's 'wandering about for victuals'.[51] Despite its attractions for explaining why York and his men left the safety of their camp to give battle, it would be surprising if the Yorkists did not do so in search of supplies and de la Torre is the only contemporary to suggest that this somehow contributed to York's defeat.

A third explanation for the Lancastrian triumph is that they were able to conceal large portions of their army in the woods around Sandal Castle, hiding the true size of their army, and then ambushing York and his men as they left the safety of their fortress.[52] This was the crux of Polydore Vergil's and Hall's accounts of the battle: York came out of his stronghold and, unaware of thousands of Lancastrians hidden in the woods either side of the castle, was soon 'enuironed on euery side, like a fish in a net, or a deere in a buckestall'.[53] The nineteenth-century historians of Wakefield embraced this notion, with Markham even adding the erroneous detail that the main gate of Sandal Castle faced south, further complicating York's manoeuvre, instead of looking north towards Wakefield. The 'Men in the Woods' theory has been comprehensively refuted by Helen Cox and Richard Knowles.[54] It stretches credulity that the Yorkists could have allowed thousands of Lancastrians to secrete themselves in the leafless woods either side of Wakefield Green unseen. Moreover, it seems clear that there were in fact only small areas of woodland around Sandal Castle, with most of the land down to Wakefield and the River Calder enclosed ridge-and-furrow fields. Wavrin places Somerset 'in the fields' facing Sandal on the eve of the battle, while the antiquarian John Leland recalled the 'sore Batell fought in the south Feeldes by this [Wakefield] Bridge' on his visit to the battlefield in the 1540s.[55]

Finally, York himself has been blamed for the debacle at Wakefield. Goaded by the taunts of the Lancastrians, his impetuosity got the better of him and, against the advice of his captains, he left the safety of Sandal Castle and rashly engaged a larger force. This account has been dismissed by some recent commentators, part of a more general rehabilitation of the Duke's reputation as a sound administrator and good soldier who would have made a fine late medieval king. It was, however, an explanation favoured by one of the earliest commentators on the battle. The papal legate, Coppini, wrote on 9 January 1461 urging his correspondent, Lorenzo de Florencia, then with Queen Margaret, to counsel Somerset to 'not be arrogant because of the trifling victory they have won, owing to the rash advance of their opponents'.[56] No other fifteenth-century source mentions York's impetuosity, however, until the Crowland Chronicle continuator, writing around

50 *Calendar of State Papers, Milan*, pp.42–3.
51 *Letters and Papers*, ii (2), p.775; Whethamstede, p.382.
52 Sadler, *The Red Rose and the White*, pp.94–95.
53 *Hall's Chronicle*, p.250.
54 Cox, *Wakefield*, pp.60–68; Knowles, 'Wakefield', pp.259–60.
55 *Leland's Itinerary in England and Wales*, ed. Lucy Toulin-Smith (5 vols., London, 1907–8), iv., p.40.
56 *Calendar of State Papers, Milan 1385–1618*, p.39.

1471.[57] From there it was bound into Vergil's and Hall's account and featured prominently in the accounts of later historians. Vergil wrongly placed Queen Margaret at Wakefield and in the Tudor accounts the Lancastrians goaded York to emerge from the safety of Sandal Castle. Hall had York proclaim that if he shut the gates of the castle 'al men might of me wounder and all creatures maie of me report dishonor, that a woman hathe made me a dastard, whom no man euer to this daie could yet proue a coward'.[58] Yet while York's speech was imagined, the sentiments expressed may have had some basis in truth. Throughout the 1450s York had demonstrated a willingness to face his enemies and settle his disputes through the threat of violence and direct confrontation. At Dartford in 1452, he had gathered arrayed for war against the King, demanding Somerset's removal, only to be dissuaded from an act of obvious treason by his fellow lords. At St Albans in 1455 he was resolved to settle the matter through violence, leading to Somerset's death. At the 'Loveday' in 1458 he had agreed to 'eschew the wey of fayt', but within less than a year he had assembled an army against the King again and was forced to retreat without giving battle at Ludford Bridge. Equally, as protector in May 1454 he had travelled north to enforce royal justice when the Duke of Exeter and Lord Egremont had attempted to seize the city of York. In December 1460, with the Earl of Northumberland and others in open defiance of royal authority, the Duke may have felt compelled to repeat this display of force.

The 'Battle' of Wakefield Reconsidered

All these accounts, however, are predicated upon the assumption that York took refuge in Sandal Castle. In fact, the evidence for that is far from clear. As we have seen, Sandal was not the stronghold it is often presented as. The earliest accounts of Wakefield, both chronicles and letters, make no mention of Sandal and instead place the Duke's defeat and death at Wakefield itself or nearby at Pontefract. Crucially, Wavrin and the continental accounts, drawing on the now lost newsletters, make no mention of Sandal, instead stating that Trollope tricked York into leaving the *town* of Wakefield. These early accounts also present York's death as murder, rather than the Duke being killed in battle. In his letter of 9 January, Coppini spoke of the 'countless acts of cruelty' of the Lancastrian lords, while the London chronicler Robert Bale wrote that 'the duke of york, the Erle Rutland his sone and the Erle Salesbury wer trayterously and ageinst lawe of armes be taking of Tretys graunted, mordered and slain'.[59] The 1461 Act of Attainder similarly identifies Wakefield as the place where Somerset and his confederates 'horribly, cruelly and tyrannously murdered the same noble prince'.[60] The genealogical roll known as the *Chronicle of England from Rollo to Edward IV*, written between 1461 and 1465, recounts how the Duke of York was 'innocent goyng towarde Yorke at Wakefeld [when his enemies] sette vpon hym oute of array and kelled hym and his sonne the Erle of Routeland, the Erle of Salusbury and Lord Harington with othir diuers gentills and comoners'.[61] The first mention of Sandal in relation to York's death is to be found in John Benet's

57 *Ingulph's Chronicle of the Abbey of Croyland*, ed. H.T. Riley (London: George Bell, 1908), p.421.
58 *Polydore Vergil*, p.108; *Hall's Chronicle*, p.250.
59 *Calendar of State Papers*, p.39; *Six Town Chronicles*, p.152.
60 *Parliament Rolls of Medieval England*, Parliament of November 1461, item 19.
61 Raluca Radelescu, 'Yorkist Propaganda and *The Chronicle from Rollo to Edward IV*', *Studies in Philology*, 4 (2003), pp.420–1; Noah Peterson, 'New Dating for *The Chronicle from Rollo to Edward IV*', *Notes and Queries*, 64 (2017), pp.230–1.

chronicle and *An English Chronicle*, which were probably written in the late 1460s. Sandal was not identified as the site of the battle again until Edward Hall did so in the 1540s.[62]

That York and his companions had not died in battle but had somehow been ambushed and subsequently murdered in cold blood is also suggested by the unusual number of legal cases that later arose from events at Wakefield. Crucially, these pleadings support the pseudo-Worcester *Annales*' statement that York was attacked not on the generally accepted date of 30 December but a day earlier, on the 29th. The *Annales* is quite explicit on this: 'On 29 December, at Wakefield, while the men of the Duke of York were wandering through the country seeking provisions a dreadful battle occurred.'[63] While, as we have seen, the author of the *Annales* was confused on who was present, his dating is significant. On 17 February 1462, Thomas Colt, one of the Duke's closest servants, who had accepted the administration of his will when the executors had refused, brought a case in the Exchequer against the collectors of customs in Hull for money owed for York's annuities granted by the crown. In it, he stated that York and Richard Anson, who was also one of the collectors of customs in Hull, had been killed at Wakefield on 29 December 1460. He repeated this claim the following year against Anson's widow and executrix, Elizabeth.[64] Colt later alleged that he was beaten and wounded at Wakefield by Roger Thorpe, whose father, Thomas, Colt had helped to imprison after the battle of St Albans in 1455. In February 1463, Colt claimed he was assaulted by Thorpe, in league with 20,000 other unknown assailants, at Wakefield on 29 December 1460. The perpetrators had then murdered the Duke of York and stolen his goods, including various weapons, household items and a suit of armour, to the value of £1,000, for which Colt, as administrator of the Duke's estates, claimed damages.[65] Soon afterwards Colt's own estates in Northumberland were also plundered.[66] There seems little doubt that what Colt was describing was the attack on the 'foraging party', in fact the Duke, his household men and his baggage train, that led directly to York's capture and subsequent murder.

These early accounts were also in agreement in stating that York, Salisbury and Rutland were all first taken prisoner and then killed. If York was indeed taken prisoner and subsequently murdered, this explains why Edward IV chose to commemorate 30 December as the date of his death. Rutland may have suffered a similar fate to his father or been killed while trying to flee (although the elaborate account of his murder on Wakefield bridge at the hands of Lord Clifford was probably a product of Edward Hall's imagination).[67] York and Rutland's bodies – or least their hearts – were initially laid to rest in the Dominican friary of St Richard of Chichester in Pontefract, strongly suggesting that the Duke at least had died in Pontefract rather than at Wakefield.[68] The circumstances around Salisbury's death seem less controversial. Most sources agree that he was taken to Pontefract and beheaded on 31 December. *An English Chronicle* recounts how his captors 'tooke hym owte of the castelle by violence and smote of his hed'.[69] The pseudo-Worcestre *Annales*, however, states that Salisbury was captured in the evening of 29 December and murdered the next day by one of

62 *John Benet's Chronicle*, p.49; *English Chronicle*, p.97 ; *Hall's Chronicle*, p.250.

63 *Letters and Papers*, ii(2)., p.775.

64 TNA, E13/147, rots. 80–1; 148, rots. 55–6. See also E13/167, rot. 10.

65 TNA, KB27/803, rot. 16d.

66 TNA, CP40/802, rot. 442.

67 *Letters and Papers*, ii(2)., p.775; *Hall's Chronicle*, p.251.

68 P.W. Hammond, Anne F. Sutton and Livia Visser-Fuchs, 'The Reburial of Richard, Duke of York, 21–30 July 1476', *The Ricardian*, 10 (1994), pp.122–65.

69 *An English Chronicle*, p.97.

the illegitimate brothers of the Duke of Exeter.[70] The short chronicle of events between 1431 and 1471 copied into the commonplace book of the Londoner John Vale stated that York, Rutland and Salisbury were captured at Wakefield 'and there beheded'. Significantly, he differentiates their deaths from those of 'the twoo lordis of Haringtonys the older and the yonge slayne in battell the same day'.[71] Abbot Whethamstede described how York and Rutland were overwhelmed by superior numbers and captured 'contrary to the promised faith and before the appointed day of battle'. Duke Richard was mocked by his captors. A crown of 'marsh grass' was set upon his head and, 'no differently than the Jews before the Lord, his captors bowed their knees before him, saying delusionally, "Hail, king, without government. Hail, king, without inheritance. Hail, leader and prince, completely without all people and possessions."'[72]

While Whethamstede was making an obvious analogy between York and the martyred Christ, his account was echoed by continental sources drawing on the lost Yorkist newsletter. Some continental authors added that York was killed on the orders of the Queen, while the Flemish chronicler Andriaan de But, in an otherwise confused account of the events in 1460–61, named Andrew Trollope as the man who cut the Duke's throat.[73] Trollope may well have been present at the Duke's death. On 6 March 1461 Edward IV offered £100 to anyone who could capture and kill eight named men, including Trollope, William Grimsby and 'the two bastards of Exeter'.[74] The Yorkist regime seemed in no doubt who had been involved in the murder of Duke Richard. On 3 December that year the Earl of Warwick was appointed as steward of England to preside over the trial of those accused of murdering the King's father.[75] Among those attainted in November 1461 for their participation in the events at Wakefield had been the West Country knight Sir James Luttrell. Luttrell had allegedly been knighted after Wakefield by the Duke of Somerset but had died of wounds suffered at the Second Battle of St Albans. In May 1475, a commission into Luttrell's lands following a complaint by his widow, Elizabeth, rehearsed how Sir James had been attainted for 'his murder of the King's father Richard, late Duke of York'. Luttrell's attainder was eventually reversed in 1485, during Henry VII's first Parliament, for the 'true faith and allegiance' he had shown to Henry VI.[76]

Several sources, both English and continental, agree that the Yorkist lords' heads were then mounted on spears, Duke Richard's adorned with a paper crown. The brief notes of historical events during the reigns of Henry VI and Edward IV compiled in the 1460s and now Lambeth Ms 448 stated that the severed heads were placed on the walls of Pontefract Castle, while the contemporary 'Short Latin Chronicle' claims it was the walls of York. Yet as both chroniclers noted in the margin '*ut dicitur*' ('as it is said'), these statements merely reflected London gossip in the months after the Duke's death.[77] The pseudo-Worcestre *Annales* stated that the heads of York, Salisbury, Rutland and all those killed or subsequently murdered at Wakefield 'were placed on various parts

70 *Letters and Papers*, ii(2)., p.775.

71 *John Vale's Book*, p.179.

72 Whethamstede, p.382.

73 *Chroniques Relatives a L'Histoire de la Belgique sous la Domination des Ducs de Bourgogne*, ed. Kervyn de Lettenhove (Brussels: L'Academie Royale de Belgique, 1870), p.432.

74 *CCR 1461–1467*, pp.56–7. Intriguingly, the final name on the list was Clapham the Younger. Was this the son of John Clapham, York's constable of Sandal in December 1460? TNA, DL29/560/8890, m. 1d.

75 *Calendar of Patent Rolls 1461–1467*, p.63.

76 *Calendar of Patent Rolls 1467–1477*, p.522; *Parliament Rolls of Medieval England*, Parliament of November 1485, item 28.

77 *Three Fifteenth Century Chronicles*, p.154, p.172.

of York'. It was the London chronicler Robert Fabyan, whose *New Cronicles of England* were first published in 1516, who established the story of York's head, adorned with a paper crown, mounted over the Mickelgate in York, a story later immortalised through Vergil and Hall by Shakespeare.[78] The story had widespread credence: the Frenchman Jean de Roye, writing his *Chronique scandeleuse* in the 1480s, recorded that the Duke of York was killed, and then 'they chopped off his head, which they put at the end of a spear; and around his head they placed a crown of needs in the form of a royal crown, in mockery of the fact that he wanted to make himself king of the said kingdom'.[79] Similarly, Andriaan de But reported that Duke Richard's head was displayed on the walls of York with a crown in mockery of his regal pretensions.[80]

Whatever the truth of events at Wakefield, the fighting took a heavy toll on the Yorkist lords, knights and esquires close to York. There is no contemporary estimate of the duration of the fighting, but sixteenth-century accounts say it lasted no more than an hour. Fifteenth-century sources give the number of Yorkist dead at between 700 and 2,500, with only 'Gregory's Chronicle' providing a figure – 200 – for the Lancastrians killed.[81] *An English Chronicle* lists Salisbury's son, Sir Thomas Neville, Sir William, Lord Harington and his brother, Sir Thomas, as well as Sir Henry Radford among the other prominent Yorkist casualties. Clement Paston, writing to his brother in January 1461, feared, albeit wrongly, that Thomas Colt, Sir James Strangeways and Sir Thomas Pickering had either fallen or been taken prisoner.[82] According to the *Brut* chronicler, the Mayor of Hull, Richard Anson, was captured along with the London mercer John Harowe, 'capitayn of þe foot-men', and brought to Pontefract and beheaded. A legal case in 1482 stated that Anson had died 'on 29 December 1460 at Wakefield', suggesting that he too was taken and killed alongside York.[83] Other sources suggested that Sir Thomas Harrington's son, John, was killed, while sixteenth-century chroniclers added more spurious names – such as Edward Hall's putative grandfather, Davey – to the list of Yorkist dead.[84] The savagery of the encounter is suggested by the later petition of John Sclatter, who was rewarded by Edward IV for the 'great injuries and mutilations suffered in the wars of our noble father at Wakefield, where he lost his right hand and badly injured the other, so that he may neither clothe nor feed himself'. Sclatter received an annual pension of four marks for his troubles.[85]

The most high-profile legal case in the wake of events at Wakefield case was brought by Alice, dowager Countess of Salisbury. Early in 1462 she accused 10 men of being the principals in the murder of her husband. This attack did not occur on the 29th but on 30 December, suggesting that the Earl was not with York when he had been attacked. Most of Salisbury's assailants were yeomen from Pontefract and Ripon, and none were of local or national prominence, but Alice also named some 30 other men, including leading Lancastrians like Sir Gervase Clifton, Sir Ralph Percy and Sir William Plumpton, as accessories. Writs were sent out to the sheriffs in various counties to arrest the accused, but each failed to bring any of the men to Westminster to answer for their crimes. One wonders if Alice ever thought there was a realistic chance of justice and what remedy

78 *Letters and Papers*, ii(2)., p.775; *New Chronicles*, ed. Ellis, p.638; *Henry VI Part 3*, Act 1 Scene 4.
79 [Jean de Roye], *Chroniques scandaleuse* (Paris, 1620), pp.9–10.
80 *Chroniques Relatives*, ed. Lettenhove, p.432.
81 *Contemporary English Chronicles*, p.69.
82 *An English Chronicle*, p.97; *Paston Letters and Papers*, ed. Davis, i., p.197.
83 *The Brut*, i. 531; TNA, E13/167, m. 10.
84 *Hall's Chronicle*, p.250.
85 *Parliament Rolls of Medieval England*, Parliament of April 1463, item 40.

she expected against men of little consequence or against those who had already been attainted for their adherence to the House of Lancaster. The case quietly disappeared from the courts as the Countess died before the end of the year.[86] Around the same time, Countess Alice and Salisbury's other executors sued Sir William Plumpton, Sir George Darrell and others for removing livestock and grain from the lordship of Middleham.[87] Other legal cases concerned with Wakefield suggest that what occurred was not a battle as we would understand it, but an extreme example of aristocratic violence. One of Salisbury's servants, Robert Percy of Scotton, near Knaresborough, was captured after the attack on York and claimed that his neighbour, the Lancastrian knight Sir William Plumpton, had laboured to have Percy's head 'stryken of' and then used his incarceration to rob him of livestock and goods valued at more than 100 marks.[88] In December 1461 Sir Thomas Ferrers, who had served with York 'with grete feliship', was released from his debts as sheriff of Leicestershire and Warwickshire to pay a 300 mark (£200) ransom he had been made to pay after being captured at Wakefield.[89] Other men also brought legal actions in the first months of Edward IV's reign seeking redress for their imprisonment and ransoming after Wakefield.[90] The immediate impact of Wakefield went beyond those present on the field. The widow of Geoffrey Southworth, who had been killed fighting with York, claimed to have been imprisoned in the days following and held to ransom by the Lancashire esquire William Syngulton. Soon after her release, she married one of Edward IV's sergeants-at-arms, John Conyers, and together the two pursued her captor at law for redress.[91]

In the aftermath of York's death, the Lancastrians celebrated their victory. According to lists compiled in the nineteenth century from various heraldic and genealogical sources, 20 men were knighted by Somerset, Northumberland, Devon, Roos and Clifford. These included their leading retainers like Alexander Hody, Robert Whittingham and Henry Bellingham, but also family members like Devon's brother John and Roger Clifford, Lord Clifford's brother. The veracity of this list may be in doubt, but dubbing knights would have given the victory a military and chivalric symbolism it otherwise lacked.[92] If they had not already done so, the Lancastrians plundered York's manor of Wakefield and Salisbury's lordship of Middleham. The Wakefield accounts record that Northumberland and Clifford took possession of Sandal Castle and drove York's tenants from the demesne lands. The fulling mill on the River Calder and various water mills were destroyed 'in the time of Edward, lately Duke of York', that is after Duke Richard's death, and deer removed from the park. No coal was mined from the coal pits near Wakefield 'because no one dared to occupy the said pits on account of various rebellions in the northern parts', while Lord Clifford removed various carts belonging to the Duke.[93]

As Richard Knowles observed over 30 years ago, Wakefield was 'in all probability ... more of a brutal skirmish than a set-piece battle.'[94] Rather than heroically – or foolishly – leaving the safety of Sandal Castle to engage a larger Lancastrian force, the Duke and a few dozen companions

86 TNA, KB27/804, rot. 65.
87 TNA, CP40/802, rot. 441.
88 TNA, C1/31/485.
89 TNA, E159/238, *brevia directa baronibus*, Mich 1 Edw IV, rot. 29.
90 TNA, C1/27/340, 456; 31/358.
91 TNA, C1/27/202.
92 W.A. Shaw, *The Knights of England* (2 vols, London, 1906), ii., pp.12–13.
93 TNA, DL29/560/8899, rots. 1, 4, 5.
94 Knowles, 'Wakefield', p.264.

were probably surprised by a larger Lancastrian force on 29 December, led by Northumberland and Clifford, just outside Wakefield. York was on the road, perhaps heading towards York, with a small force when he appears to have been ambushed. Was this the origin of the 'foraging party' story or did York's hubris, believing a show of force in the Lancastrian heartland would bring the rebellious lords to heel, finally get the better of him? Clifford and Northumberland, along with Somerset, who may have been at Pontefract when York was captured, now reaped their revenge for events at St Albans five years earlier. Hall's account of Clifford's merciless execution of Edmund, Earl of Rutland, on Wakefield Bridge may have been apocryphal, but it captured something of the Lancastrian lords' bloodthirsty orgy of violence, fuelled by their personal hatred of York and Salisbury. Their treatment of their enemies was reflected in the behaviour of their retainers and servants towards York's men, the suspension of the accepted laws of war, and the destruction and theft of Yorkist property.

* * *

York's and Salisbury's deaths were a major, but far from fatal, blow to the Yorkist cause. London and many in the surrounding counties now rallied behind the Earl of Warwick. Coppini, writing to the Duke of Milan in January 1461, seemed confident still of victory with Warwick assembling a large army, 'though the perils are great'. Warwick's own letter to Pope Pius II, written on 11 January, expressed his confidence in 'either a fair and sure peace or victory'.[95] The Earl had Henry VI still in London and Yorkist propaganda now worked overtime to present the conflict in terms of north versus south, rather than Lancastrian versus Yorkist. Clement Paston echoed these sentiments towards the end of the month when he assured his brother that 'my lordys þat ben here haue as moche as þey may doo to kep down all thys cwntre more þan iiij ore v schers, fore þey wold be vp on þe men in northe, fore it ys fore þe welle of all þe sowthe.'[96] Wakefield changed the political landscape in two important ways: first, it confirmed the struggle as one that could easily be presented as a clash of regional cultures and, second, it ensured that there could be no more pretence of political compromise between the scions of the houses of Lancaster and York.

Sources and Further Reading

The sources for events at Wakefield in December 1460 are fully described and put into context in Paul L. Dawson and David Grummit, 'The "Battle" of Wakefield of 1460 Reconsidered', Battalia 3 (2025), pp.1–26. All previous secondary sources wrongly present Wakefield as a set-piece battle. Helen Cox's *The Battle of Wakefield Revisited* is the fullest account, although the conclusions differ fundamentally from those presented here.

95 *Calendar of State Papers, Milan*, pp.41, 44.
96 *Paston Letters and Papers*, ed. Davies, i., pp.197–8.

7

The Battle of Mortimer's Cross

Edward, Earl of March, spent Christmas 1460 at either Gloucester or Shrewsbury. He was in the latter, however, when he received news of his father's death early in January.[1] By then the new Duke of York, as Edward became on his father's death, was already busy raising troops by virtue of commissions of array issued in the name of Henry VI. It was probably for service with him that the city of Salisbury raised 130 men after receiving letters in the King's name on 3 January.[2] Other towns and cities across the Midlands and Welsh marches were similarly put on notice. On 20 January the bailiffs of Shrewsbury were ordered to repair their walls and guard the city's gates to prevent the Duke of Somerset, the earls of Devon and Northumberland, and lords Clifford, Neville and Roos from entering. The Yorkist administration in Westminster must have feared that the Lancastrian lords, fresh from their surprise victory at Wakefield, would march towards the Midlands, rendezvousing with the earls of Pembroke and Wiltshire, and converge on London. A similar commission on the same day to the bailiffs of Leicester suggests that this was indeed the case.[3] On the 28th of that month the bailiffs of Salisbury received a second demand for troops. This letter, sent in the name of Henry VI and copied to towns, counties and individuals throughout England, explained 'that thoo mysrewlie and outerageous people in the north partes of this land been comyng hiderwardes purposyng the vtter destrucion aswell of the contre of you and other oure trew subgittes and also the subuersion of the comen weell of alle the londe the whiche wee in noo wise may nor well suffre but defende in alle wise'. The city fathers hastily assembled a further 92 men and immediately despatched them to London.[4]

Edward was almost certainly aware that Jasper Tudor, Earl of Pembroke, and James Butler, Earl of Ormond and Wiltshire, were assembling men in Wales and intending to march and meet the Lancastrian army in Yorkshire. As well as raising men himself in the marches, he knew of the efforts of three of his father's staunchest supporters in the principality – Walter Devereux, William Herbert and Roger Vaughan – to recruit in south and west Wales. Confident of the size of his host and probably filled with a desire to avenge his father's death and assert his own leadership of the Yorkist cause and his position as heir to the throne, Edward now set out to bring Pembroke and

---

1 *Six Town Chronicles*, p.167; *Three Fifteenth Century Chronicles*, p.76.
2 Salisbury Leger Book B 1452–1567 (G 23/1/2), fos. 44v–46v.
3 *Calendar of Patent Rolls, 1452–1461*, p.657
4 *Proceedings and Ordinances of the Privy Council*, vi., pp.307–10.

Wiltshire to battle and destroy their army before they could join forces with Queen Margaret and other Lancastrian lords.[5]

A New Duke of York and Old Quarrels

The build-up to and events of the Battle of Mortimer's Cross have left little trace in the historical record, rendering it one of the more obscure battles of the Wars of the Roses. There is confusion over when it was fought; there is no certainty over where it was fought; and no contemporary source provides any information on the disposition of the two sides or the course of the fighting. All that can be said with any certainty is that at the beginning of February 1461 a Yorkist army led by Edward, the new Duke of York, defeated a Lancastrian army commanded by the earls of Pembroke and Wiltshire near Mortimer's Cross in Herefordshire. As they were for Wakefield, the mainly London-based pro-Yorkist chroniclers of the 1460s were poorly informed about the battle, while the usually imaginative Tudor historians have relatively little to say.[6] It appears to have featured but briefly in the various newsletters that reached the continent, and the accounts based upon them note little more than that the Earl of March, as they consistently referred to Edward, defeated the Earl of Wiltshire. Similarly, the Welsh poets, although they lamented the death of Owen Tudor, had very little to say about the battle itself.[7]

In January 1461 Edward, Duke of York, had around him a small but able and loyal band of men. His three chief captains were Sir William Herbert of Raglan, Walter Devereux of Weobley, and Sir Roger Vaughan of Tretower. They had joined him in the marches after their largely unsuccessful efforts to bring the principality to heel throughout the previous autumn. According to a list compiled by William Worcestre around 1479, he was also joined by three lords: Reynold, Lord Grey de Wilton, Sir John Radcliffe, Lord Fitzwalter, and John, Lord Audley. The remainder of names in Worcestre's list very much suggest that the core of the men York gathered around him were those who had served his father in Wales and the marches. These included Herbert's brother, Richard, John Milewater, whose father had been the Duke's receiver of Wigmore and several lordships in Wales, and Sir Richard Croft of Croft Castle, Herefordshire (alongside whom Edward had grown up at Ludlow Castle), along with two other knights from the same county, Sir John Lynell and Sir William Knylle. There was significant military expertise among York's men. Herbert, Devereux and Vaughan had proved themselves defending Yorkist interests in Wales during the 1450s, while in Worcestre's list several esquires were noted as 'a man of war'. One of those listed, Philip Vaughan of Hay, was described as 'a man of war of France, the most noble esquire of lances'. His service in France is obscure, but he was perhaps a son of the Philip Vaughan killed at Agincourt in 1415 and a kinsman of the Devereuxs. One omission from Worcestre's list was John Dwnne of Kidwelly. A close associate of William Herbert and kinsman of the great Welsh rebel Owain Glyn Dŵr, he had been a longtime servant of Richard, Duke of York, in West Wales.[8] According to the pseudo-Worcestre *Annales*, Sir William Hastings and Sir John Wenlock were with Edward in Gloucestershire in the days after the battle and some historians have assumed

5 Wavrin, v., p. 327; Evans, *Wales and the Wars of the Roses*, pp.122–3.

6 *Polydore Vergil*, p.109; *Hall's Chronicle*, p.251.

7 Evans, *Wales and the Wars of the Roses*, pp.128–9; BNF, MS Français 88, fo. 141v.

8 William Worcestre, *Itineraries*, ed. John Harvey (Oxford: Clarendon Press, 1969), pp.202–5; Johnson, *Duke Richard*, p.235; Evans, *Wales and the Wars of the Roses*, p.58.

they too fought at Mortimer's Cross.[9] No contemporary source offered an estimate for the size of the Yorkist army except for the 'Short English Chronicle', which provided the unlikely number of 30,000, and the pseudo-Worcestre *Annales* with an even more nonsensical 51,000.[10] Given the size of the known urban contingents and the relatively few nobles who joined Edward's army, it seems unlikely that it would have exceeded a couple of thousand men in total.

The composition and size of the army assembled by Pembroke and Wiltshire is even less clear. After Northampton, Pembroke had garrisoned the castles of Carreg Cennen and Kidwelly, as well reinforcing his own castles of Pembroke and Tenby, and the royal castles of Aberystwyth, Denbigh, Carmarthen and Harlech, which he held. The Duke of York's own castles in the Principality and in the marches, such as Montgomery and Wigmore, continued to be held by men loyal to the Lancastrians. The order given to Herbert, Devereux and Vaughan to recover these places seems to have had little effect.[11] The movements of the two Lancastrian commanders in the autumn of 1460 are obscure. Wiltshire almost certainly remained in the Low Countries, and he may have sailed to Wales via Ireland, where he enjoyed some support both as Earl of Ormond and by virtue of his appointment as lieutenant there by Henry VI in December 1459. Pembroke's travels are altogether more mysterious. According to the Welsh poet Lewis Glyn Clothi, he had sailed to Ireland and then onto France when Margaret had left Wales for Scotland and only returned to Milford Haven on 27 December 1460. This suggestion was dismissed by R.S. Thomas, who insisted Jasper remained in Wales throughout, but the 'Short English Chronicle' also suggests that Edward received news of the earls' arrival 'by see' early in the new year.[12]

If indeed Pembroke had only returned to Wales at the end of the year, then he worked quickly to assemble an army. Perhaps Wiltshire, accompanied by his French, Breton and Irish mercenaries, did not arrive until mid-January, but this is speculation.[13] Once again William Worcestre provides the fullest list of those who fought alongside the Lancastrian earls at Mortimer's Cross. Most of the Welshmen named came from Carmarthenshire and Pembrokeshire: Lewis ap Rhys of Carmarthen, Philip Mansel and Hopkin ap Rhys from Gower, and two sons of the notorious Gruffudd ap Nicholas, 'the eagle of Carmarthen', who had terrorised much of West Wales in the 1450s. Also with the earls was Jasper Tudor's father, Owen, although whether he fought in the battle or was simply captured afterwards is unclear. The men were recruited from across Wales if the presence of Llewellyn ap Hulkyn, an esquire from Anglesey, the Tudors' homeland, who was captured during the battle, is anything to judge by.[14] A substantial proportion of the army appears to have come from Herefordshire. It was led by Sir John Scudamore of Kentchurch, supported by his sons, James and Sir Henry, and his brother, William. Another prominent Lancastrian present at Mortimer's Cross was the Warwickshire knight Sir John Throckmorton. According to the author of 'The Short English Chronicle', the earls had also recruited 'Frensshemen and Brettons, and Iresshemen' for their army, and while this has been noted by almost every modern historian writing on the battle, there is no other evidence for the presence of foreign mercenaries at Mortimer's Cross. There is no

9 *Letters and Papers*, ii(2)., p.777.
10 *Three Fifteenth Century Chronicles*, p.76; *Letters and Papers*, ii(2), pp.775–6.
11 Dan Spencer, *The Castle in the Wars of the Roses* (Barnsley: Pen and Sword, 2020), pp.56–7.
12 Evans, *Wales and the Wars of the Roses*, pp.74–5; *Three Fifteenth Century Chronicles*, p.76; R.S. Thomas, 'The Political Career', pp.188–99.
13 Geoffrey Hodges, *Ludford Bridge and Mortimer's Cross* (Almeley: Logaston Press, 1989), pp.39–40.
14 Michael J. Bennett, 'Memoir of a Yeoman in the Service of the House of York, 1452–1461', *The Ricardian*, 8 (1989), pp.259–64.

real sense from contemporary sources of how many men Pembroke and Wiltshire had mustered (only the pseudo-Worcestre provides a figure of 8,000, which is probably an exaggeration), but given what followed it seems likely that they were outnumbered by the Yorkists.

The Battle of Mortimer's Cross

None of the contemporary sources provide any indication of how the two sides arrayed their forces or how the fighting progressed once battle had joined. The site of the battlefield has eluded recent archaeological investigation. Its traditional location was based largely on local tradition and the rather spurious discovery of artefacts. These concentrated on the crossroads between the ancient road which runs west–east from Easthampton to Lucton, and Watling Street, the Roman road now known as Hereford Lane, which runs north–south. An alternative site, further south about a mile and a half from Mortimer's Cross itself, in the parish of Kingsland, was marked by the erection of a stone monument in 1799.[15] William Worcestre, in an unusually precise description, located the battlefield as eight miles from Hereford and three miles from Wigmore.[16] Given that the location of the battlefield and disposition of the armies is unclear, most scholarly debate has revolved around the direction from which the Lancastrians and Yorkists approached Mortimer's Cross. This would suggest the armies' positioning and the terrain features that would have influenced the tactical thinking of the opposing commanders.

It would have taken at least five days, probably several more, for the Lancastrians to make their march from Pembroke to Mortimer's Cross, a distance of well over 100 miles whichever route they took. It has been argued that their likely intent was to attack York's castle of Wigmore before moving onto Ludlow, rather than heading north to rendezvous with Queen Margaret's forces, although this seems unlikely. Laying siege to these strongholds would have required a sizeable artillery train and would have squandered the advantage Wakefield had handed the Lancastrians.[17] Moreover, there is nothing to suggest that the Yorkists had regained control of Wigmore Castle by January 1461. In March the previous year, the Lancastrian household knight Sir William Catesby had been appointed receiver of Wigmore, while in May John, Lord Dudley, had been made constable and porter of the castle.[18] In 1461, Dudley was in Yorkist custody after his capture at Blore Heath, but Catesby or their deputies may still have been holding the castle at the beginning of 1461. If that was the case, it would have been a convenient place for the Lancastrian earls to rest and resupply before meeting Margaret somewhere in the Midlands. Two routes have been suggested for the Lancastrian march to Mortimer's Cross. The shorter route took them from Llandovery over the mountains through Sugarloaf Pass to Builth Wells and New Radnor. A second, longer route would have involved leaving the Usk Valley and marching to Brecon, from where they followed the north bank of the River Wye through Weobley towards Leominster. The Brecon route would have allowed many more opportunities to victual the army and avoided crossing the mountains in the dead of winter.

The Lancastrians' route to Mortimer's Cross is important as historians have used it to determine the disposition of the two armies. H.T. Evans favoured the shorter route through the mountains

15 Brooke, *Visits to Fields of Battle*, pp.74–5, 80.
16 Worcestre, *Itineraries*, ed. Harvey, pp.202–3.
17 Hodge, *Ludford Bridge and Mortimer's Cross*, p.40.
18 *Calendar of Patent Rolls, 1452–1461*, pp.550, 586.

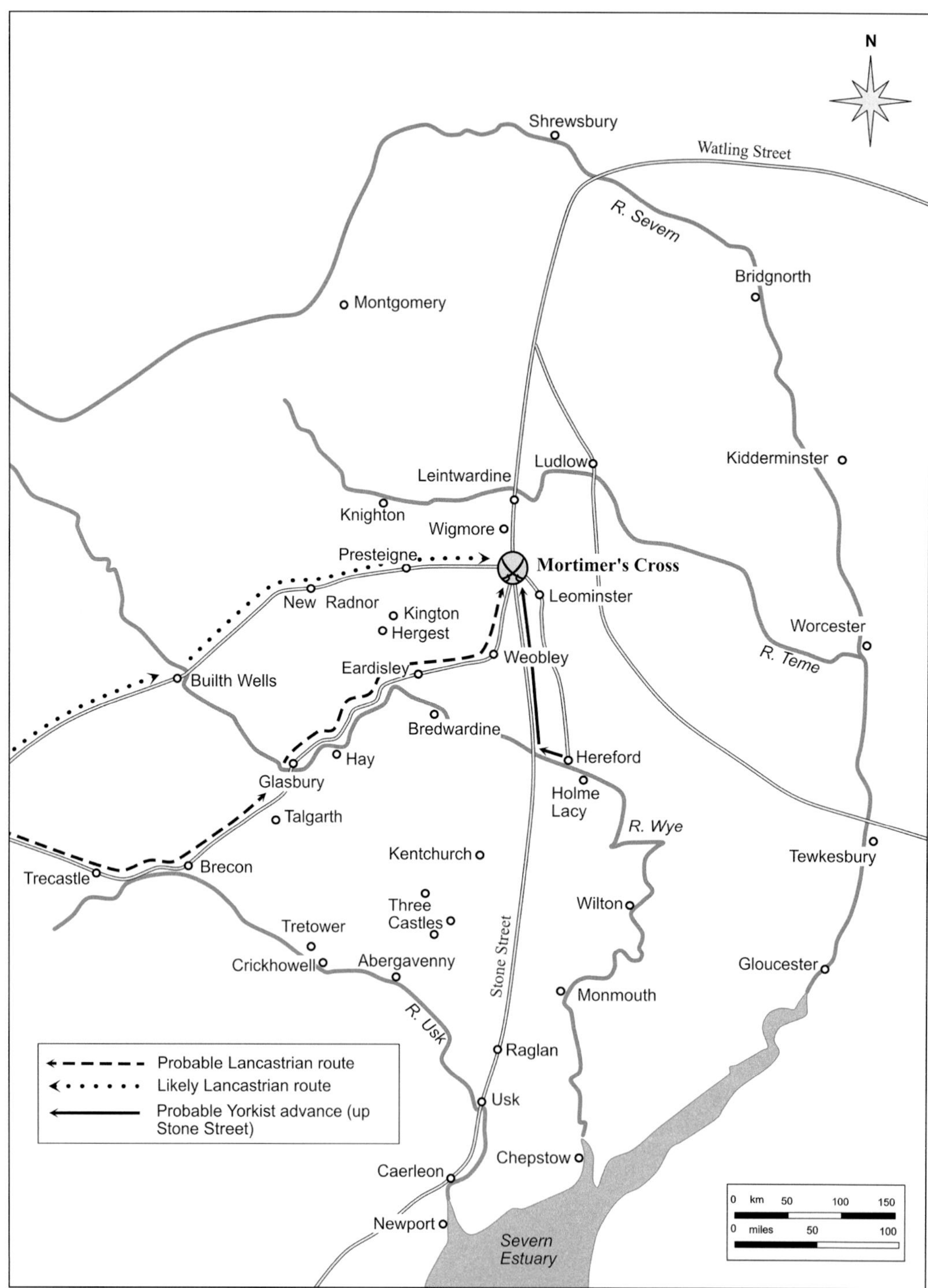

The Mortimer's Cross campaign, 1461. This map shows the two possible Lancastrian routes from Wales to Mortimer's Cross.

and thus had the Lancastrians approaching Mortimer's Cross from the west, with the two armies deployed facing each other across the Roman road. The Yorkists faced west, with their backs to the River Lugg, while the Lancastrians were arrayed along the top of a ridge near 'Mortimer's Rock'.[19] This would have been a difficult position from which the Lancastrians could deploy and descend the slope to engage Edward's army, while the Yorkists would have been unwise to deploy with the river to their back. Hodges argued that Pembroke and Wiltshire came via Brecon along the River Wye and thus marched to Mortimer's Cross from the south. In Hodges's account the battlelines were rotated through 90 degrees, with the Yorkists straddling the Roman road, just south of the former Mortimer's Cross Inn and the tree known locally as 'Battle Oak', their flanks secured by the River Lugg on their left and high ground to the right. The Lancastrians advanced north from Kingsland, the relatively narrow frontage between the river and the high ground forcing the two armies to employ their battles in columns rather than line abreast.[20] Both interpretations assume that the battle was fought at or near Mortimer's Cross itself. A third possibility, assuming the Lancastrians took the longer, southerly route through Wales, is that the battle was fought further south, in the parish of Kingsland, in the area around the stone monument erected in 1799. The manor of Kingsland was held by the Mortimer family, and they had held a weekly market and annual fair there since the late thirteenth century. The 'cross' referred to by contemporaries may have been a market cross. This site accords with a late seventeenth-century description of the battle taking place in the parish of Kingsland in 'a field called ye Great West Field near Mortimer's Cross', to the south of Evans's and Hodge's battlegrounds.[21] Hodge also suggests that the narrowness of the terrain if the Lancastrians advanced to Mortimer's Cross from the south would have forced both armies to deploy their three battles in columns rather than line abreast. Yet if, as he suggests, the Yorkists had only 2,000 men and the Lancastrians still fewer, they could have deployed in a more conventional manner if the battle was fought closer to Kingsland.[22] Nevertheless, given the complete lack of documentary or archaeological evidence locating the battlefield firmly in the landscape, any identification of the site or putative deployment of the two armies remains purely speculative.

While the Lancastrian approach to battle remains unclear, there is evidence of the Yorkist preparations for battle. At the beginning of February Edward moved to Hereford. The 'Short English Chronicle' describes how, upon learning that Pembroke and Wiltshire were approaching, York abandoned his plan to march to London, and 'he with all his men torned a yene bacwarde in to Walis'.[23] 'Gregory's Chronicle' tells us that at Hereford, 'he mousterd hys many with owte the towne wallys in a mersche that ys callyd Wyg mersche'.[24] Widemarsh Common, to the north-west of Hereford, was an obvious place for the Yorkists to muster, and it was here on the cold morning of 2 February that the army witnessed the natural phenomenon of a parhelion. The refraction of ice crystals in the air caused two mock suns to appear either side of the sun itself. The author of *An English Chronicle* provided the fullest description of what happened:

19 Evans, *Wales and the Wars of the Roses*, p.125; Haigh, *Military Campaigns*, pp.42–3; Sadler, *The Red Rose and the White*, p.99.

20 Hodges, *Ludford Bridge and Mortimer's Cross*, pp.49–51; Bicheno, *Battle Royal*, pp.265–7.

21 *The 1675 Thomas Blount Manuscript History of Herefordshire*, ed. Richard Botzum, Catherine Botzum and Norman C. Reeves (London: Lapridge Publications, 1997), p.97.

22 Hodges, *Ludford Bridge and Mortimer's Cross*, pp.43, 50.

23 *Three Fifteenth Century Chronicles*, p.76.

24 *Contemporary English Chronicles*, p.71.

The stone monument, erected in 1799, in Kingsland parish may suggest a site further to the south than the crossroads at Mortimer's Cross for the battle fought on 3 February 1461. (Battlefields Trust, used with permission)

> And the Monday before the daye of the batayle, that ys to say, in the feest of the Puryficacion of Oure Blessed Lady [Candlemas, 2 February], abowte x atte clocke before none, were seen iij sonnys in the firmament shynyng fulle clere, whereof the people had grete meruayle, and therof were agast. The noble Erle Edward thaym comforted and sayde, "Beeth of good comfort, and dredeth not; thys ys a good sygne, for these iij sonys betokene the Fader, the Sone, and the Holy Gost, and therefore late vs haue a good harte, and in the name of Almyghty God, go we agayns our enemyes."[25]

It was a masterstroke of leadership if the 18-year-old Duke of York was able to turn the parhelion to his advantage there and then, but it certainly soon became a defining moment of young Edward's career and the so-called 'sun in splendour' was adopted as one of the principal Yorkist badges. A scene depicting the appearance of the parhelion, showing Edward addressing his army with the three suns and three crowns in the sky and showing the town of Hereford in the background, was included in a Yorkist propaganda roll made in the summer of 1461. Edward looks to the heavens and asks, 'Lord, what wilt thou have me to do?' God's response, taken from the scriptures, is a clear foretelling of York's eventual accession to the throne: 'Thou shalt be crowned from the top of Amana, from the top of Sanir and Hermon.' [26] From Hereford, the Yorkist army then marched the 16 miles or so to array themselves across the Roman road somewhere between Mortimer's Cross and Kingsland. From there, they awaited the arrival of the Lancastrians.

No contemporary writer left any description of what happened when the two armies met on 3 February. In his *Recueil*, Wavrin introduced the detail that Edward attacked the Lancastrian camp, but this did not feature in the earlier accounts that seem to have been Wavrin's exemplar.[27] Even the later Tudor writer Edward Hall was unusually brief, saying only Edward 'fiercely set on his enemies'.[28] Most detailed descriptions of the fighting at Mortimer's Cross are based upon the long and imaginative account contained in Michael Drayton's epic poem *The Miserie of Queene Margarite*, published in 1627. His emphasis on the failure of Wiltshire's Irish in the face of disciplined marcher bowmen probably owed more to early Stuart prejudice against the Gaelic inhabitants of Ireland than any genuine memories of the fifteenth-century battle.[29] Most modern accounts of the fighting are pure fiction, not supported by any contemporary evidence or later chronicles.[30] The outcome of the battle was, nevertheless, very clear. On 11 March the Milanese ambassador wrote to his master, Francesco Sforza, Duke of Milan, stating simply that on 3 February Edward had won a battle against two lords of the Queen's party. In the fighting, 8,000 men fell, including 200 or more knights and esquires.[31] The Yorkist chroniclers of the 1460s gave differing figures for the numbers of dead: both 'Gregory's Chronicle' and the 'Short English Chronicle' stated 3,000 Lancastrians had died, while *An English Chronicle* ventured 4,000. Jean de Wavrin inflated the

25 *An English Chronicle*, p.99.

26 BL, Harley MS. 7353; Sonja Drimmer, 'A Political Poster in Late Medieval England: British Library Harley MS 7353', in *Performance, Ceremony and Display in Late Medieval Britain: Proceedings of the 2018 Harlaxton Symposium*, ed. Julia Boffey (Donington: Shaun Tyas, 2020), pp.333–59.

27 Wavrin, v., p.328; BNF, MS Français 88, fo. 142.

28 *Hall's Chronicle*, p.251.

29 Michael Drayton, *The Battaile of Agincourt Fought by Henry the Fift of that Name, King of England, against the Whole Power of the French …* (London, 1627), STC 7190; Hodges, *Ludford Bridge and Mortimer's Cross*, pp.49–55; Saintuste, *Edward IV and the Wars of the Roses*, pp.39–41; Bicheno, *Battle Royal*, pp.266–9.

30 Sadler, *The Red Rose and the White*, pp.98–101; Haigh, *Military Campaigns*, pp.42–3.

31 *Calendar of State Papers, Milan*, p.57.

number of dead to between 6,000 and 7,000. Both Pembroke and Wiltshire escaped the slaughter, but Owen Tudor was less fortunate. He was taken alive to Hereford, where he was beheaded. According to 'Gregory', Owen believed he would be pardoned 'tylle he sawe the axe and the blocke'. Then, in a moment of literal gallows humour, he quipped, '"That hede shalle ly on the stocke that was wonte to ly on Quene Kateryns lappe" and put hys herte and mynde holy unto God, and fulle mekely toke hys dethe.'[32]

Beside Owen Tudor and the two earls, the precise fate of those who served in the Lancastrian ranks at Mortimer's Cross is more difficult to establish. William Worcestre identified ten other Lancastrians who were beheaded alongside Tudor at Hereford, while the pseudo-Worcestre *Annales* states eight 'captains' were put to death.[33] The most prominent among them was the Lancastrian knight Sir John Throckmorton. Five or probably six of the others named were Welshmen, including Reginald Gwyneth, chamberlain of Gwynedd, while the two sons of Sir John Scudamore – James and Sir Henry – were also beheaded. Worcestre's list should be treated with some caution. Among the men he named was the Herefordshire lawyer Thomas Fitzharry of Poston in Vowchurch. Fitzharry was associated with the Scudamores and had clashed with William Herbert and Walter Devereux in 1456 over the murder of Herbert's kinsman, Roger Vaughan. Fitzharry had sat in the Commons for Herefordshire in the Coventry Parliament that had attainted the Yorkist lords, and a commission for his arrest had been issued in the wake of the Yorkist victory at Northampton. Worcestre was mistaken, however, in naming him among those Lancastrians executed after Mortimer's Cross. Fitzharry had, in fact, escaped with Pembroke and continued to resist the Yorkists in Wales into 1462 before travelling to Scotland. He survived to be restored to a position of local authority as a justice of the peace in Herefordshire during Henry VI's Readeption and may even have fought at the Battle of Tewkesbury in 1471.[34] At least one prominent Welsh Lancastrian was captured and put to ransom. Llewellyn ap Hulkyn was taken by Hugh Wiot, a Yorkist man-at-arms. Hulkyn offered £100 for his release, but Wiot handed him over to Edward, who allegedly ransomed him for the unlikely sum of 1,000 marks (£666 13*s.* 4*d.*). We only know of this incident through the chance survival of a later petition from Wiot seeking recompense for his long service to the House of York, but it likely points to a practice that was more widespread than assumed in the battles of the Wars of the Roses.[35] We know of no prominent Yorkists who died at Mortimer's Cross, although those who had fallen fighting alongside Edward on 3 February were subsequently remembered in some of the chantry chapels erected in the 1460s to pray for those killed in Yorkist service.[36]

After the battle Jasper, Earl of Pembroke, retreated into Wales. On 25 February he wrote from Tenby to Roger Puleston and John Eyton, keepers of Denbigh Castle, promising to avenge 'the great dishonour and rebuke that we and yee now late have by traitor Marche, Herbert, and Dunns, and their affinityes'. John Dwnne of Kidwelly may have earned Pembroke's rancour by shadowing the Lancastrians' march from South Wales and informing the Yorkists of their route, allowing Edward to intercept them at Mortimer's Cross. Jasper remained at Tenby until the summer. On 24 July he wrote to Puleston imploring him to hold Denbigh and to do his utmost 'to your faithful diligence for the safeguard of hit'. Jasper also asked him for reassurance of the disposition of the

32 *Contemporary English Chronicles*, p.70; *Three Fifteenth Century Chronicles*, p.76; *An English Chronicle*, p.99; Wavrin, v., p.328.
33 Worcestre, *Itineraries*, ed. Harvey, pp.202–3; *Letters and Papers*, ii(2), p.776.
34 *The House of Commons, 1422–1461*, iv., pp.381–6.
35 Bennett, 'Memoirs', pp.261–3.
36 *Calendar of Patent Rolls, 1461–1467*, pp.516–7.

local people 'towards my Lord Prynce', Henry's and Margaret's son, who had emerged as the figurehead of Lancastrian resistance after Towton.[37] Wiltshire's movements are obscure. Rather than lingering in Wales or crossing to Ireland, he may have moved to join Queen Margaret and the other Lancastrian lords in the north. According to Wavrin, Margaret was devastated when she heard news of Mortimer's Cross, 'because she greatly loved the Earl of Wiltshire'.[38] The victorious Yorkists remained in the marches in the immediate aftermath of the battle. On 12 February Edward was commissioned to call together the King's loyal subjects in the counties of Staffordshire, Shropshire, Herefordshire, Gloucestershire, Worcestershire, Somerset and Dorset to march against and resist the King's enemies and rebels.[39] He was still engaged in raising more men when his uncle, the Earl of Warwick, met the Lancastrian army at St Albans.

* * *

Militarily, the Battle of Mortimer's Cross changed little. The Lancastrians' main strength lay in the retainers and tenants of the northern lords, helped by men from the West Country. The defeat of Pembroke's Welsh followers and the few European mercenaries and Irishmen that Wiltshire may have cobbled together did little to alter the balance of forces. Equally, while Edward was clearly active in raising men from the marches, the ultimate success of Yorkist plans depended on the men they could raise from the south-eastern counties and London. Politically and symbolically, however, Mortimer's Cross was significant. We do not know why Edward tarried in the marches and Midlands after the battle – perhaps, as Michael Bennett suggested, 'ensconced in Hereford castle, in the aftermath of his victory, Edward can be seen as a latter-day warlord, presiding over the trials of his enemies, garnering booty and ransoms, and giving gifts to his followers'.[40] His delay meant, however, that he avoided the defeat at St Albans later in the month. He could then meet the Earl of Warwick and return to London victorious, the saviour of the realm from the depredations of the Lancastrians and their foreign allies. It was a powerful propaganda opportunity that the Yorkists would exploit to the full.

Sources and Further Reading

Geoffrey Hodges's *Ludford Bridge and Mortimer's Cross* (Almeley, 1989) remains a good introduction to the complexities of studying the battle but see also the articles by Adam Lamkowski and Dave Lanchester in *The Hobilar* 23 (1997). The Mortimer's Cross 1461 Battlefield Project, sponsored by the Battlefields Trust, attempted to locate the battlefield through a thorough archaeological survey and review of the documentary evidence. The reports, by Glenn Foard and Tracey Partida, are excellent and represent the current state of understanding. The project nevertheless failed to securely locate the battlefield in the landscape. The reports can be downloaded at www.mortimerscross1461.co.uk.

37 John Williams, *Ancient and Modern Denbigh* (Denbigh: J. Williams, 1836), pp.86–7.

38 Wavrin, v., p.328.

39 *Calendar of Patent Rolls, 1452–1461*, p.659.

40 Bennett, 'Memoir', p.261.

8

The Second Battle of St Albans

The repercussions of what had happened at Wakefield at the end of December 1460 were seismic. They transformed the political landscape, especially in the north of England, overnight. Some sense of the abrupt change in attitudes forced by Northumberland's and Clifford's actions can be gained from the payments made by the chamberlains of Hull. Between Michaelmas and Christmas 1460, the burgesses spent their money on fortifying the town walls, purchasing guns and gunpowder, making gunstones, and appointing keepers of the four town gates, as well as placing a great chain across the mouth of the harbour. They were determined, it seems, to deny access to Hull to the Lancastrians or anyone else for that matter. Between Christmas and Easter 1461, however, the accounts record messengers sent to Wressle Castle, as well as gifts of wine and fish to Northumberland, Clifford, Sir Ralph Percy and men of the Earl's household. The chamberlains paid for a horse given to Queen Margaret, purchased more gunpowder, and equipped men who rode to St Albans with the Queen.[1]

After Wakefield, Margaret had made her way south from Lincluden in Scotland. There, on 5 January, she had signed some sort of agreement with the regent, Mary of Guelders, possibly including a promise of marriage between Prince Edward and James III's sister, Mary. The main tenet of their agreement, however, as Michael Hicks suggests, was probably a promise that the Scots would cease their attacks on the border, allowing the northern lords to concentrate their efforts on the Yorkists. On 20 January Margaret met with her supporters in York. There they signed a document promising 'that they shal laboure by alle moynnes reasonable and withoute in convenient' to uphold the agreement made between the two queens at Lincluden earlier in the month. As well as the known Lancastrian partisans, the dukes of Exeter and Somerset, the earls of Northumberland and Devon, and Lord Roos, Margaret was joined by John, Lord Neville, and his brother, the Earl of Westmorland, Ranulph, Lord Dacre, Henry, Lord Fitzhugh, the Bishop of Carlisle and the Bishop of Coventry and Lichfield.[2] The latter, as we have seen, had given the Queen and Prince Edward shelter after the Battle of Northampton and may have accompanied her into Wales and Scotland. The Lancastrian party, it seems, had grown significantly in numbers and confidence in the immediate aftermath of York's death.[3]

1 Hull City Archives, BRF2/371.

2 Michael Hicks, 'A Minute of the Lancastrian Council at York, 20 January 1461', *Northern History*, 35 (1999), pp.214–21.

3 John Whelpdale, a residentiary canon at Lichfield cathedral from 1454 until his death in 1490, was among those attainted in November 1461 for his presence at Towton and he probably accompanied the bishop and

News of Wakefield soon reached the continent and both the Yorkists and Lancastrians sought to reassure their friends abroad. On 9 January Francesco Coppini assured the Duke of Milan that the Earl of Warwick had the support of the people in the south of England, and that he was assembling a large army to march on the King's enemies, a sentiment reinforced by Antonio de la Torre in his own letter to the Duke. Two days later, Warwick himself wrote to reassure the Duke of Milan of the situation and to Pope Pius II asking the pontiff not to be worried by the news coming out of England and assuring him that 'all will end well'.[4] Queen Margaret's plans, however, appear to have been dealt a blow by news of the Yorkist victory at Mortimer's Cross. On 26 February, Pierre de Brézé, her cousin and Seneschal of Normandy, wrote to Charles VII with news brought to him by one of his agents, who was with the Queen. De Brézé told the French king that Margaret had instructed him to do what he could to hamper Warwick's ships operating out of Calais, and that the Queen and her son intended to take ship to Antwerp, for which she desperately needed Charles's help.[5]

The Lancastrian March on London

It was probably at their January meeting that the Lancastrian lords agreed to march south. Their progress south along the Old Great North Road has become synonymous with pillaging, looting and the destruction of property. Yet, as we have seen, the trope of the barbarian-like northerner had been recurrent in Yorkist propaganda for several months by the beginning of 1461. In fact, there is very little documentary evidence of Lancastrian depredations. In 1463 the Stamford merchant William Colom brought a suit against a group of northerners, led by the Cumberland knight Sir William Martingdale. He alleged that 'during the reign of Henry VI', presumably when the Lancastrians passed through the town in 1461, they had broken into Colom's house, stealing goods worth £40.[6] Another plea involving the Lancastrian knight Sir William Plumpton and his brother-in-law Sir George Darrell concerned the theft of certain cloth and books from a Stamford man which was alleged to have taken place on 5 March, *after* the Battle of St Albans.[7] In 1461, the town of Stamford petitioned Edward IV for a new charter, which was duly granted the following year, citing the damage caused during the Lancastrian march south. Yet, as Alan Rogers has pointed out, this was a convenient way for a group of wealthy merchants, many of whom had lent money to the Yorkist cause, to gain further local power and influence at a time of political crisis. Indeed, it seems likely that the Lancastrians took more than one route south. In October 1461 Edward IV remitted £65 5*s.* 4*d.* due from the burgesses of Nottingham for their loyalty and due to the 'thaire grete persecucion losse and trouble ... susteigned by oure enemies and rebelles by the space of half yere and more', suggesting that Lancastrian forces passed through the town on

the queen throughout this period: *Parliament Rolls of Medieval England*, Parliament of November 1461, item 20; Carol M. Southworth, 'The Canons of Lichfield Cathedral in the Last Quarter of the Fifteenth Century' (University of Birmingham, MPhil thesis, 2012), p.30.

4 *Calendar of State Papers, Milan*, pp.41–4.

5 T. Basin, *Histoire de Charles VII et Louis XI,* ed. J. Quicherat (Paris: Societe de l'histoire de France, 1859), iv., pp.358–60.

6 Alan Rogers, 'Stamford and the Wars of the Roses', *Nottingham Medieval Studies*, 53 (2009), p.92.

7 TNA, KB27/804, rot. 50.

more than one occasion and may have remained there after the Second Battle of St Albans.[8] From Nottingham a portion of the army marched to Northampton, from there taking another main route south, Watling Street, towards St Albans.[9] Northampton too may have suffered at the hands of a Lancastrian force. In May 1462 the townsmen successfully petitioned for a remission of £20 of the fee farm, suggesting a degree of economic hardship, and two months later they had their charter renewed.[10]

The most powerful case for the Lancastrian 'sack' of the towns along the Great North Road was made by John Whethamstede, writing in the mid-1460s, and by the second continuator of the Croyland Chronicle, writing a decade or more later. Southern distrust of 'northerners' had a long history, dating to at least the thirteenth century, but the Yorkists had exploited this, stressing how Queen Margaret had promised her followers the freedom to plunder the south of England if they marched with her against the Act of Accord made in the 1460 Parliament.[11] Whethamstede joined this chorus in his account of the Second Battle of St Albans, but he did so to show off his classical learning and frame his later panegyric to Edward IV as much as to faithfully record the actions of the Lancastrians. Quoting the classical author Lucanus, he claimed that men from the south suffered from the 'excessive mildness of the climate', which made them 'too soft', while every northerner, coming from colder climes, was 'wild, a lover of war and death'.[12] The Croyland Continuator, who was prone to exaggerate the impact of the wars generally, claimed that after the Duke of York's death at Wakefield, 'the northmen, sensible that the only impediment was now withdrawn … swept onwards like a whirlwind … and universally devoted themselves to spoil and rapine, without regard of place or person'.[13] The Lancastrian army did not make the diversion of a dozen or so miles from the Great North Road to pillage the abbey, however, and although the Lancastrians may have attacked the Duke of York's town of Grantham, just as they had Wakefield and Middleham, and would subsequently loot the town of St Albans after the battle, there is no real evidence that the worst fears of Yorkist propagandists were realised.[14]

The army that marched with Margaret towards London was by no means exclusively northern, although the men raised by the Percys and Clifford probably accounted for the bulk of the force. As well as characterising them as northerners, the contemporary chroniclers, especially those close to the Earl of Warwick, presented the Lancastrian army at the Second Battle of St Albans as that of the Queen and the Prince of Wales. As the continuator of 'Gregory's Chronicle' observed, 'every man and lorde bare the Pryncys levery, that was a bende of crymesyn and blacke with esteryge [Ostrich] ys fetherys'.[15] The Lancastrian army also contained contingents supplied by at least one religious house, if an entry in the commonplace book of the Londoner John Vale is correct. Vale copied a signet letter from Edward IV written in the wake of the Battle of Towton ordering an

8 TNA, E159/238, *brevia directa baronibus*, Mich 1 Edw IV, rot. 9.

9 *Calendar of State Papers, Milan*, p.48.

10 *The Records of the Borough of Northampton*, ed. Christopher A. Markham and J. Charles Cox (2 vols., London: Elliot Stock,1898), i., pp.91–3.

11 Andy King, 'The Anglo-Scottish Marches and the Perception of "The North" in Fifteenth Century England', *Northern History*, 49 (2012), pp.37–50.

12 Whethamstede, pp.391–2.

13 *Ingulph's Chronicle*, pp.421–2.

14 B.M. Cron, 'Margaret of Anjou and the Lancastrian March on London, 1461', *The Ricardian*, 11 (1999), pp.597–601.

15 *Contemporary English Chronicles*, p.71. A bend was a sash, worn over the shoulder, bearing the livery device and badge of a lord.

unnamed prior to be removed from office for 'trying to secure our overthrow at St Albans and elsewhere with men in his livery, and agreeing to men's deaths in the town of St Albans'.[16] Most accounts agree that Margaret and Prince Edward were accompanied by the Duke of Somerset, although again the stress on Somerset's part in the battle was as much designed to demonstrate his faithlessness, having previously promised not to take up arms against Warwick. The Latin 'Brief Notes', 'Gregory', Robert Bale's chronicle and Jean de Wavrin also gave prominence to Andrew Trollope, who was among those knighted after the battle, and Wavrin even made him commander of the Lancastrian vanguard.[17] Yet precisely which other lords stood alongside Margaret and Somerset is less clear. Robert Bale's chronicle provided an extensive list of Lancastrian lords, ten in all (including the earls of Oxford and Westmorland, who are not named in any other source), while the pseudo-Worcestre *Annales* named eleven. The latter was alone in identifying the twelve-year-old Earl of Shrewsbury (who was supposedly knighted after the battle by Prince Edward) and lords Welles, Grey of Codnor and Fitzhugh as present on the Lancastrian side. 'Gregory', despite his detailed account of the fighting, merely stated that Margaret was accompanied by the lords who had been with her in the north, a list which, as we have seen, was based more upon later perceptions of which northern lords had supported Henry VI's cause.[18]

Few contemporaries ventured an estimate for the size of the Lancastrian army at St Albans in 1461. The *Annales* gave a preposterous number of 80,000, and the only other estimate – that made by the Milanese ambassador to the court of the Dauphin Louis – was of an equally unlikely 60,000. The contemporary compiler of the 'Brief Notes' noted it was a great army, but there is no evidence to support his claim that it comprised Scots, Welsh and 'other aliens' alongside the 'Northernmen'. In this he was probably merely repeating the charge levelled against the Lancastrians in the 1461 Act of Attainder.[19] 'Gregory' is probably our best guide to the size of the Lancastrian host. He reported that there were no more than 5,000 men in the Queen's army, as many had fled at the beginning of the battle. Those that remained were the retainers and household men of the Lancastrian lords and Prince of Wales. 'Gregory's' estimate, as we shall see, may indeed represent the bulk of the Lancastrian forces engaged at the Second Battle of St Albans.[20]

We can be much more confident of the identity of Yorkists lords who fought at the Second Battle of St Albans. The Earl of Warwick, the Duke of Norfolk and the Earl of Arundel left London on Thursday, 12 February. They took with them Henry VI and marched under the royal banner. With them went John Neville, Warwick's brother, who had recently been created Lord Montagu, Henry, Viscount Bourchier, and his brother, John, Lord Berners, as well as William, Lord Bonville, and the veteran of the French wars Sir Thomas Kyriel, elected one of the knights of the Garter just four days previously. According to *An English Chronicle*, Richard, Duke of York's son-in-law, the 18-year-old John de la Pole, Duke of Suffolk, was also among the Yorkist ranks.[21] One of the versions of the *Brut* chronicle added William, Lord Faucounberg, but he was almost certainly still in Calais acting

16 *John Vale's Book*, pp.161–2.

17 *Three Fifteenth Century Chronicles*, p.154; Hannes Kleineke, 'Robert Bale's Chronicle and the Second Battle of St. Albans', *Historical Research*, 87 (2014), p.750; Wavrin, v., p.327.

18 See appendix. *Letters and Papers*, ii(2)., p.776. The *Annales'* account of the battle itself is missing from the manuscript.

19 *Letters and Papers*, ii(2)., p.776; *Calendar of State Papers, Milan*, p.53; *Three Fifteenth Century Chronicles*, p.155.

20 *Contemporary English Chronicles*, p.71.

21 *An English Chronicle*, p.98. See appendix.

as Warwick's lieutenant, while 'A Brief Latin Chronicle' also names Lord de la Warre among the Yorkist ranks, a curious addition as the author of *An English Chronicle* had numbered him among the Lancastrian defenders of the Tower the previous July.[22] Like the Lancastrians, the Yorkists split their forces. The Duke of Norfolk, with the King, advanced up the Great North Road and then Watling Steet to St Albans, while Warwick marched directly north along the Old North Road (Ermine Street) towards Ware. This allowed the Yorkists to block two of the principal roads to London, while the third, the Great North Road at Hatfield, lay between them.[23] There are no reliable estimates for the size of the Yorkist army. Both Prospero Camulio, the Milanese ambassador to the French court, and Abbot Whethamstede numbered Warwick's force alone at some 4,000–5,000, although this may not account for the men under Norfolk's command. This was a more credible figure than the total of 200,000 Yorkists claimed by the author of the 'Brief Notes.'[24] Indeed, the Yorkists may have assembled more than 10,000 men in total and, if the combined Lancastrian armies were also around this size, there is an argument to be made that the Second Battle of St Albans witnessed the largest assemblage of forces in this stage of the Wars of the Roses.

The Second Battle of St Albans

The Second Battle of St Albans has attracted much attention from military historians. Alfred Burne considered it a remarkable battle that featured not only a night march to contact, but also an audacious flank attack by the Lancastrians and a battleline that stretched several miles. He was at a loss to explain the tactical innovation on the Lancastrian side, which was 'so unpredictable that a feminine hand may be detected in it.' He suggested that Margaret of Anjou was behind the Lancastrian plan and that she may have been 'striving to emulate' her heroine, Joan of Arc! [25] It seems unlikely that the battle displayed such startling feats of female generalship, and the reality may have been more mundane. Norfolk's men reached St Albans on 13 February, while Warwick probably reached Ware the following day.[26] Most historians from Burne onwards have assumed that the Lancastrians marched south from York to Royston, which they reached on 10 February, before turning west and taking the Icknield Way towards Dunstable. This, it has been suggested, was because of intelligence given by Richard Lovelace, one of Warwick's men, who had agreed to betray the Yorkists in return for his life after being captured at Wakefield. Instead of attacking the Yorkists at St Albans from the north-east, as expected, the Lancastrians now marched to Dunstable with the intention of attacking from the north-west. While this explanation may have satisfied Burne's notion of 'Inherent Military Probability', it assumes, first, that the Lancastrian army had marched south as a single body and, second, that they had won the intelligence battle through treachery and the failure of the Yorkists to identify their position and movements.[27] The first of these assumptions is almost certainly false, while the second is based on a selective reading of the sources. On 16 February a small Yorkist force led by the Sussex esquire Robert Poynings was

22 *The Brut*, i., p.602; *Three Fifteenth Century Chronicles*, p.172; *An English Chronicle*, p.89.

23 Penny Tucker, 'The Second Battle of St Albans', *Battalia*, 2 (2024), pp.39–40.

24 *Calendar of State Papers, Milan*, p.54; *Three Fifteenth-Century Chronicles*, p.154; Whethamstede, p.391.

25 Burne, *Battlefields*, p.232.

26 *John Benet's Chronicle*, p.49.

27 Burne, *Battlefields*, pp.232–5; Burley, Elliott and Watson, *The Battles of St Albans*, pp.59–61; Haigh, *Military Campaigns*, pp.47–9; Sadler, *Red Rose and the White*, pp.104–5; Bicheno, *Battle Royal*, pp.275–82.

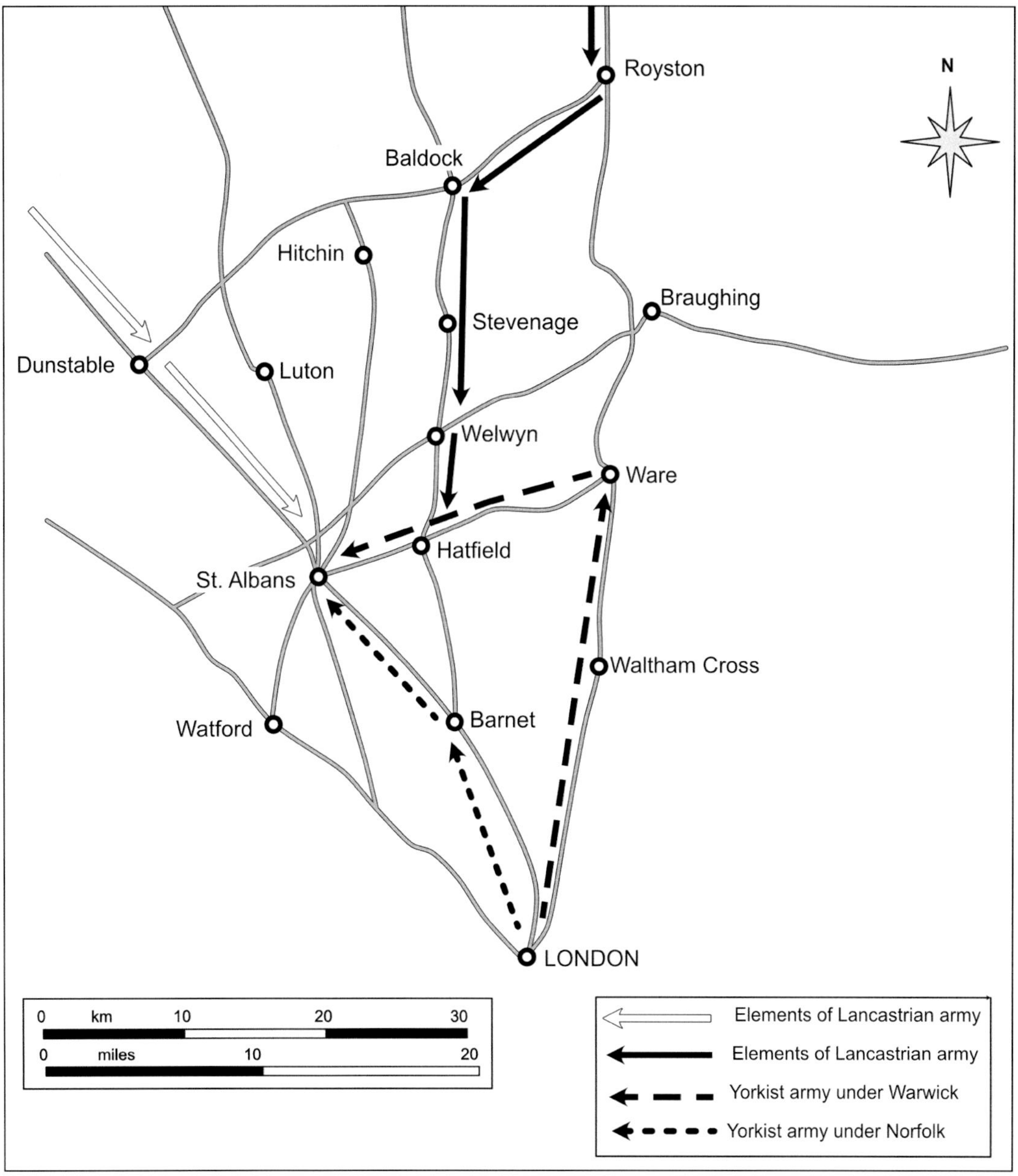

The main approach routes to St. Albans and the probable routes taken by the Yorkist and Lancastrian armies in February 1461.

attacked and routed in Dunstable. According to his inquisition *post mortem*, Poynings died the following day, while 'Gregory' claimed, improbably, that the part of the Yorkist force at Dunstable was led by a local butcher, who hanged himself out of shame for the costly defeat.[28] Rather than the main Lancastrian force taking the 28-mile detour from Royston to Dunstable, it seems more likely that Poynings and his men were defeated by a separate Lancastrian force approaching St Albans from Northampton.

The surviving sources for the following battle, fought on 17 February in and around St Albans, are fuller than most battles of the Wars of the Roses but confused and contradictory. None allow the historian to recreate what happened with the precision presented in some modern accounts. Each contemporary writer reported the battle from their own narrow perspective or tried to make sense of the confused events in the aftermath. One explanation that has been given undue prominence was that of the alleged treachery of Richard Lovelace, one of Warwick's Kentish captains.[29] The story appears to have originated in the now lost newsletters that were sent to Calais and disseminated in France and the Low Countries during the early months of 1461. They were designed to exonerate the Earl of Warwick for any blame in the disaster at Wakefield and the Yorkist defeat at St Albans. The story of Lovelace's treachery appears prominently in Jean de Wavrin's exemplar, and it was later incorporated into and formed the main thrust of his account of the battle in the *Recueil*.[30] It was a convenient explanation of events that tied together Wakefield and St Albans, underlining the perfidy of the Duke of Somerset and those involved with him, and deflecting any blame for the Yorkist defeat away from Warwick's leadership.[31] Lovelace's treachery featured in the otherwise bland narrative of the London-based author of *An English Chronicle*, but no other English source mentions him, although Robert Bale thought the Yorkists were put to flight 'by treson wrought in the Kinges ost'.[32] Similarly, much has been made of the detailed account contained in the continuation of 'Gregory's Chronicle.' The author provides a vivid picture of the Burgundian contingent which fought on the Yorkist side and the failure of their new-fangled gunpowder weapons and other novelties, as well as the apparent failure of the Yorkist mounted scouts. The importance given to 'Gregory's Chronicle' derives largely from the assumption that he was an eyewitness to the battle. Yet, as Penny Tucker has shown, that was almost certainly not the case, and his somewhat confused description of the battle appears to have been cobbled together from various half-heard rumours and colourful tales.[33]

One man who was an eyewitness to the battle – or at least present in the town during the fighting – was John Whethamstede, Abbot of St Albans. Whethamstede's account was coloured by his disdain for and fear of the Lancastrian army, which he characterised, as we have seen, as undisciplined northerners intent on destruction. The Abbot gave no indication of the time or even the day when 'the northerners' entered the town 'desiring to take a route through its middle and direct their army against the King's army [that is, the Yorkist army].' Near the Eleanor Cross in the

28 *Letters and Papers*, ii(2), p.776; *Contemporary English Chronicles*, p.71. See *The House of Commons, 1422–1461*, v., p.231 for the correct identification of Robert, and not Edward, Poynings as the Yorkist captain killed at Dunstable. Robert's fate remained unknown to his widow as late as May 1461.

29 Burley, Elliott and Watson, *Battles of St Albans*, pp.74–5; Haigh, *Military Campaigns*, pp.52–3.

30 BNF, MS Français 88, fos. 141v–142v.

31 BNF, MS Français 88, fo. 142v; Wavrin, v., pp.328–9. Wavrin reports how later, in March, Lovelace was captured, brought before Warwick in London and conveniently executed: Wavrin, v., p.334.

32 *An English Chronicle*, p.98; Kleineke, 'Robert Bale's Chronicle', p.750.

33 Tucker, 'St Albans', pp.30–3.

Market Place, 'they were compelled to retreat by a few archers … and flee with dishonour to the western end of the town; where, by the lane leading from the very end towards the north, as far as St Peter's Street, they obtained entrance and there engaged in a great conflict with a certain band of the army of the lord king'. From there, after some fierce fighting, 'they escaped to a heath called "Barnet" [Bernards] Heath', near the northern end of the town, where they encountered with some larger forces, four or five thousand of the vanguard of the king's army, a much greater, indeed a very great, conflict for the time being'.[34] There is nothing in the sources to suggest that this assault was led by Andrew Trollope nor that this force had conducted a night march from Dunstable to reach their objective. Indeed Carlo Gigli, writing to Bishop Coppini, and the writer of the newsletter sent to the Dauphin Louis, reported by the Milanese ambassador at his court, both stated that the fighting did not start until after midday.[35] Whethamstede may have been describing just one of the Lancastrian forces converging on St Albans that day. His description of some of the Lancastrians fleeing after encountering the Yorkist archers may be the same incident that 'Gregory' described in his account: 'For þe moste parte of northeryn men fledde away, and sum were take and spoylyed owte of hyr harnesse by the way as they fled.'[36]

Whethamstede's account seems to bear little relation to the other contemporary English accounts of the fighting. The missing account of the battle by Robert Bale was only discovered in Trinity College Dublin in 2013. Bale described how on 17 February 'the King being in a feld beside Seint Albons called Sandell and his Baner displaied' was confronted by the Lancastrian army. The Lancastrians were 'weell horsed and arraied and there overe threwe þe Kynges Baner'. Flushed with victory, the Lancastrians then sacked the towns of St Albans and Barnet.[37] *An English Chronicle* reported that the Yorkist lords with the King 'took hys felde beside a lytell towne called Sandryge, nat fer from Seynt Albonys, in a place called Nomannesland, and there he stoode and sawe his peple slayn on bothe sydes'.[38] The Latin 'Brief Notes' placed the battle a mile-and-a-half outside of St Albans at 'Nomannyslond'.[39] The only other contemporary source to locate the fighting was the Yorkist poem *The Rose of Rouen*, written shortly after the Battle of Towton in praise of Edward IV and the other Yorkist lords. One of its stanzas states: 'Upon a shrof Tuesday on a grene leede,/ Be-twix Sandricche & saynt Albons, many man gan blede.'[40]

Thus, as Penny Tucker has recently pointed out, most of the contemporary accounts are at odds with Burne's account of the battle, which has been favoured by recent historians. Burne argued that the Yorkists deployed their main force on Bernards Heath, with perhaps three other detachments covering some four miles to Nomansland Common, between Sandridge and Wheathampstead. In formulating this narrative, Burne largely followed Whethamstede, but he also applied his notion of 'Inherent Military Probability'. Bernards Heath dominated the northern roads into St Albans and was protected by a formidable Iron Age earthwork known as Beech Bottom Dyke. Behind this protection, it is presumed, the Yorkists erected their field fortifications and artillery as described by 'Gregory.'[41] Yet, in the absence of consequential archaeological evidence and the

34 Whethamstede, pp.390–1.
35 *Calendar of State Papers, Milan*, pp.49, 54.
36 *Contemporary English Chronicles*, p.71.
37 Kleineke, 'Robert Bale's Chronicle', p.750.
38 *An English Chronicle*, p.98.
39 *Three Fifteenth Century Chronicles*, p.154.
40 Robbins, *Historical Poems of the XIVth and XVth Centuries*, p.216.
41 Tucker, 'St Albans', pp.41–3; Burne, *Battlefields*, p.233; Burley, Elliott and Watson, *Battles of St. Albans*, pp.84–5.

confused and contradictory nature of the sources, it is impossible to determine with any confidence precisely where the Yorkists had assembled their forces. As John Benet's chronicle suggests, the Yorkist lords were probably in the town on the morning of 17 February and, on hearing of the approach of a Lancastrian force, probably a different one to that which approached St Albans from Dunstable, 'the king went to meet them in the eastern part of St Albans with something like 1,000 men'.[42] It is unclear whether Benet meant that King Henry physically accompanied the Yorkist force or whether his royal authority was being used figuratively. While the fighting on Nomansland Common, north-east of Sandridge, had been characterised as the Yorkist retreat from the town, it was more likely a separate engagement with a different Lancastrian force. It was this, and not the fighting in the town described by Whethamstede, that caught the attention of the London-based chroniclers.[43]

The most detailed and immediate account of the battle was probably that contained in a newsletter written to the Dauphin Louis 'by one who was at the great battle on Shrove Tuesday'. This was probably one of several newsletters circulated via Calais and designed in part to exonerate the Earl of Warwick of any blame for the Yorkist defeat. A copy came into the hands of Prospero Camulio, the Milanese ambassador to the Dauphin's court in exile in the Burgundian town of Jemappes. He described its contents in a letter, written on 9 March, to Francesco Sforza, Duke of Milan. The original newsletter upon which Camulio based his account has not been found. It gave 'full particulars of the princes, the numbers engaged, the assaults, the blows, the wounded and the rumours circulating that day on one side and other'. Camulio began by describing how the King's Yorkist army was camped in St Albans, but had suffered considerable desertion among its ranks because of the lack of victuals. After midday, Somerset attacked Warwick's position 'with 30,000 horse ... and wore them down with his attack'. This forced the Earl to 'quit the field'. Then, Camulio continued, Warwick moved into St Albans where he encountered another Lancastrian force of roughly equal strength, allegedly led by Queen Margaret herself. At this, Warwick, 'seeing himself alone and the day far spent', returned to the camp. Camulio does not reveal the location of the Yorkist camp, but stated that when Warwick arrived there, closely pursued by the Lancastrians, 'he heard some shouting from camp to the enemy. Fearing some act of treason, he got away as best he could.' Henry VI was discovered by Somerset, 'under a tree a mile away, where he laughed and sang'. The Duke took custody of the King and rode with him to St Albans to be reconciled with the Queen and Prince Edward.[44]

Camulio's account makes sense when read alongside the other sources for the battle. In its essentials, it was corroborated by letters written on 19 February by an Italian merchant in London, Carlo di Gigli, to his master, Michele Arnolfini, in Bruges and to the papal legate Coppini. Gigli too reported the fighting began around midday and lasted until dark. Warwick and the Yorkists, 'when they saw the victory incline to the other side, took flight'.[45] The other important point made by Camulio was that the Lancastrians who attacked Warwick from the north-west, forcing him to retreat *towards* St Albans, were mounted. Whethamstede makes the same observation that a significant proportion of the Lancastrian army was mounted, albeit this was probably a separate group. As the Yorkists fled, the Lancastrians 'pursued them with great speed on horseback; and seizing many of them, pierced them with their lances, and forced them to pay their due fate through mortal wounds'. It was only

42 *John Benet's Chronicle*, p.49.
43 Burley, Elliott and Watson, *Battles of St Albans*, pp.76–7.
44 *Calendar of State Papers, Milan*, pp.54–6.
45 *Calendar of State Papers, Milan*, pp.48–9.

nightfall that prevented a greater slaughter.[46] Robert Bale also noted the Lancastrians were 'weell horsed and arraied', probably the same 'howseholde men and feyd men' that 'Gregory' said 'gate that fylde'.[47] The use of mounted men may have been pivotal in the outcome of the battle. First, being mounted allowed the Lancastrians to cover quickly the 13 or so miles between Dunstable and St Albans and onwards towards Wheathampstead through Sandridge and Nomansland Common. Second, as 'Gregory' suggests, most of the Yorkist army was on foot and the sudden appearance of the mounted Lancastrians in the rear of their camp at Bernard's Heath could have caused the confusion and panic that led to Warwick's decision to abandon the field. The Yorkist defeat was, then, in some respects due to a failure of intelligence, but the swift movement of the Lancastrians armies might, to some degree, mitigate Warwick's culpability in the debacle.

As far as the Yorkists were concerned, there is no doubt that the Second Battle of St Albans was a debacle. Bale stated that the Duke of Norfolk was wounded and that the earls of Arundel and Warwick were put to flight. His chronicle numbered those slain at 4,000 on both sides. Other English chroniclers accounted for between 5,500 and 1,916 killed, while Camulio reported that some 4,500 men 'in one skirmish and another' lost their lives in fighting that lasted from midday to midnight. Writing in April to Coppini, George Neville, Bishop of Salisbury, gave the death toll at 3,000 on both sides.[48] In reality, the death toll was probably fewer and most of the Yorkists probably fled in the confusion. Rumours abounded of where the leading Yorkists were and as late as 4 March Coppini was told, quite wrongly, that Warwick had fled to Calais.[49] There were very few prominent men among the casualties and no Yorkists were named among those killed in the fighting on 17 February. The pseudo-Worcestre *Annales* named Sir James Luttrell and Arnold Savage among the Lancastrian dead.[50] The Tudor chronicler Edward Hall claimed that Sir John Grey, whose widow Elizabeth Woodville would go on to marry Edward IV, was also killed on the Lancastrian side at St Albans. The author of 'Warkworth's Chronicle', writing in the 1470s, however, claimed Grey died at Towton, while a Hanseatic merchant reported later rumours that Grey had variously been killed in battle, thrown off Rochester Bridge or executed for treason.[51] The aftermath of battle also afforded an opportunity for the settling of scores. The Londoner Thomas Myrdale later claimed that his father had been murdered by the Lancastrian Robert Whittingham on account of a debt. Myrdale stated his father had paid Whittingham the sum owed but, nonetheless, Whittingham's servants had 'stroke off his head' in the confusion after the battle.[52] There were also, it was alleged, those who had taken advantage of the confusion and laid in wait 'to robbe the people coming home from the feld of Seynt Albonys'.[53]

In the retreat the Yorkists also surrendered one of their most important political advantages: the custody of Henry VI. The King was almost certainly with the Yorkist vanguard, commanded by his chamberlain, Warwick's brother, John, Lord Montagu. Whethamstede provided a detailed account of Henry's last moments under Yorkist control. As darkness fell 'and understanding that in

46 Whethamstede, p.392.

47 Kleineke, 'St Albans', p.750; *Contemporary English Chronicles*, p.71.

48 Kleineke, 'St Albans', p.750; *Three Fifteenth Century Chronicles*, p.155; *Contemporary English Chronicles*, p.71; *An English Chronicle*, p.98; *Calendar of State Papers, Milan*, pp.55, 61.

49 *Calendar of State Papers, Milan*, p.54.

50 *Letters and Papers*, ii(2), p.776; *Calendar of Fine Rolls, 1461–1471*, pp.1–2.

51 *Hall's Chronicle*, p.252; *Contemporary English Chronicles*, p.114; Livia Visser-Fuchs, 'English Events in Caspar Weinrich's Danzig Chronicle 1461–1495', *The Ricardian*, 7 (1986), p.313.

52 TNA, C1/27/478.

53 TNA, C81/1547/154.

the King himself there was neither spirit nor courage, indeed, neither countenance nor speech, to console or encourage their people, rather a heart inclined to the opposite side, and to the Queen, his wife', the Yorkists around the King withdrew. Henry was advised by Thomas Hoo, a Sussex lawyer who had close professional connections to both the Duke of Norfolk and Earl of Northumberland, to send a message to the Lancastrian lords. Hoo himself approached Northumberland, and the King was brought to Lord Clifford's tent, where he was reunited with his wife and son.[54]

Whethamstede's account of Henry's reconciliation with the Queen is at odds with the narrative found in Camulio's letter and elsewhere. Camulio reported that the King had been placed under a tree a mile from the Yorkist camp. Upon hearing the news of Warwick's flight, he asked two 'princes', probably Montagu and Bonville, to remain with him before the Duke of Somerset arrived to convey him to St Albans to be reunited with the Queen.[55] Camulio's account, as we have seen, was based upon the newsletters sent to the continent shortly after the battle and designed to exonerate Warwick from blame. These newsletters formed the basis of Jean de Wavrin's account and that found in *An English Chronicle*. In the latter, Richard Lovelace led the Kentish contingents away from the Yorkist vanguard, thus presaging the collapse of the Yorkist position. Wavrin developed this story of treachery. As Somerset's men attacked the Yorkist camp, 'Lovelace approached the King and said, "Sire, all our men are in disarray."' Henry asked Lovelace where Warwick was and was told the Earl had fled, while Sir Thomas Kyriell, who was with the King, 'asked where his [Lovelace's] men, and Lovelace answered that they had all fled'. Echoing the account in Camulio, suggesting a common source, Wavrin goes on to say that upon hearing the news, the King, who was 'beneath a large oak tree … laughed heartily at the turn of events'. Lovelace, 'the treacherous traitor', then led the King and Kyriell to the Queen, 'who was very pleased with the king's arrival'.[56]

Whatever the true circumstances of Henry's reconciliation with his wife and son, the events that followed clearly shocked contemporaries. As was usual in the aftermath of a battle, men were knighted. Henry first knighted his seven-year-old son, who in turn knighted 30 prominent Lancastrians, beginning with Andrew Trollope and including Robert Whittingham, Thomas Tresham and William Tailboys, as well as the young Earl of Shrewsbury.[57] Thereafter the Lancastrians turned to vengeance. Almost all the sources agree that William, Lord Bonville, and Sir Thomas Kyriell were beheaded on the orders of Prince Edward. The Yorkist chroniclers captured something of the indignation of those 'who bode with the kynge and trusted on him, for he graunted to save them'. The author of *An English Chronicle* claimed that notwithstanding the King's promise of safety, the Queen, the Duke of Exeter and the Earl of Devon pressed for their execution. 'Gregory' reported of Bonville, 'the comyn sayynge that hys longage causyd hym to dye'.[58] Wavrin's account contains a speech, probably invented, delivered by Kyriell. Queen Margaret accused him of being a traitor, to which Kyriell replied: 'My most revered lady, I never once thought of, or committed treason, nor has anyone ever been able to accuse me of any villainous deed; it would grieve me to be marked as such in my old age.'[59] In the Parliament of November 1461, it was recalled how King

54 Whethamstede, pp.392–3.

55 *Calendar of State Papers, Milan*, p.55.

56 *An English Chronicle*, p.98; Wavrin, v., pp.328–9.

57 Shaw, *Knights of England*, ii., p.13; *Contemporary English Chronicles*, p.73.

58 *An English Chronicle*, p.98; *Contemporary English Chronicles*, p.71; *Three Fifteenth Century Chronicles*, pp.76, 155, 172; *Letters and Papers*, ii(2)., p.777.

59 Wavrin, v., p.329.

Henry had 'wilfully allowed' Bonville, Kyriell, and the unfortunate bearer of one of the King's banners that day, an esquire named William Gower, 'to be murdered and after that tyrannously beheaded' notwithstanding the 'faith and assurance on the word of a king, by his own lips'.[60] At least three other prominent Yorkists were captured: John, Lord Montagu, John, Lord Berners, and the Middlesex knight and comptroller of the King's household Sir Thomas Charlton. According to Carlo di Gigli, Montagu escaped Bonville's and Kyriell's fate as he was needed as a hostage and surety for the life of Somerset's brother, Edmund, then held as a prisoner in Calais, and because the King had declared himself satisfied with his chamberlain. Instead, Montagu was conveyed to York and placed in the custody of the Mayor.[61] Nevertheless, the execution of Bonville and Kyriell confirmed the reputation of the Lancastrians, and the King in particular, as oath breakers and reinforced the Londoners' fears of their own treatment at the hands of the 'northern' army.

Snatching Defeat from the Jaws of Victory

The success of Yorkist propaganda in creating a climate of fear around the Lancastrian northern army may have contributed to the collapse of their position at St Albans, but it was also central to what happened next. From St Albans, the Lancastrian army was expected to immediately march on London. Instead, Henry, Margaret and the rest of the Lancastrian lords advanced only as far as Barnet. Some historians have criticised the Lancastrian inaction, especially Queen Margaret's leadership, accusing her of 'throwing away her chance of success'.[62] Yet, as Barbara Cron has pointed out, that is to fundamentally misunderstand the Lancastrian position and read their actions through the lens of Yorkist propaganda. The Lancastrians had neither the means nor the inclination to take London by force. Instead, they asked the Mayor and aldermen for supplies. This request was granted, but the carts were prevented from leaving the city by a mob.[63] According to 'Gregory', the victuals and a sum of money the Mayor and aldermen had pledged to the Queen were stopped by a group led by Sir John Wenlock's cook. Rather than being the actions of 'an unruly element among the poorer classes', this was probably a concerted effort by a Yorkist element within the city to deny help to the Lancastrians.[64]

Next, the Mayor despatched the dowager duchesses of Bedford and Buckingham, as well as Lady Scales (the widow of the defender of the Tower murdered the previous year). All three women were well known to the Queen. They, along with a delegation of aldermen, met the Queen at Barnet on 20 February and returned with promises that the Lancastrian army would not harm anyone in the city, except the 'evildoers'. It seems that few in London believed the Lancastrian promises of goodwill. A Lancastrian force, led by Alexander Hody and Baldwin Fulford, was sent to Westminster, presumably to assume control of the law courts, chancery and exchequer, and two days later proclamations were issued from there in the King's name declaring Edward, 'Earl of March', a traitor.[65] On 21 February further negotiations between representatives of the aldermanic council and three Lancastrian knights, Edmund Hampden, John Heron and Robert Whittingham, resulted in an

60 *Parliament Rolls of Medieval England*, Parliament of November 1461, item 18.

61 *The Brut*, i., p.602; *Calendar of State Papers, Milan*, p.61.

62 J.R. Lander, *The Wars of the Roses* (Stroud: Alan Sutton, 2000), p.96.

63 Cron, 'Lancastrian March', pp.604–5.

64 *Contemporary English Chronicles*, p.73; J.L. Bolton, 'The City and the Crown', *The London Journal*, 12 (1986), pp.11–24.

65 *Letter and Papers*, ii(2)., p.777; *The Brut*, i., p.531; Cron, 'Lancastrian March', p.605.

agreement that they, with 400 men, should be allowed to the enter the city. The Mayor issued a proclamation that they should not be harmed, but when they arrived outside Aldgate two days later, they found the gates barred. It may be this incident that was described in *An English Chronicle*, although the author describes the Lancastrians as being led by the Duke of Somerset: 'And anon, hereupon, certayn speres and men of armes were sent by the sayde Duk, forto haue entered the cyte before his commyng, whereof some were slayn, and some sore hurte, and the remnant put to flyght.'[66] Carlo Gigli related a different story: on 22 February a group of Lancastrian horsemen had appeared at the Aldgate and been refused entry to the city. Upon hearing this and rather than risking a confrontation, the Lancastrian knights decided to abandon their plans to enter London.[67] Whatever the truth of the matter, the voices of conciliation within the city were quashed, and the Londoners' Yorkist sympathies prevailed. The city stood resolute in refusing entry or succour to the Lancastrians. By 26 February, when the city received messengers from the Warwick and York requesting entry, the Lancastrians were already making the long return north to York.

In the immediate aftermath of St Albans, the fate of the scattered Yorkists was unclear. Warwick, wisely, decided against returning to London and instead travelled west to rendezvous with Edward, Duke of York. Edward has been criticised for not marching towards London immediately after his victory at Mortimer's Cross, but he was still recruiting troops in the marches and in the Midlands. On 12 February he had been given a wide-ranging commission throughout the counties of Shropshire, Stafford, Hereford, Gloucester, Worcester, Somerset and Dorset to call together the King's faithful subjects and proceed against the Lancastrian rebels.[68] From Gloucester, he began the march along the old Roman road, now the A40, towards London. Probably on 23 or 24 February York met Warwick at Burford (or further north at Chipping Norton according to the *Annales*) in Oxfordshire. It is not clear how many men Warwick had brought with him from St Albans, but York appears to have added considerably to his army. According to the pseudo-Worcestre *Annales* it had grown to 8,000.[69] Prospero Camulio wrote with characteristic exaggeration when he told the Duke of Milan the two Yorkist lords had assembled 150,000 men, but he probably captured something of the excitement and confidence that surrounded York and Warwick's rendezvous when he described their army as 'the finest troops ever seen in England'.[70] John Benet estimated the Yorkist army at 20,000 horsemen and 30,000 on foot, again an exaggeration but a statement that reaffirms the sense of the anticipation around York's and Warwick's impending arrival in London. They probably entered London on Friday, 27 February. Duke Edward took up lodgings at Baynard's Castle, where he took counsel.[71] The Yorkist lords now set about assembling an army and 'anone fyll ynto hym peple innumerable, redy forto go with hym into the north to venge the noble Duke Richard, hys fadre'.[72] There could be no more negotiation or compromise. York had to realise his claim to the throne and destroy the Lancastrians in battle.

* * *

66 Helen Maurer, *Margaret of Anjou* (Woodbridge: Boydell and Brewer, 2003), pp.198–9; *An English Chronicle*, p.99.

67 *Calendar of State Papers, Milan*, p.51.

68 *Calendar of Patent Rolls, 1452–1461*, p.659.

69 *Letters and Papers*, ii(2)., p.777; *Contemporary English Chronicles*, p.73.

70 *Calendar of State Papers, Milan*, p.55.

71 Maurer, *Margaret of Anjou*, p.201. John Benet and 'Gregory' give 26 February; *John Benet's Chronicle*, p.50; *Contemporary English Chronicles*, p.73. *An English Chronicle*, p.100 gives 28 February.

72 *An English Chronicle*, p.100.

Despite the relative abundance of sources, the Second Battle of St Albans remains one of the most enigmatic battles of the Wars of the Roses. History, they say, is written by the victors, and there is no doubt that our understanding of the battle is distorted through the lens of Yorkist, and especially Warwick's, propaganda. The events of 17 February were a disaster for Warwick: his intelligence failed him, and he was caught unawares by the speed of the Lancastrian advance; his army fled from the field amidst confusion and possible rumours of treason; and he lost custody of King Henry and whatever legitimacy that gave the Yorkist cause. In the battle's aftermath, Warwick was quick to disseminate a narrative that blamed events not on any failure of leadership on his part, but on treason which crystallised in the person of Richard Lovelace. The other powerful strand of Yorkist propaganda was the myth of the rapacious northerner. This had been the mainstay of their messaging throughout the autumn and winter. It was also the core of Abbot Whethamstede's account of the battle, but in explaining Second St Albans in this way he was principally setting up his later portrayal of Edward IV as saviour of the realm rather than trying to accurately recount the events of 17 February. Paradoxically, it was the success of Yorkist propaganda that, in part, led to their defeat at St Albans but which also prevented a debacle turning into a disaster. The myth of the northerner steeled the Londoners against the Lancastrians and allowed York and Warwick to enter the city with their armies largely intact.

The Lancastrians, and Queen Margaret in particular, have attracted much criticism for their failure to press their advantage after St Albans. Realistically, however, they had few, if any, options. They had realised their principal objective, regaining control of Henry VI. Their army was probably exhausted and running short of supplies, not to mention a doubtless waning desire to remain on campaign, and its commanders could not be confident of defeating York's and Warwick's combined forces in battle. The Lancastrians had little choice but to return to the north, attempt to recruit more men, and await the inevitable Yorkist response.

Sources and Further Reading

The account of the Second Battle of St Albans in Peter Burley, Michael Elliott and Harvey Watson, *The Battles of St Albans* (Barnsley: Pen and Sword, 2007) was heavily influenced by Alfred Burne's account in *The Battlefields of England* (London, 1950), pp.232–44. The authors subsequently revised their battleplan in the light of the discovery of the missing fragment of Robert Bale's chronicle (*Battlefields*, 25:3 (Winter 2021), pp.14–21). Penny Tucker's 'The Second Battle of St Albans', *Battalia* 2 (2024), pp.27–48 is a thorough review of the sources and main interpretations of the battle and offers an in-depth analysis of the strategic priorities of both sides. An invaluable account, with an incisive discussion of the sources, of the Lancastrian march south and their attempts to gain access to London can be found in B.M. Cron, 'Margaret of Anjou and the Lancastrian March on London, 1461', *The Ricardian* 11 (1999), pp.590–615. The Kentish captain Richard Lovelace, Warwick's scapegoat for the defeat at St Albans, has continued to fascinate contemporaries and recent historians alike. His identity remains obscure but see Revd A.J. Pearman's two essays on the family: 'The Kentish Family of Lovelace', *Archaeologia Cantiana* 10 (1876), pp.177–184 and 'The Kentish Family of Lovelace No. 2', *Archaeologia Cantiana* 20 (1893), pp.54–63.

9

Ferrybridge and Towton

On Thursday, 26 February 1461, just nine days after the Lancastrian victory at St Albans, Edward, Duke of York, and his cousin the Earl of Warwick, accompanied by a few other Yorkist lords and their respective bands of men, entered London.[1] It was a remarkable turnaround in fortune from the disaster at Wakefield less than two months previously. By murdering the Duke of York at Wakefield, the Lancastrians, and by extension King Henry VI, had committed treason, rendering the Act of Accord of the previous year null and void. With the capital secure and the financial and political support of the Londoners assured, the Yorkists now set about enacting what the logic of their situation demanded. Edward lodged at Baynard's Castle on the river and from there planned his next move. The following day, 27 February, he issued a signet letter promising his good lordship to the provost and fellows of Eton College. In it he made his royal pretensions clear, declaring himself 'vray [true] and just heire, Duc of York, Erl of March, and Ulvestre'. Despite being in law still a minor and not having possession of his father's estates, Edward's claim to his father's titles, to be heir to the throne, and by extension now rightful King of England, was made explicit in a matter-of-fact way.[2]

In the afternoon of 1 March some 3,000 to 4,000 people, both Londoners and men from Edward's and Warwick's armies, assembled in St John's Fields to hear George Neville, Bishop of Exeter, proclaim Henry VI's misdeeds and outline York's claim to the throne. He asked the crowd if they renounced Henry as their king, which they answered in the affirmative, and then called for their acclamation of Edward as king. The message was carried to Edward at Baynard's Castle and the following day his claim to the throne was proclaimed in the city. On Tuesday, 3 March a hastily convened council of lords, led by Archbishop Bourchier and the bishops of Exeter and Salisbury, the Duke of Norfolk and Earl of Warwick, met and 'elected' Edward as their king. Later that day, proclamation was made that the people should meet Edward at St Paul's at nine the following morning. On 4 March, he processed to the cathedral, where he made offerings, and a *Te Deum* was sung. Then Bishop Neville preached from St Paul's Cross, rehearsing Edward's title and inviting

1 There is some debate over whether it was 25 or 26 February, but see C.A.J. Armstrong, 'The Inauguration Ceremonies of the Yorkist Kings and Their Title to the Throne', *Transactions of the Royal Historical Society*, fourth series, 30 (1948), pp.51–73, which this section largely follows.

2 Alex Brondarbit, '"Into our Defense and Saveguarde": Eton College and the Good Lordship of Edward, Duke of York', *Royal Studies Journal*, 4 (2017), pp.1–14.

the crowds to follow their new king to Westminster, where he took up his estate in Westminster Hall. The reign of Edward IV had begun.[3]

The correspondence contained in the archives of Milan reveals much about the mood in London at this time. Although the flow of news from England was heavily mediated through the Earl of Warwick's men and the foreign observers were largely sympathetic to the Yorkist cause, their letters reveal a widespread confidence that Edward would prevail amid a fear of the bloodshed that would inevitably follow from the climactic clash of York and Lancaster. On 4 March Nicolo Darabatta informed the papal legate, Bishop Coppini (then in Bruges having, it was reported, fallen out with the Earl of Warwick over plans to excommunicate the Lancastrians), that Edward had been chosen as king and planned shortly to march north to confront Henry, Queen Margaret and Prince Edward. 'There is a great multitude,' he continued, 'who say they want to be with him to live and die. These are great matters sufficient to fill every man with fear.' Prospero Camulio, the Milanese ambassador at the court of the Dauphin Louis, had heard that Henry VI had resigned the crown in favour of his son and even that the old King had been poisoned to facilitate Edward of Lancaster's accession. Edward IV and Warwick had amassed an army of 150,000 men, 'the finest troops ever seen in England'. Another of Coppini's correspondents put the size of the Yorkist army at 200,000. On 11 March Camulio provided more details to his master: Warwick had been placed in charge of an army of 120,000 men, divided into three divisions of 20,000, 40,000 and 60,000, whereas the Lancastrians had only 30,000 men. Warwick had put a strong fleet to sea to prevent Queen Margaret from escaping to France, but poor weather had also made the Channel unnavigable. On 27 March Camulio updated the Duke further, explaining that Edward had accepted all the trappings of regal authority, 'except the unction [anointing with oil] and the crown … until he has annihilated the other king and reduced the island and realm to a stable peace and, among other things, exacted the vengeance due for the slaughter of his father and of so many knights and lords, who have been slain of late'.[4]

We know relatively little of the Yorkist preparations before they left London to march north. On 6 March Edward ordered the sheriffs of London and counties throughout the realm to make proclamation detailing the treasons of Henry VI, the dukes of Somerset and Exeter, the earls of Pembroke, Wiltshire, Northumberland and Devon, and lords Roos, Welles and Neville. All men aged between 60 and 16 were to assemble, defensively arrayed, to wait upon the Yorkist king and resist the rebels. On the same day, letters close to the captains, masters and men of the fleet assembled to sail to the 'northern parts of the realm' ordered them to make proclamation to the effect that anybody adhering to the party of the Lancastrian rebels who departed from them within ten days would receive a royal pardon. Twenty-two named individuals and anyone having lands to the value of £100 per annum were to be excluded, while eight men – Andrew Trollope, the illegitimate brothers of the Duke of Exeter, William Grimsby, Robert Whittingham, Thomas Tresham, Thomas Fitzharry and 'Clapham the Younger' – had bounties placed on their heads of £100 each. This may have been for their personal involvement in the murder of Richard, Duke of York. The proclamation also ordered that no one was to rob and distress Ranulph, Lord Dacre of Gilsland, the Northumberland knight Sir Ralph Gray or John Widdrington. The prohibition against seizing Dacre's lands was designed to protect them for one of Edward's supporters, Sir Richard Fiennes, Lord Dacre of the South, who had a claim to the barony of Gilsland. The reasoning behind the other

3 Armstrong, 'Inauguration Ceremonies', pp.55–64.
4 *Calendar of State Papers, Milan*, pp.53–9.

two names is unclear, although Gray had custody of the Neville estates at Middleham after the murder of Warwick's father, while Widdrington was married to one of the daughters of Warwick's retainers Sir Robert Ogle.[5] On 8 March commissions were issued to purvey carts to transport the King's ordnance north and victuals for the royal army, while commissions of array were issued for Essex, Gloucestershire, Shropshire and those counties the Yorkists would pass through on their way north. Four days later Edward instructed Warwick, who had left London to raise men in the Midlands on 7 March, to receive Lancastrian deserters and seize the property of those who refused to submit.[6]

In London, Edward set about raising further loans to pay for the new campaign. On 8 March, for example, the prior and convent of Christchurch in London lent the King 500 marks (£333 6*s*. 8*d*.) in ready cash, while the prior of St Bartholomew's in West Smithfield advanced £40. The principal lenders, however, were the London merchants, especially those who shipped wool to Calais. Between July 1460 and April 1461, they lent various sums at different times amounting to 16,500 marks (£11,000), of which £4,000 was lent immediately before Edward's departure north in anticipation of the Towton campaign. As the King travelled north, he collected further loans. In Cambridge, for example, the Abbot of Bury St Edmunds provided him with £100 in cash.[7] Others helped raise the money to send an army north: Bishop Neville pawned some of his jewels to a London grocer, never to see them again as they were taken to Sandwich, where they were stolen by pirates![8] On 11 March William, Lord Fauconberg, left London with the mass of Yorkist foot soldiers, mainly from Kent and the Welsh marches. Meanwhile Sir John Wenlock was sent to Thorpe Waterville in Northamptonshire, where the Duke of Exeter's castle was held by a group of Lancastrian diehards. Two days later, the King himself marched out of the city, accompanied by the Duke of Norfolk, at the head of the Yorkist mounted men-at-arms, which included a contingent of Burgundians, led by Seigneur de la Barde and carrying the banner of the Dauphin Louis (then still in exile under the protection of the Duke of Burgundy).[9]

The Battle of Towton: Myths and Misunderstandings

The Battle of Towton, fought in the fields between the villages of Saxton and Towton some 15 miles south-west of York, is often heralded as the largest and bloodiest battle on English soil. Few battles, however, can have attracted the mythology, misunderstandings and misinformation that have dogged our understanding of the clash of arms that took place on Palm Sunday, 29 March 1461. Perhaps the principal reason for this is the lack of contemporary evidence: we have no eyewitness accounts and very few documentary records pertaining to the battle, while most of the contemporary English chronicle sources, all Yorkist in their sympathies, are laconic in their descriptions of the events. The contemporary sources, such as they are, appear to have relied heavily on now lost newsletters distributed in the wake of the battle. Indeed, the Yorkists' – and especially the Earl of Warwick's – attempt to control the narrative in the battle's

5 *Calendar of Close Rolls, 1461–1467*, pp.54–7; *House of Commons, 1422–1461*, iv., pp.3–6; vii., pp.491–3.

6 *Calendar of Patent Rolls, 1461–1468*, pp.7, 9, 28, 31.

7 TNA, E404/72/1/16, 19, 22–3, 29, 80.

8 Scofield, *Edward IV*, i., p.158.

9 *Contemporary English Chronicles*, p.74; *Calendar of State Papers, Milan*, pp.61, 64; Basin, i., pp.301–2; ii., pp.231–3.

aftermath is evident from the correspondence preserved in the Milanese and Venetian archives and from the records of the Duke of Burgundy. Given the paucity of contemporary sources, historians from the seventeenth century onwards relied excessively on the colourful description contained in Edward Hall's chronicle, written in the 1540s. These same historians weaved local legend, family stories and other Tudor and Stuart accounts into their narratives of the battle to leave today a generally accepted understanding of Towton that probably has little basis in fifteenth-century reality.

Contemporaries and later historians alike offered incredibly, and often ridiculously, large estimates for the size of the armies involved. 'Gregory's Chronicle' numbered the Yorkist army at 200,000 men. The 'Short English Chronicle' stated merely that Edward had a 'grete multitude of pepul' with him against 100,000 Lancastrians, while John Benet's account is confused: he also stated Edward, Warwick, Norfolk and Fauconberg left London with 200,000 men. When Warwick met Edward at Doncaster, he brought with him 60,000 'well-armed' men. By contrast, the Lancastrians had only 40,000 men.[10] These pro-Yorkist chroniclers writing in the 1460s were, as we have seen, prone to exaggeration when enumerating armies, and the large numbers featured in their description of Towton were designed to underline the battle's importance in the Yorkist imagination. Significantly, in contrast to the Tudor chroniclers and later historians, where they enumerated the two armies, the Yorkists outnumbered the Lancastrians. Writing in the 1540s, Edward Hall's statement on the size of the Yorkist army – 48,980 men – claimed a payroll as its authority, but it was a number not inconceivable for European armies of the mid-sixteenth century (although the Lancastrian army of 60,000 would have dwarfed even the largest force assembled by any of Hall's contemporaries).[11] Hall's figures were accepted without question by Richard Brooke in 1857 and in the first scholarly account of Towton by Cyril Ransome, published in 1889, as well as, after some spurious reasoning, by Colonel Alfred Burne in his influential *Battlefields of England*.[12] More recent historians have tended to revise down Hall's figures to between 25,000 and 40,000 men on each side.[13] Yet if true, this would still mean that the armies at Towton were at least twice the size, if not more, than any other army assembled by an English king during the fifteenth century and were almost certainly the largest assemblage of armed men anywhere in Europe during the late Middle Ages.[14]

Given the month or so that Edward had to assemble his forces and considering most of the north and westernmost counties were hostile to the Yorkist cause, an army approaching anywhere near 20,000 men would have been a monumental effort by the new King and his followers. Equally, given the demands of the Margaret of Anjou's St Albans campaign, which had ended in ignominious retreat the previous month, it seems unlikely that the Lancastrians could have raised anywhere near that number in the north and the West Country. Similarly, there is little evidence, outside of a concerted campaign by Yorkist propagandists, that the Lancastrian army comprised large numbers of 'Frenchmen and Scots'. A newsletter written in Bruges on 9 April and received in Dijon 10 days later stated that the Lancastrians had raised a large army 'both Scots, French,

10 *Contemporary English Chronicles*, p.74; *Three Fifteenth Century Chronicles*, p.77; *John Benet's Chronicle*, p.50.

11 *Hall's Chronicle*, p.253.

12 Brooke, *Visits to Fields of Battle in England*, p.101; Cyril Ransome, 'The Battle of Towton', *English Historical Review*, 4 (1889), pp.462–3; Burne, *Battlefields of England*, pp.247.

13 Boardman, *Towton 1461*, pp.165–7, but see the cautionary words of Bicheno, *Battle Royal*, pp.298–9.

14 Grummitt, *War and Martial Culture*, pp.217–8.

Bretons, English and others'.[15] It is possible that some French troops may have been brought into England by the Seneschal of Normandy, Pierre de Brezé, in the two galleys he commissioned in Rouen in February 1461, but that remains speculation.[16]

Indeed, what little concrete evidence we have of troops raised for the Towton campaign on both sides suggests much smaller numbers. The city of Coventry, for example, probably the fourth or fifth largest and wealthiest town in England, had ignored the Lancastrian demand for men and instead sent men to Edward in London at the end of February, raising £100 to pay their wages. On 12 March the King sent a privy seal letter asking for more men, in response to which the city sent a further 100 men and £80 to meet their expenses.[17] Urban contingents probably made up a sizeable proportion of the Yorkist army. The poem known as *The Rose of Rouen* named ten towns and cities, from Canterbury to Bristol and Nottingham, that sent men to Towton to fight for Edward, and soldiers are known to have also served from Bury St Edmunds.[18] Yet it is unlikely that urban contingents were important for their size or prowess. They mattered because of the relative ease with which the apparatus of urban government allowed men to be assembled, armed and paid. Few town contingents, if any, would have exceeded 100 men and we can safely discount the city of York's claim made in 1485 to Henry VII that it had sent 1,000 men to fight for Henry VI at Towton.[19] If true it would have probably represented more than a quarter of the total male population of England's second city. Other Lancastrian towns seem not to have helped at all. There is no evidence that the burgesses of Exeter or Kingston-upon-Hull sent men to serve at Towton, although the townsmen of Beverley spent a shilling sending off their small contingent with a fortifying cup of wine.[20]

Other factors point to the conclusion that the armies engaged at Towton were significantly smaller than usually thought. As well as men, fifteenth-century armies comprised large numbers of horses. One recent estimate puts the numbers of horses involved in the Towton campaign at some 16,000 but supplying this number of animals would surely have been beyond the capacity of any of the communities through which they passed at the end of a particularly long and hard winter.[21] Indeed, as Wavrin noted, on the eve of the battle the Yorkist army was suffering both from the cold weather and a lack of supplies.[22] Nevertheless, as we have seen, Englishmen rode to battle rather than marched on foot, and the ability to provide fodder doubtless limited the size of the armies. The Towton battlefield itself is relatively unusual for the Wars of the Roses in as much as it is securely identified by both archaeological and documentary evidence. The current registered battlefield on and around Towton Dale is some 6.8 km^2 in area but contains landscape features erroneously identified with the fighting on Palm Sunday. The location of most of the verified archaeological finds relating to the battle is in a much smaller area on Towton Dale between 'Bloody Meadow' and 'North Acres' and comprises some 2 km^2 with a smaller deposit to the south-east around 'Dintingdale.'[23] Given the usual division of a fifteenth-century host, the armies,

15 *Coventry Leet Book*, i., p.314; *Parliament Rolls of Medieval England*, Parliament of November 1461, item 20; Archives Départementales de la Côte-d'Or, Archives Municipales de Dijon, B 450 fol. 26v.

16 Charles de Beaurepaire, *Notes sur six voyages de Louis XI à Rouen* (Rouen: Alfred Pèron, 1887), p.37.

17 *Coventry Leet Book*, i., pp.313–15.

18 *Historical Poems*, ed. Robbins, p.217.

19 *The York House Books, 1461–1490*, ed. Lorraine Attreed, 2 vols (Stroud: Alan Sutton, 1991), i., p.390.

20 Poulson, *Beverlac*, i., p.238.

21 Jonathan Riley, 'Logistics and Supply in Renaissance Armies', *Arms and Armour*, 8 (2011), pp.139–51.

22 Wavrin, v., p.338.

23 Anne Curry and Glenn Foard, *Bosworth 1485: A Battlefield Rediscovered* (Oxford: Oxbow, 2013), p.191; Tim Sutherland, 'The Archaeological Investigation of Towton Battlefield', in *Blood Red Roses*, ed. Veronica Fiorato,

if anywhere near the size suggested by Hall or even the more conservative estimates of modern historians, would have been required to deploy in columns, rather than the usual line abreast, and then the men would have had to stand many more than the accepted six ranks deep based on the standard one-yard frontage per man calculation. Of course, not every man who agreed to serve would have been present at once on the field or even have made it to the battlefield. It is clear from John Paston III's undated letter of early 1461 that many of the men raised for the Yorkist cause in Norfolk simply wandered about the county without being assigned captains amid a general reluctance to serve. Fewer than 400 seem to have made it to London to march north.[24]

Even if contingents did make it to the vicinity of battle, they were by no means assured of taking part in the fighting or even locating their comrades. The sixteenth-century Welsh chronicler Ellis Gruffyd tells the story of a soldier who lost his way while marching to join the Lancastrian army before Towton. He came across a group of Yorkists, who beat him for his Lancastrian allegiance. He continued his march only to come across some Lancastrians who mistook him for a Yorkist and meted out the same treatment! He then came across a third group of soldiers, who questioned him and then spared him, laughing at his misfortune.[25] While the tale is almost certainly apocryphal, it demonstrates how commanders could be prevented from deploying the full might of their forces at Towton and other battles of the Wars of the Roses. Nevertheless, Towton was certainly a large battle by the standards of the time. The Lancastrian army at Ludford Bridge, given the number of lords who appear to have turned out for Henry VI, may have been larger than either the Lancastrian or Yorkist army at Towton, while the combined number of men who took the field at St Albans the previous month may have been more than assembled for Towton. Yet the series of battles on Palm Sunday 1461 that culminated at Towton were almost certainly the largest battle of the period 1455 to 1461 in terms of the number of men engaged in the fighting. The Dijon newsletter claimed the Yorkists had 11,000 'well-armed combatants', and this is certainly the upper end of any probably army size.[26] Ultimately, unless new documentary evidence emerges, we will never know for certain the size of the armies that fought on Palm Sunday, but if we take the fighting on Towton Dale it seems likely that true number of men involved was closer to Graham Evans's estimate of 7,000 on each side than the 23,000 to 25,000 suggested by Boardman. Even if we suppose that the engagements at Ferrybridge, near Sherburn-in-Elmet and Towton Dale involved several separate forces, their numbers probably did not exceed 10,000 on either side.[27]

If the numbers engaged at Towton were likely much smaller than has previously been assumed, then it follows that the extraordinary number of casualties – reported by contemporaries at between 28,000 and 38,000 dead – was also a product of the Yorkist propaganda campaign in the battle's aftermath. The first mention of 28,000 dying on the field was made in a letter from William Paston to his brother on 4 April. The figure 'nomberd by harraldys' apparently originated in a letter written by Edward IV to his mother, Duchess Cecily. It was repeated in the newsletters sent by Bishop Neville and Nicholas O'Flanagan, Bishop of Elphin, to Bishop Coppini three days later, and by Camulio writing to the Duke of Milan on 18 April. Twenty thousand of those killed were

Anthea Boylston and Christopher Knüsel (Oxford: Oxbow Books, 2007), pp.155–68.

24 *Paston Letters and Papers*, ed. Davis, i., pp.519–20.

25 T.G. Hunter, 'The Chronicle of Ellis Gruffyd' (Harvard University, PhD thesis, 1995), pp.191–3, 299–300.

26 Archives Départementales de la Côte-d'Or, Archives Municipales de Dijon, B 450 fol. 26v.

27 Graham Evans, *The Battle of Edgcote 1469: Re-Evaluating the Evidence* (Northampton: Northamptonshire Battlefield Society, 2019), pp.27–8; Boardman, *Towton 1461*, pp.165–7. For a more detailed discussion of army size in this period see Grummitt, *War and Martial Culture*, pp.78–86.

Lancastrians, while the Yorkists lost only 800 according to Bishop O'Flanagan, or 8,000 according to Camulio and the Milanese merchant in Bruges, Pigello Portinaro. Soon the number began to creep up: on 17 April Bishop Coppini's physician, Master Antonio, claimed 30,000 were killed between Pontefract and York.[28] The earliest chronicle accounts written on the continent, by the so-called Monstrelet Continuator and the Burgundian Jacques du Clercq, increased those killed to 30,000 or even 36,000 (the figure repeated by Wavrin).[29] The London chroniclers of the 1460s inflated the number of those killed still further: both John Benet and 'Gregory's Chronicle' had 35,000 dead, while 'A Short English Chronicle' accounted for 36,777.[30] The author of *The Rose of Rouen* settled on 27,000, which rhymed better than 28,000, while the anonymous author of the verse copied into an East Anglian manorial document in the early 1460s numbered the dead at 35,000.[31] Yet not all the contemporary sources placed the death toll so high. The pseudo-Worcestre *Annales* stated that 9,000 Lancastrians had perished, 'some in battle and some in flight', while the author of the newsletter sent to the Mayor of Dijon in April 1461 had heard that 10,000 had died at the battle, only 300 of whom were Yorkists.[32] By the late 1460s, the enormous figures had, however, gained official recognition. In his bull of 1467 promoting a battlefield chapel at Towton, Pope Paul II stated that 'about 30,000 men were slain'.[33]

By the beginning of the sixteenth century, it seems generally accepted that some 30,000 men had fallen at the Battle of Towton, and by the 1540s efforts were made to verify this through the identification of mass graves on or near the battlefield. The antiquarian John Leland visited Towton and Saxton between 1535 and 1542 and recorded that a 'great multitude of men' had been slain and buried on the battlefield. Many of their bones had then been moved by a local landowner, Richard Hungate, to Saxton churchyard. John Stow, writing in 1615, stated that the 33,000 bodies (or, he noted, 35,091 as some said) were buried in five large grave pits half a mile from Saxton church.[34] The York antiquarian Francis Drake testified to seeing open graves containing many bones, as well as arms and armour, in 1734.[35] In 1792 Daniel Defoe visited Towton as part of a tour of Wars of the Roses battlefields. In Letter Nine of his *Tour Tho' The Whole Island of Great Britain*, he described how he was led to the battlefield and how 'Tradition guided the Country People, and they us, to the very Spot' where 36,000 men had died. Paraphrasing Vergil, he recalled how the ploughs turned up 'arrow-heads and Spear-heads, and broken Javelins, and Helmets, and the like', yet no memorials or physical traces of the battlefield remained in the landscape. He and his friends 'cou'd only give a short Sigh to the memory of the Dead, and move forward'.[36] The search for the missing bodies

28 *Paston Letters and Papers*, ed. Davis, i., p.165; *CSP, Venice*, i., pp.64–6, 68, 72; *CSP, Milan*, i., pp.62–65.

29 BNF, MS Français 88, fo. 146; MS Français 20354, fo. 116v; Wavrin, v., p.341; *Mémoires de Jacques du Clercq*, iii., p.119.

30 'John Benet's Chronicle', ed. Harriss and Harriss, p.229. *John Benet's Chronicle*, p.50 wrongly translates the number of dead as 45,000.

31 *Historical Poems*, ed. Robbins, p.218; Richard Beadle, 'Fifteenth-Century Political Verses from the Holkham Archives', *Medium Aevum*, 71 (2002), pp.101–21.

32 *Letters and Papers*, ii(2)., p.778; Archives Départementales de la Côte-d'Or, Archives Municipales de Dijon, B 450, fo. 26v.

33 *Calendar of Papal Registers Relating to Great Britain and Ireland: Volume 12, 1458–1471*, ed. J.A. Twemlow (London, 1933), p.623.

34 Leland, i., p.43; John Stow, *The Annals or General Chronicles of England* (London: Thomas Adams, 1615), p.415.

35 Francis Drake, *Eboracum or the History and Antiquities of the City of York* (London: William Bower, 1736), p.111.

36 Daniel Defoe, *A Tour Thro' the Whole Island of Great Britain*, ed. John McVeagh (3 vols. London: Pickering & Chatto, 2001), iii., p.94.

was taken up in the late 1840s by Richard Brooke. He claimed that in June 1848 the bones interred in Saxton churchyard had been exposed by workmen digging a trench, yet he did not find any evidence of mass graves on his own visits to the battlefield. In 1889 another historian, Alexander Leadman, wrote an influential account of Towton in which he discussed mass graves still visible on the battlefield. Yet, as Tim Sutherland has recently pointed out, these were most likely Romano-British burial sites.[37]

The extraordinary carnage on Palm Sunday 1461 is one of the most persistent myths about the battle, yet it is not borne out by any contemporary documentary evidence. The contemporary newsletters and pro-Yorkist chroniclers listed a dozen or so of the most prominent Lancastrians who fell and a couple of Yorkists, while the evidence of writs of *diem clausit extremum* (instructions to escheators to make inquisition into the lands of deceased tenants in chief), testamentary records and other documents add a few more names to those who died at Towton. Many more men said to have fallen at Towton, either in family legend or in seventeenth-century heraldic visitations, can be shown to have survived the battle by many years.[38] Assessing the evidence for those who fought and may have died at Towton among the men who sat in the House of Commons during Henry VI's reign, Simon Payling could identify 36 Parliamentarians who fought for Lancaster at Towton but only eight who were slain. For the Yorkists, the death toll was even smaller: only two of 10 MPs – John Stafford and Robert Horne – who are known to have fought at Towton were killed.[39] Given that the alleged death toll was some four times larger than the entire population of York at the time, it is surprising that the Battle of Towton left little or no trace on the economy or demography of northern England. The dead from medieval battlefields are notoriously difficult to locate and much has been made of the discovery in the mid-1990s of some 60 skeletons of those killed at the battle at Towton Hall. While their remains may testify to the savagery of fifteenth-century warfare, they are hardly conclusive evidence of mass graves or of a death toll anywhere near that propagated by Yorkist sources in the immediate aftermath of the battle. A more realistic death toll for the fighting on Palm Sunday could well be between 2,800 and 3,800, a figure 10 times fewer than that claimed by contemporaries and later historians.[40]

If the 'bloodiest battle' moniker owed its origins to Yorkist propaganda, the blame for another persistent myth – that the battle was thought in a blizzard – can be laid squarely at the feet of the Tudor chronicler Edward Hall. Hall explained that as the two sides approached Towton, 'their fell a small snyt or snow, which by violence of the wyn was driven into the faces of them which were of kyng Henries parte, so that their sight was somewhat blemished and minished'. He went on to describe how Lord Fauconberg cleverly positioned his Yorkist archers so that when the Lancastrians shot their arrows, they fell short. 'When their shot was almost spent,' Hall continued, 'the lord Fawconbridge marched forwarde with his archers, which not onely shot their awne whole sheues, but also gathered the arrowes of their enemies, and let a greate parte of them flye agaynst

37 Brooke, *Visits to Fields of Battle in England*, pp.92–4; A.D.H. Leadman, 'The Battle of Towton', *Yorkshire Archaeological Journal*, 10 (1889), pp.298–300; T.A. Sutherland and A. Schmidt, 'Towton 1461: An Integrated Approach to Battlefield Archaeology', *Landscapes*, 4 (2003), pp.15–25.

38 Graham A. Darbyshire, *The Gentry and Peerage of Towton* (2 vols., Lincoln: Freezywater Publications, 2010-11).

39 Simon Payling, 'Was the Battle of Towton as Bloody as All That?', *The History of Parliament*, www.historyofparliament.com/2020/03/29/was-the-battle-of-towton-bloody, accessed 5 May 2025.

40 Tim Sutherland, 'Killing Time: Challenging the Common Perceptions of Three Medieval Conflicts – Ferrybridge, Dintingdale and Towton – "the Largest Battle on British Soil"', *Journal of Conflict Archaeology*, 5 (2009), p.23.

their awne masters.'[41] For many historians, this incident defined the battle and led directly to the eventual Yorkist triumph. Yet, it was a pre-modern commonplace that having in the wind in your opponent's face and the sun in their eyes were advantages that any good commander would know and aim to facilitate when drawing up for battle.[42] The origins of the Towton story are seldom explored, but many historians have assumed that Hall's description is 'so precise … it smacks of a story passed down of a novel battle situation' or that the Tudor chronicler had access to information and sources about the battle now lost to us.[43]

In fact, no contemporary made the connection between the weather conditions and the Yorkist triumph. Indeed, the icy conditions and snow were not mentioned at all by the earliest commentators on the battlefield. The author of Bibliothèque Nationale de France, Manuscrit Français 88 and Wavrin were the first to mention the extreme cold and a storm, but placed it immediately after the Yorkists had taken the crossing at Ferrybridge.[44] Yet it was not until the 1470s that the continuator of the Crowland Chronicle mentioned that the battlefield was covered in snow: noting the 38,000 dead, he described how 'the blood, too, of the slain, mingling with the snow which at this time covered the whole surface of the earth, afterwards ran down in the furrows and ditches along with the melted snow, in a most shocking manner, for a distance of two or three miles'. The only other source to mention the snow was the author of 'Howard's Chronicle', writing in the early 1520s, who merely noted that 'all the season it snew'.[45] None of the chronicle sources mention the wind affecting the battle. Abbot Whethamstede, however, made the weather central to his account of Towton. Whethamstede wrote how:

> The Lord Himself was also present, and gave [Edward] power against his enemies, and such grace, that the wind blew in his face, as soon as he was about to fight against his enemy, turned in the opposite direction in such a way that it slowed down and blunted the entire enemy barrage, causing it to do no harm, or very little, to him and his, and inflict no injury.

The failure of the Lancastrian archery so frustrated Edward's enemies that their morale soon collapsed when it came to hand-strokes. Yet in his description of Towton, Whethamstede was simply reinforcing the parallels he had made earlier in the passage between Edward IV and the Roman Emperor Theodosius the Great (379–395 CE). Over two days, on 5 and 6 September 394, Theodosius had won a celebrated victory over the rebel emperor Eugenius and his military commander Arbogast at the Battle of the Frigidus in modern-day Slovenia. Theodosius's victory was reputed to have been due to a wind that had blown the spears and arrows of his enemies back in their faces. Whethamstede described the emperor's victory at the Frigidus river and Edward's victory at Towton as 'similarly, and in almost all respects' the same.[46] Whether Hall knew of Whethamstede's account is unclear, but the manner of Theodosius's victory over his rivals was well-known to educated fifteenth and sixteenth-century writers and readers and was a common trope in medieval and early modern battle narratives.

41 *Hall's Chronicle*, pp.255–6.
42 Christine de Pizan, *The Book of Deeds of Arms and of Chivalry*, ed and trans. Sumner Willard and Charity Cannon Willlard (University Park, PA: The Pennsylvania State University Press, 1999), pp.64–5.
43 Christopher Gravett, *Towton 1461: England's Bloodiest Battle* (Oxford: Osprey Publishing, 2003), p.56.
44 BNF, Manuscrit Français 88, fo. 145; Wavrin, v., p. 338.
45 *Ingulph's Chronicle*, p.425; *Contemporary English Chronicles*, p.101.
46 Whethamstede, p.409; Nic Fields, *The Battle of the Frigidus River AD 394* (Barnsley, 2024), pp.101–21.

Hall is responsible for other commonly accepted aspects of the Towton story for which there is no other contemporary evidence. His is the first account to mention the fight at Dintingdale where John, Lord Clifford, was supposedly killed by an arrow in the throat (a familiar motif repeated in other sixteenth-century accounts of battle deaths and injuries during the Wars of the Roses). There is similarly no evidence, other than in Hall's chronicle, for the assertion that Edward made proclamation before battle commenced that 'no prisoner should be taken, not one enemie saued'. Hall, like Polydore Vergil, stressed the unusually long duration of the battle – 10 hours – in contradiction to some of the earlier fifteenth-century sources, but it is he alone who describes the 'bridge of bodies' that allowed the Lancastrians to escape across the swollen Cock Beck.[47] Hall claimed to have been repeating local legend, but we do not know that he visited the battlefield. There is the possibility that Hall had access to the now-lost newsletters sent to the continent in the aftermath of the battle, or at least some of the accounts written from them. He is the only English source, for example, to describe how the Earl of Warwick killed his horse at Ferrybridge. This story formed the cornerstone of the Burgundian Jacques du Clercq's account of Towton and of the narrative of the Monstrelet Continuator.[48] Whatever his sources, Hall's account of the battle, designed above all to stress the savagery and tragedy of civil war, was popularised further by Holinshed and Shakespeare. It formed the basis of Sir Richard Baker's *A Chronicle of the Kings of England*, published in 1684, of Francis Drake's 1736 account, and the Leeds antiquarian Thomas Dunham Whitaker's influential description of the battle published in 1816.[49] From there Hall, or those who paraphrased him, have provided the mainstay of almost all academic and popular narratives of the Battle of Towton.

While Hall's account has dominated the overall understanding of the course of the battle on Towton Dale and the earlier actions at Ferrybridge and Dintingdale, other sources mythologised the conduct and deaths of individuals. The widely believed story that Ranulph, Lord Dacre, was killed when he was shot in the neck by a small crossbow-wielding boy hidden in a bur tree was popular by the mid-sixteenth century. The story can be traced back to at least 1585 when it was reported by Somerset Herald Robert Glover in his visitation of Yorkshire. He described the local legend of a 'bur tree … decayed within this few years' in North Acres which had given rise to the rhyme 'The Lord of Dacres was slayne in the North Acres.' Glover's story was picked up again and popularised by Whitaker in 1816 (although he pointed out the coincidence that Dacre apparently suffered the same fate as Lord Clifford had at Dintingdale a few hours before).[50] The supposed site of the bur tree appeared on mid-nineteenth-century Ordnance Survey maps, and around the same time the current memorial cross, 'Dacre's Cross', was erected, allegedly using stone from the demolished battlefield chapel. It languished in a hedgerow for decades until it was resurrected in its current location in 1927 by Harrogate archaeologist James Ogden.[51] Another example of a widely disseminated Towton myth is that of the Welsh knight David Matthew. Matthew allegedly saved Edward IV's life at Towton, for which he was granted the right to bear the augmentation 'Towton' on his heraldic arms. According to the story, Matthew stood six feet eight inches and was aged 60 when he performed this heroic deed, and he remained active until he was killed in a riot in Neath in 1484!

47 *Hall's Chronicle*, pp.253–5; *Polydore Vergil*, p.111.

48 *Mémoires de Jacques du Clercq*, iii., pp.116–18; Visser-Fuchs, *History as Pastime*, pp.476–7.

49 Sir Richard Baker, *A Chronicle of the Kings of England* (London: H. Sawbridge, 1684), p.203; Drake, *Eboracum*, pp.109–10; Thomas Dunham Whitaker, *Loidis and Elmete* (Leeds: C. Davison, 1816), pp.154–6.

50 Whitaker, *Loidis and Elmete*, p.156.

51 Martin Hickes, 'Rally to the Cross', *Towton Battlefield Society*, www.towton.org.uk/wp-content/uploads/2022/05/rally_to_the_cross.pdf, accessed 5 May 2025.

The stone cross associated with the death of Ranulph, Lord Dacre, at the Battle of Towton. Its provenance is unknown, but Paul Dawson has suggested it was a medieval boundary marker. The memorial was moved to its current location in 1927. (Author)

The story that Matthew had carried Edward IV's standard appears to date from the early eighteenth century, when it was mentioned in a description of the Matthew tombs at Llandaff Cathedral. It was not until the 1850s, however, that the claim that he had saved the King's life appeared.[52] In fact, there are no contemporary records of a David Matthew serving, let alone being rewarded for such a deed, at Towton. The man whose tomb can still be seen in Llandaff Cathedral died before 1470 and does not appear ever to have been knighted or recognised at the time for his martial exploits.[53]

The Battle of Towton: The Contemporary Evidence

On leaving London, Edward made his way north via Royston and Cambridge along the Great North Road. From Grantham he seems to have travelled to Nottingham, where a portion of the Lancastrian army may have lodged after St Albans, before rejoining the Great North Road at Newark for the final leg of the journey to rendezvous with Warwick at Doncaster. The Earl had marched north on Watling Street, through Northampton to Coventry, where he had apparently caught up with and executed one of the illegitimate brothers of the Duke of Exeter. From Coventry, he had travelled on to Lichfield and from there to Doncaster. The order of march is unclear, but it seems that the Yorkist army was split into at least three separate forces under Edward and Fauconberg, Warwick and Norfolk.[54] There is no firm evidence of how the Lancastrians spent the days before Towton. The royal household, referred to as the 'Queen's household', appears to have stayed in Beverley on its return from St Albans, occasionally joined by the Duke of Somerset and Lord Clifford, while other Lancastrian lords were lodged in York.[55] What efforts were made to raise men or retain those who marched with Queen Margaret to St Albans is unclear. Wavrin reported that the Lancastrians had moved to Nottingham in early March, recruiting men, but no other source confirms this, although it may explain Edward's detour there on his way north.[56] The Yorkists' advance guard appears to have reached Pontefract by Friday, 27 March, clearly abandoned by their opponents, with the rest of the army the following day.

Our knowledge of what happened next is almost entirely mediated through a series of extant letters written in the battle's immediate aftermath and by now-lost newsletters distributed in England and Burgundy that were incorporated into chronicle accounts both at home and on the continent. These accounts were Yorkist in their sympathies, and seem initially to have been written from Warwick's point of view, stressing the Earl's central role at Towton rather than Edward's. The first news of Towton, brought by Warwick's pursuivant of arms, reached the Duke of Burgundy and the towns of Ghent and Bruges on 9 April. In May Walter Wrottesley, one of Warwick's most trusted servants, who had been pricked as sheriff of Staffordshire in October 1460 and who had carried the Earl's banner at Towton, travelled to the Low Countries with Warwick Pursuivant and further news of the battle. These accounts, which appear to have differed from the narratives

52 Browne Willis, *A Survey of the Cathedral Church of Landaff* (London: R. Gosling, 1719), p.25; John and John Bernard Burke, *A Genealogical and Heraldic Dictionary of the Landed Gentry of Great Britain and Ireland* (2 vols., London: Henry Colburn, 1847), ii., p.844.

53 'David Mathew of Llandaf, *fl. c.*1424–58', *Guto's Wales: The Life of a Poet in Fifteenth-Century Wales*, www.gutporglyn.net, accessed 5 May 2025.

54 TNA, C81/782; *John Benet's Chronicle*, p.50; Hicks, *Warwick the Kingmaker*, pp.218–19.

55 Poulson, *Beverlac*, i., pp.235–7. See appendix for the Lancastrian and Yorkist lords who may have fought at Towton.

56 Wavrin, v., pp.336–7.

of the battle contained in the letters written on 7 April to Bishop Coppini, seem to have found their way into the accounts of continental chroniclers. Their pro-Warwick bias is suggested by the Burgundian receiver-general's description of the news as relating to a battle fought between the Earl and the Duke of Somerset.[57]

The newsletters described separate actions at Ferrybridge, near Sherburn-in-Elmet (what may have later become known as the fight near 'Dintingdale') and between Saxton and Towton. This is suggested by the evolving names by which the battle was known. In the days immediately following it was identified as an event in time rather than something that was located in a specific place. It was the day, Palm Sunday, rather than the location that mattered to early commentators, such as the bishops of Elphin, Exeter and Salisbury, or the writer of the newsletter that came into William Paston's possession. In official records and chronicle accounts of the 1460s the battle was variously known as 'Palm Sunday Field called York Field', the 'battle at Shirborne beside York', the battle fought 'between the towns of Sherburn in Elmete and Tadcaster, in the shire of York, called Saxtonfield and Towtonfield' or simply 'our last field in the north parts'. These names identified a general locality but located the battle firmly in time, on Palm Sunday, 29 March 1461.[58] Traditionally historians have placed the action at the crossing of the River Aire at Ferrybridge on Saturday, 28 March and the main battle at Towton as taking place the following day. However, the place name and other evidence points to an initial clash for the crossing over the Aire on the Saturday, then another series of encounters fought over different locations on Palm Sunday. Indeed, Tim Sutherland has argued convincingly that historians have misunderstand the description of time in the various battle narratives. The day began at dawn, the hour of Prime or 6 a.m., and was followed by 12 hours of 'day' and 12 hours of 'night.' Thus, when the Howard chronicler stated the battle began at 'four of the clock at night' they meant at 4 a.m. If the fighting continued 'all night until tomorrow afternoon', it meant it began in the early hours of the morning and continued into the afternoon *on the same day*. The Bishop of Exeter, George Neville's letter to Coppini stated that the fighting to secure the crossing at Ferrybridge began 'with the rising of the sun', so at dawn on Palm Sunday, and continued 'until the tenth hour of the night', that is until 4 a.m. on Monday, 30 March. This was corroborated by Bishop Beauchamp's letter to Coppini, which stated the result of the battle, which had begun at Ferrybridge and ended with the Lancastrian flight from Towton, 'remained doubtful *the whole day*', that is from dawn on Palm Sunday until the same time on the Monday.[59] John Benet's chronicle also makes it clear that there were three distinct 'battles' fought between the Lancastrians and Yorkists on Palm Sunday.[60] The telescoping of three separate actions fought in different locations into a single battle at Towton on Palm Sunday also makes sense of Hall's assertion that the fighting lasted 10 hours. In fact, as Sutherland points out, it was the early nineteenth-century historian Thomas Dunham Whitaker who first insisted that the action at Ferrybridge began in the morning of Saturday, 28 March, and was concluded that day, and it is his misunderstanding that has shaped the accounts of modern historians.[61]

57 Archives Départementales du Nord, *Registre* of the Receiver General of the Duke of Burgundy, 1 Oct. 1460–30 Sept. 1461, B.2040, fos. 237, 267, 268.

58 Grummitt, *War and Martial Culture*, p.205.

59 Sutherland, 'Killing Time', pp.1–26.

60 *John Benet's Chronicle*, p.50.

61 Whitaker, *Loidis and Elmete*, pp.154–5; Sutherland, 'Killing Time', p.5. For the general acceptance of 28 March as the date of the 'battle' of Ferrybridge, see Clement Markham, 'The Battle of Towton', pp.8–9, Leadman, 'Battle of Towton', p.291.

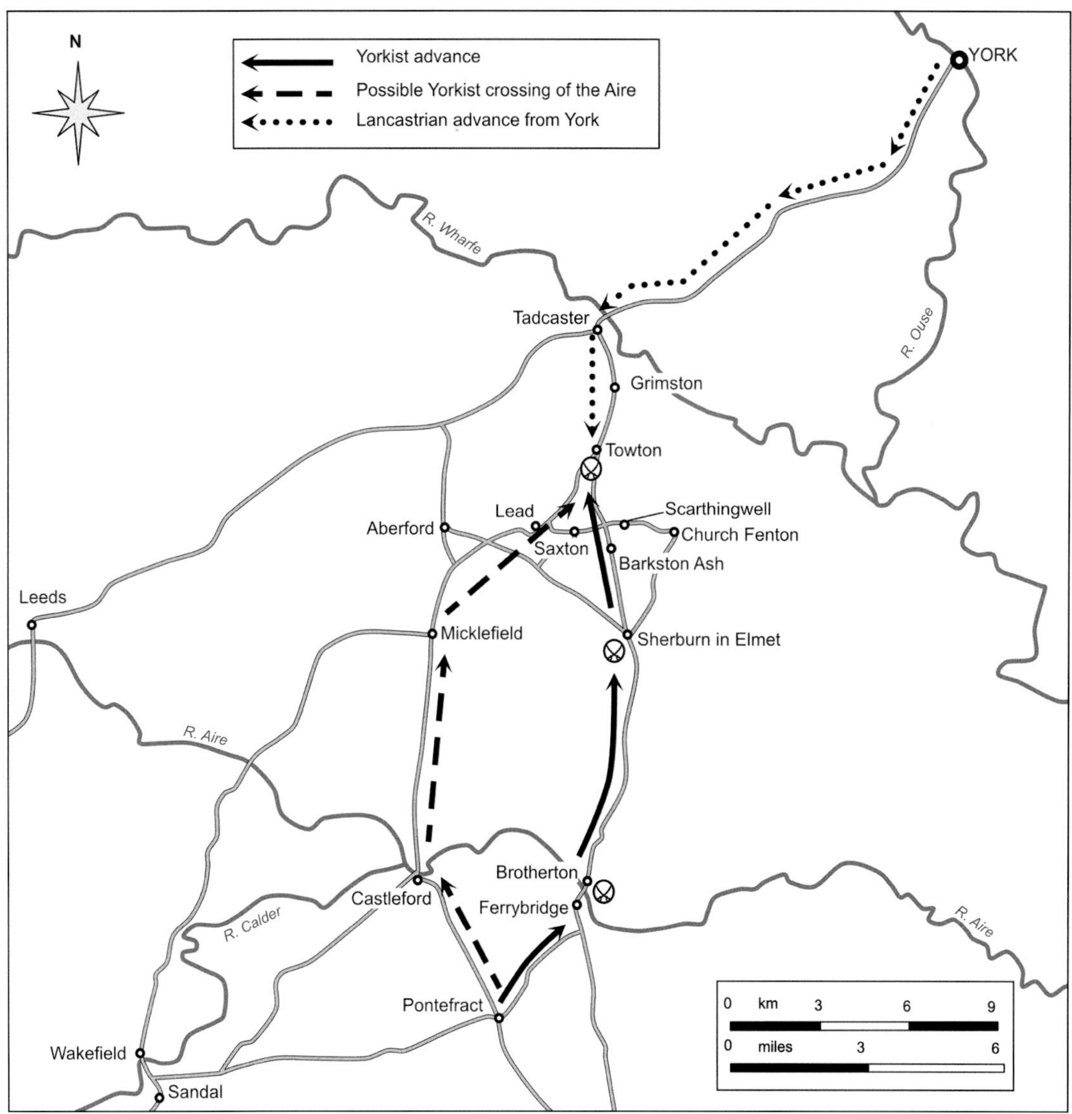

Palm Sunday, 1461: before dawn on Sunday, 29 March the Yorkists began the action to secure the crossing over the River Aire at Ferrybridge. Once across the river, they fought two distinct actions near Sherburn-in-Elmet and on Towton Dale amid what was probably a fluid pursuit of the Lancastrians.

The letters sent to Coppini on 7 April, and a reconstruction of events described in the now-lost newsletters, allows us to identify distinct Yorkist narratives of the fighting on Palm Sunday 1461. There seems no doubt that that the first action occurred at the crossing of the River Aire at Ferrybridge, just two miles from Pontefract. Bishop Neville's letter written on 7 April stated clearly that the fighting on Palm Sunday began at 'Feurbirga', while the pseudo-Worcestre *Annales* stated the battle begun 'around Palm Sunday' at 'Ferybrygge'. 'Gregory' wrote that the battle at Ferrybridge was fought 'on the xxviij daye of Marche, that was þe Palme Sunday Euyn'.[62] As we have seen, 'eve' in this context means the hours before Prime, when the new day was deemed to have begun, suggesting that battle was joined before dawn on 29 March. Bishop Neville's description of the action seems straightforward: the Yorkists arrived at Ferrybridge 'about sunrise' and found the crossing destroyed. The Yorkists were forced to repair it and, in fierce fighting, routed the Lancastrians who were arrayed on the other bank.[63] Neville's account, however, may obscure what may have been a much larger encounter than has previously been supposed. It is clear that the stone bridge at Ferrybridge was not destroyed in March 1461 – it survived intact until it was replaced by a new structure in the eighteenth century – and Neville may have been referring to a temporary crossing further upstream at Knottingley or even Castleford. The Battle of Ferrybridge then was not a mere skirmish in prelude to the main battle fought at Towton, but a significant clash of arms in its own right. Most historians, following Hall, characterise Ferrybridge as an encounter between the Yorkist vanguard led by John, Lord Fitzwalter, then guarding the crossing, which had already been destroyed by the retreating Lancastrians, and a small, mounted Lancastrian force, led by John, Lord Clifford. Clifford's appearance took Fitzwalter by surprise, and he was soon overwhelmed and killed. The Lancastrians then destroyed the makeshift bridge made by Fitzwalter's men. The shock galvanised the Earl of Warwick into action and he advanced and retook the crossing.[64]

The earliest continental sources, however, described a different course of events, one that made no mention of Clifford. According to Jacques du Clercq and the Monstrelet Continuator's chronicle, the Yorkist vanguard met a large Lancastrian force led by the Duke of Somerset, on 28 March, guarding the stone bridge. The two sides engaged, and the Yorkist vanguard was destroyed. 'An uncle of the Earl of Warwick' and 'other great lords' (presumably including Fitzwalter, although he is not explicitly named) were killed. John, the illegitimate son of Thomas Montagu, Earl of Salisbury, had served as a knight in the retinue of the Duke of York in 1441, but his identity was clearly unknown to Hall, who mistakenly wrote of the death of Warwick's illegitimate brother.[65] When the rest of the Yorkist army heard of the disaster at Ferrybridge they were 'very discomfited, and almost everyone wanted to flee'. Edward responded by allowing those wanted to depart to do so, but offered those who would remain 'a certain large sum of money'. It was Warwick, however, who rallied the troops. Moved to tears by the death of his uncle and the other lords, he offered his cause to God, drew his sword and kissed the cross on its hilt. Addressing the Yorkist troops, he cried, 'Whoever wants to return, do so ... as for me, I will die and live with those who remain with me.' He then dismounted and, with his sword, killed

62 *Calendar of State Papers, Milan*, p.61; *Calendar of State Papers and Manuscripts, Relating to English Affairs, Existing in the Archives and Collections of Venice and other Libraries in Northern England, Volume 1, 1202–1509*, ed. R. Brown (London: HMSO, 1947), p.99; *Letters and Papers*, ii (2)., p.777; *Contemporary English Chronicles*, p.74.

63 *Calendar of State Papers, Venetian*, pp.99–100 contains the fullest version of Neville's letter.

64 Boardman, *Towton 1461*, pp.110–12; Haigh, *From Wakefield to Towton*, pp.67–73.

65 TNA, E101/53/33; William Dugdale, *The Baronage of England* (London: Thomas Newcombe, 1675), i., p.652.

his horse. Du Clercq stated the fighting that followed occurred 'the next day', but as we have seen, this probably simply meant that it began after dawn.[66] The account was copied into the manuscripts of the so-called Monstrelet Continuator. It was this account, probably through the 1502 printed edition of Monstrelet's chronicle, which found its way into Edward Hall's chronicle.[67] 'Gregory's Chronicle' also recorded that it was Warwick who had carried the crossing at Ferrybridge, noting that the Earl 'was hurte yn hys legge whythe an arowe at the same jornaye'.[68] Indeed, Warwick's injury at Ferrybridge on the morning of 29 March may have been sufficient to render him *hors de combat* for the remainder of the day. A later Chancery petition presented by the Earl's surgeon, Richard Knyght, explained that he had been commanded by Edward and Warwick to 'attend upon his seid lord and other diverse of the kynges people the which where hurt at the same feld'.[69]

Wavrin, drawing on the unique account in Bibliothèque Nationale de France, Manuscrit Français 88, but also presumably on his conversations with Warwick's servants and others, offered a different account of the fighting at Ferrybridge and shifted the emphasis from Warwick to Edward. He stated how, while at Nottingham on 27 March, Edward learned that Somerset and Richard Woodville, Lord Rivers, were holding the crossing over the Aire. The Yorkist king appointed the young Duke of Suffolk as marshal and commander of the vanguard and sent him north with Lord Fauconberg and 14,000 men. Reaching Pontefract the next day, Suffolk sent his scouts to Ferrybridge where, in the evening, they were pushed back by the Lancastrians. Hearing this, Edward, 'as a brave and confident knight', realised that it was vital to secure the crossing and marched out to take it. Wavrin characterised the ensuing encounter as a 'scarmuche' or skirmish, but conceded it lasted for six hours, 'from noon until six o'clock in the evening', and cost 3,000 killed on both sides. He went on to say that the Yorkists then 'passed their entire army across it that same night'. Following his manuscript source, Wavrin omitted Warwick completely from his narrative of Ferrybridge, did not mention Lord Fitzwalter or any other casualty by name, and seemed to suggest that the action took place the day *before* the battle of Towton. Wavrin's rewriting of the 'battle' of Ferrybridge is significant. It did not follow the version in the manuscript of the Monstrelet Continuator he owned himself, but instead he copied from Manuscrit Français 88. This manuscript was owned by Louis of Bruges, Lord of Gruuthuse. Gruuthuse had himself been present in England in 1461 and played host to Edward IV during his exile in 1470. It was during a visit to Bruges during this period that Wavrin met Edward IV and may have compiled his account of Palm Sunday.[70] Neither of these Yorkist narratives – which we might term the 'Du Clercq' and the 'Wavrin' accounts of Ferrybridge – mention Lord Clifford, but both make clear that the action at crossing of the Aire was a large encounter and not merely a prelude to the main event at Towton the next day. Indeed, John Benet's rather confused but important account of the events of Palm Sunday 1461 may have been echoing the 'Wavrin' narrative of the Battle of Ferrybridge when he described the first of three clashes that day: 'King Edward fought valiantly and … he killed [many], or put them to flight. Many knights on the king's side fled, and so the king fought on foot.'[71]

66 Du Clercq, *Mèmoires*, iii., pp.116–7; *The Chronicles of Enguerrand de Monstrelet*, ed. Thomas Johnes (2 vols., London: Routledge, 1867), ii., pp.272–3.

67 *Hall's Chronicle*, pp.252–3.

68 *Contemporary English Chronicles*, p.74.

69 TNA, C1/28/397.

70 Wavrin's manuscript of the Monstrelet Continuator's chronicle was Lille BM E20. It contains the 'du Clercq' account of Ferrybridge (fos. 150–2): Visser-Fuchs, *History as Pastime*, pp.530, 569–70.

71 *John Benet's Chronicle*, p.50.

In Hall's account, Edward then dispatched Lord Fauconberg with Walter Blount and Robert Horne to cross the Aire some three miles further upstream at Castleford. The intention was to outflank Clifford and his men and trap them. Clifford realised what was happening and attempted to flee to the main Lancastrian army. He was, nevertheless, surprised by the Yorkists and 'either for heat payne, putting of his gorget, sodainly with an arowe (as some say) without an hedde, was striken in the throte' and was killed. Alongside him, 'at a place called Dintingdale, not farr from Towton', John, Lord Neville, was also killed.[72] Hall's sources, other than the Monstrelet Continuator, are unclear, but no fifteenth-century source mentioned the crossing at Castleford. Equally, none of the contemporary accounts mentioned 'Dintingdale' and, although Clifford and Neville were both named among those killed in the earliest newsletters, they were simply recorded as being slain on Palm Sunday. It is unlikely that the Clifford family tradition of the story, and of Lord John's burial in an unmarked pit, recorded by Whitaker in the early nineteenth century predated the Tudor chronicler's account. Whitaker identified 'Dintingdale' as a small valley between Scarthingwell and Towton.[73] Scarthingwell is to the south of the ancient parish of Saxton, close to the border with Barkston parish. When Leland visited the battlefield, he observed that 'this feeld was as much fought in Saxton paroch as in Towton, yet it berith the name of Towton'.[74]

Indeed, it seems likely that after the action of Ferrybridge, the Yorkists pursued the Lancastrians north along the Old Great North Road (which may have followed roughly the route of the modern-day York Road or A162) into Barkston parish. There they fought the second major engagement of the day, a fluid battle that may have begun close to Sherburn-in-Elmet and ended somewhere near Scarthingwell. John Benet, after discussing the action at Ferrybridge, described how 'other [adverse] lords fought against the king *the same day* near Sherborn in Elmet, and he similarly vanquished them'. Indeed, the 1461 Act of Attainder referred to 'a field between the towns of Sherbourne in Elmet and Tadcaster in the said county of York, called Saxton field and Towton field', perhaps pointing to two distinct engagements.[75] Hall's imagined account of Clifford's death at 'Dintingdale' thus may have recalled the flight of the Lancastrians from the second major engagement of the day, fought across the ancient parishes of Saxton and Barkston.

What most historians regard as 'the battle of Towton', fought on the plateau between the villages of Towton and Saxton was, then, the beginning of the third major engagement of the day. John Benet, although he conflates the fighting with the resulting Lancastrian rout, is explicit in this: 'And thirdly, *on the same day*, the king fought with the Earl of Northumberland and Lord Neville and others by the town of Tadcaster and conquered them and put them to flight.'[76] It was this clash of arms that Hall so memorably described in his chronicle. As we have seen, the central role given to Lord Fauconberg, the Yorkist archers and the weather conditions was almost certainly apocryphal, yet there seems little doubt that this area witnessed heavy fighting. The site has been subjected to intensive archaeological investigations, with heavy concentrations of ferrous metal and other finds just north of Saxton in the area of Towton Dale and North Acres. These finds are distinct from another concentration a little to the south-west, between Saxton and Scarthingwell, which may relate to the fighting at 'Dintingdale' described above. Most accounts present this third

72 *Hall's Chronicle*, p.255; Boardman, *Towton 1461*, pp.121–4.

73 Thomas Dunham Whitaker, *The History and Antiquities of the Deanery of Craven* (London: Nichols and Son, 1805), p.224.

74 Leland, i., p.43.

75 *John Benet's Chronicle*, p.50; *Parliament Rolls of Medieval England*, Parliament of November 1461, item 20.

76 *John Benet's Chronicle*, p.50.

engagement as a set-piece battle, with the Yorkists arriving late in the evening of 28 March, to find the Lancastrians encamped at Towton. The following morning the Lancastrians advanced towards Saxton to give battle on the area of open pasture bordered by Castle Hill Wood and the River Cock to the west, and which fell away to lower ground to the east. The fighting took place on this plateau, descending into a bloody slugging match after the initial archery exchange. It lasted some 10 hours before the Duke of Norfolk arrived and the Lancastrians were routed, their remnants fleeing towards Cock Beck and Renshaw Wood, and pursued to Tadcaster and on to York.[77]

The contemporary accounts are, however, confused and contradictory over this crucial stage of the Battle of Towton. The fifteenth-century English chronicle accounts provide little detail: 'Gregory' merely recorded that on Palm Sunday Edward met 'whythe the lordys of the Northe at Schyrborne', making no mention of either Saxton or Towton and giving this stage of the battle no great special significance. The author of a 'Short English Chronicle' similarly described the battle as taking place 'beside Shireborne', whereas 'Howard's Chronicle', written in the 1520s, provided no location for the battle that was 'sore foughten' and lasted into the afternoon.[78] By contrast, the poem known as *The Rose of Rouen* may have singled out the fighting on Towton Dale, stating it took place on Palm Sunday 'affter þe none' and lasted no more than an hour before the Lancastrians yielded and took flight.[79] The letters written on 7 April by Bishop Neville and others do not add much clarification to our understanding of events after the battle for Ferrybridge. Neville, after his description of events at the crossing, wrote that on Palm Sunday there was fought a battle that lasted from dawn until 'the tenth hour of the night' (that is, 4 a.m. on 30 March). He described 'so many dead bodies' covering an area six miles long by three broad, roughly the distance along the old Roman road from Sherburn-in-Elmet to Tadcaster. Neville then added: 'I prefer you should learn from others than myself how manfully our King, the Duke of Norfolk, and my brother [Warwick] and uncle [Fauconberg] bore themselves in this battle: first fighting like common soldiers, then commanding, encouraging, and rallying their squadrons like the greatest captains.' Bishop Beauchamp observed that the outcome of the battle 'remained doubtful the whole day' and attributed the victory to Edward himself, who had 'single-handed cast himself into the fray as he did so notably with the greatest of human courage'. None of the three bishops who wrote to Coppini in the immediate aftermath of the battle described a single decisive clash of arms on Palm Sunday but instead suggested a more fluid battle that stretched from Ferrybridge to the gates of York, and which began around dawn on Palm Sunday.

The earliest continental chronicle accounts, so clear in their two contrasting accounts of the crossing of the Aire at Ferrybridge, are much less helpful in understanding the rest of the day's action. Probably the first to be written from now-lost Yorkist newsletters was that of the Burgundian Jacques du Clercq. He merely stated that after Ferrybridge the Yorkist and Lancastrian armies met in battle. The fighting lasted for three hours 'at most; finally, the misfortune of battle fell on the Duke of Somerset and the people of the queen'. Du Clercq, like other accounts, then went on to list the Lancastrian dead. He was the only chronicler, however, to note that Sir Andrew Trollope, killed in the fighting, 'carried himself nobly, and was very valiant there; he killed there, as they say, a knight and two men-at-arms'.[80] The later manuscripts of the Monstrelet Continuator, however,

77 Boardman, *Towton*, pp.169–222.

78 *Contemporary English Chronicles*, pp.74, 101; *Three Fifteenth Century Chronicles*, p.77.

79 *Historical Poems*, ed. Robbins, p.218.

80 *Mémoires de Jacques du Clercq*, iii., pp.118–19.

who had copied the same source as du Clercq regarding the Battle of Ferrybridge, appear to have garbled their accounts of the remainder of the day's fighting. They described the fighting as lasting for three *days*, a battle 'so horrible and so deadly that the murder that took place was a horror'. They all agreed the outcome of the battle was in doubt for much of the time, but that eventually the tide turned against the 'people of the queen and the Duke of Somerset'.[81] Yet neither du Clercq nor most of the manuscripts of the Monstrelet Continuator offered any clues as to the location of this post-Ferrybridge fighting.

Bibliothèque Nationale de France, Manuscrit Français 88 offered another, and fuller, account of the post-Ferrybridge action. Its author described how when Edward and his men heard the main Lancastrian army was in the field they were 'very joyful'. Scouts were sent to reconnoitre their positions and when they returned Edward addressed his men: 'My children, I pray you to be good and loyal to one another today, for we are fighting a fair and just quarrel.' The Yorkist army answered in the affirmative and Edward awaited the attack of the Lancastrian vanguard. However, a Lancastrian cavalry charge surprised the Yorkists' mounted men-at-arms, most of whom fled 'a good six miles'. Some historians have suggested that this was a pre-planned ambush by men concealed in Castle Hill Wood. Although there is no contemporary evidence that it originated from there, the scatter of archaeological finds suggests that the Lancastrian attack may have come from that direction.[82] There is no reason to doubt, however, that this was a clash of mounted men. The battle now hung in the balance. The Earl of Northumberland's ward failed to follow up – the author of Manuscrit Français 88 suggested Northumberland was already dead – and Edward stepped forward again to save the day. The young King urged the remaining Yorkists to help him recover his kingdom, dismounting and killing his horse, promising to live or die with his men. At this point, the Lancastrians advanced again, banners displayed and crying 'King Henry!' The melee continued for some time, the advantage swinging this way and that, before God gave the Yorkists the victory. The chronicler says the most ferocious attack fell on the Earl of Warwick's battle and he was 'defeated', but the Yorkists prevailed nonetheless, and he ended by listing the most prominent men killed on each side.[83]

It is clear that Jean de Wavrin used the text of this manuscript as the basis for his own account of the 'great battle made quite close to York'. He copied some portions of it verbatim, while other passages he paraphrased. Yet he also made significant additions. Wavrin added that the two armies were just four miles apart when Edward's scouts spotted the Lancastrian army and provided important detail to his description of the cavalry attack that scattered Edward's mounted men-at-arms. The Lancastrian force, Wavrin related, was led by Richard Woodville, Lord Rivers, and his son Anthony and consisted of 6,000 or 7,000 'Welshmen' and Sir Andrew Trollope. They joined with another 7,000 men under the Duke of Somerset to attack Edward's own cavalry. According to Wavrin, the Yorkists fled and were chased for *11* miles. At this stage, Wavrin's narrative becomes a little more confused. Like his source text, he considered the failure of Northumberland's battle to follow up the attack instrumental in staving off disaster for the Yorkists, but the Earl was not dead and soon appeared again in Wavrin's narrative, carrying Henry VI's banner and engaging Edward's remaining men in a desperate melee. Warvrin agreed that the fight was long and its

81 Lille BM E20, fo, 150v; BNF, MS Français 20354, fo. 117v; BL, Harley MS 4424, fo. 158v; *Monstrelet*, ed. Johnes, ii., p.272.

82 Boardman, *Towton 1461*, pp.198–203; Gravett, *Towton*, pp.59–60. For sceptical views on the Castle Hill Wood ambush see Haigh, *From Wakefield to Towton*, pp.134–5; Bicheno, *Battle Royal*, pp.305–6.

83 BNF, MS Français 88, fos. 145–6.

outcome in question for some time, but 'in the end, through the great prowess primarily of the Earl of March, God granted him victory'. Warwick's battle, he agreed, was heavily engaged and the Earl was severely wounded. Before listing the dead, he added the conclusion that the Earl of March had triumphed over 'the king, the queen and the Duke of Somerset'.[84]

Wavrin's account must be considered our most important narrative of the 'battle of Towton.' He described the fighting that took place on Towton Dale between the villages of Saxton and Towton in unparalleled detail. The broad outline of the action – that the Yorkists approached the Lancastrians from the south and battle was soon joined, resulting in a desperate fight, the outcome of which was in doubt until the very end – concurs with the brief description in the letters of 7 April and the probable contents of the Yorkist newsletters seen by du Clercq. Wavrin's account is perhaps more important for what it omits: there is no mention of an archery duel, nothing to suggest the weather played any role, and no mention of the Duke of Norfolk's late arrival swinging the balance in favour of Edward IV. His elaborations and alterations to the account in Manuscrit Français 88, to which he almost certainly had access as a guest of Louis of Bruges in the winter of 1470/71, speak to the peculiar circumstances of the manuscript's compilation. Wavrin met Edward IV, then in exile during the Readeption of Henry VI, and the other Yorkist exiles on more than occasion, and Wavrin made the Yorkist king even more of a central figure than he had been in his exemplar. The prominence given to the Woodvilles is also significant. Like his source text, Wavrin noted that Lord Rivers and his son, Anthony, were captured at the battle, but he also gave them both a prominent role in the cavalry charge that almost broke the Yorkist army. Anthony, by then 2nd Earl Rivers after the murder of his father in August 1469, was also a guest of Lord Gruuthuse, and Wavrin's story of a knightly charge by the young Woodville bested only by a remarkable display of personal prowess by Edward IV himself would have been a fitting tribute to his Burgundian host and his Yorkist guests.[85] Indeed, following Edward's restoration to the throne in May 1471 there was a subtle shift in the way in which the fighting on Palm Sunday was described. The third engagement fought on Towton Dale increasingly became known as the Battle of Towton, downplaying and eventually erasing the importance of the earlier fighting at Ferrybridge and Sherburn-in-Elmet. In the Parliament of 1472 Ralph Vestynden, one of the yeomen of the King's chamber, had his annuity of £10 exempted from the Act of Resumption. The exemption recalled his 'goode and aggreable service which he did us, in berying and holding of our standard of the Blakbull in the *Battaill of Towton*'. Yet the original warrant 11 years previously had remembered Vestynden's service at 'Sherbourne in Elmete'. Indeed, the first grant explicitly in recognition of service at Towton seems to have been to the Kentishman John Cattys in July 1468, remembering his wounds suffered at 'Towton Felde'.[86] Had the reference to Towton in the Act of Attainder in 1461 merely recalled the place where Edward's enemies had committed treason by unfurling their banners against his royal standard, as Wavrin and the author of Manuscrit Français 88 suggested, rather than the site of the decisive encounter of Palm Sunday?

---

84 Wavrin, v., pp.339–41.

85 Livia Visser-Fuchs, 'Richard in Holland 1470–1', *The Ricardian*, 6 (1983), pp.220–28; Visser-Fuchs, *History as Pastime*, pp.69–70.

86 *Parliament Rolls of Medieval England*, Parliament of October 1472, item 14; W. Wheater, *The History of the Parishes of Sherburn and Cawood* (2nd edn, London: Longmans, 1882), p.74; *CPR, 1467–1477*, p.110.

The Battle of Towton certainly captured the Victorian imagination. John Quartey's picture showing Edward IV rallying his men amid the battle was engraved by Charles Oliver Murray for James Grant's British Battles on Land and Sea, published in 1878. The armour and weapons depicted were anachronistic, but the prominence given to cavalry was perhaps not.

From Towton to York

The fourth and final stage of the fighting on Palm Sunday was the retreat of the defeated Lancastrian army towards York. According to the Howard chronicler, the Lancastrian line finally collapsed when 'aboute the noone the forsaid John, Duke of Northfolke, with a freshe band of good men of warre, cam into the ayde of the new electe King Edward'.[87] This was the first suggestion that Norfolk's men had lagged behind and the earliest Yorkist sources, as we have seen, suggested that the Duke fought alongside the King, the Earl of Warwick and Lord Fauconberg from the onset. The chronicle's patron, Thomas Howard, elevated to the title of Duke of Norfolk following his victory over James IV of Scotland in 1513, may simply have wanted to give his namesake and ancestor, who died in November 1461, a more prominent role in the battle. Indeed, Norfolk's late intervention is not mentioned by Hall – who merely says the Duke fell sick on the eve of the battle – or any later chronicler, and it was not until 1719 that the Howard Chronicle was printed by Thomas Hearne. It was ignored by historians of Towton until it was reintroduced into the story by William Grainge in 1854, but soon thereafter Norfolk's arrival late in the day became an established part of Towton

87 *Contemporary English Chronicles*, p.101.

mythology.[88] Another Tudor elaboration on this stage of the battle that has become a commonplace in recent historiography was the bloody rout across Cock Beck and the River Wharfe. Hall wrote that the Lancastrians were:

> discomfited and ouercome, and lyke men amased, fledde toward Tadcaster bridge to saue them selfes: but in the meane way there is a litle broke called Cocke, not very broade, but of a great deapnes, in the whiche, what for hast of escapyng, and what for feare of folowers, a great number were drent and drowned, in so much that the common people there affirme, that men alyue passed the ryuer vpon dead carcasis, and that the great ryuer of Wharfe, which is the great sewer of ye broke, & of all the water comyng from Towton, was colored with bloude.

Hall claimed the 'common people' as his source, but if it was a local legend, the story of the retreat across Cock Beck and the 'bridge of bodies' escaped the notice of John Leland, who had visited the battlefield shortly before Hall wrote his chronicle and who described the Cock Beck and its confluence into the Wharfe in his *Itinerary*.[89]

Regardless of whether the Cock Beck deserves its grisly reputation or not, the pursuit of the retreating Lancastrians back to York was both protracted and doubtless bloody. Bishop Neville described how many of the Lancastrians were killed as they fled and that 'great numbers were drowned in the river [Wharfe] near the town of Tadcaster, eight miles from York, because they themselves had broken the bridge to cut our passage that way'. Many others were killed in or near Tadcaster itself 'and so many dead bodies were seen as to cover an area six miles long by three broad and about four furlongs'. The Dijon newsletter stated the 'chase … lasted from the said [Palm] Sunday to the following Tuesday, five or six leagues long', some 15 to 18 miles. This extended pursuit of the defeated Lancastrians may explain why in later versions of the Monstrelet Continuator's chronicle the length of the battle was given as three days instead of the three hours mentioned by du Clercq. Indeed, on 17 April Bishop Coppini's physician, Master Antonio, told his master that the battle had begun at six in the morning on Palm Sunday and had lasted until noon the following Tuesday.[90] English sources in the 1460s seemed less aware that the pursuit of the Lancastrians was an important part of the fighting on Palm Sunday and beyond. While 'Gregory' mentioned that many men were drowned during the fighting at Ferrybridge, he didn't mention the pursuit after the battle on Towton Dale. He recorded his sorrow at the death toll, however, lamenting that 'many a lady lost hyr beste be lovyd in that batayle'. The Crowland Continuator, probably writing in the early 1470s, noted that the Lancastrians, 'Their ranks being now broken and scattered in flight, the king's army eagerly pursued them, cutting down the fugitives with their swords, just like so many sheep for the slaughter, [and] made immense havoc among them for a distance of ten miles, as far as the city of York.'[91] Composed around the same time, the 'Brief Latin Chronicle' also stated that many Lancastrians were drowned in the retreat, suggesting that the rout towards York had become established in the historical memory as the final bloody chapter of the Towton story.[92]

88 William Grainge, *The Battles and Battle Fields of Yorkshire* (York: James Hunton, 1854), p.71.
89 *Hall's Chronicle*, p.256; Leland, i., p.43.
90 *Calendar of State Papers Milan*, pp.71–2.
91 *Chronicle of the Abbey of Croyland*, p.425.
92 *Three Fifteenth Century Chronicles*, p.174.

The view from 'Bloody Meadow' on Towton Dale looking down towards Cock Beck. (Simon Marsh)

Contemporaries were clear on the heavy price paid by the Lancastrian leadership at Towton. A remarkably consistent list of prominent casualties was appended to the Yorkist newsletters of April 1461 and found its way into almost all the chronicle accounts, both in England and on the continent, written in that decade. Most agreed that Northumberland, Clifford, Neville, Beaumont, Welles, Dacre and Trollope had been slain. William, Viscount Beaumont, had, in fact, survived. He was captured and although attainted in November 1461, he was subsequently pardoned on 23 December that year. Northumberland may have been taken to York to die of his wounds, but the others seem to have been slain in the field. The Earl of Devon was also named in these earliest despatches, although he was executed in York when captured the following day, as was Sir Ralph Bigod (who was known as Lord Mauley). The names provided in these earliest reports tally closely with those Lancastrians attainted in Edward IV's first Parliament: Exeter, Somerset, Devon, Northumberland, Beaumont, Roos, Clifford, Welles, Neville, Dacre and Richemount-Grey. In the aftermath of battle several men whose whereabouts were presumably unknown were wrongly reported dead: the Earl of Westmorland (who probably had not been there at all), Sir Richard Welles, Lord Willoughby (who was not attainted and may not have been present), Sir Henry Stafford, the brother of the first Duke of Buckingham, and Anthony Woodville, Lord Scales. William Paston seemed to suggest that Sir Ralph Gray had died fighting for the Lancastrians, although Wavrin would later list him among the Yorkist casualties. In any case, he survived and would be executed in 1464. Similarly, Bishop O'Flanagan prematurely reported the death of Sir Ralph Percy, eldest surviving brother of the Earl of Northumberland. Du Clercq had also heard that Sir Richard Percy, another of Northumberland's brothers, and 'Lord Grey', probably Lord Richemount-Grey, had also fallen. Wavrin simply copied the list of the dead from Bibliothèque Nationale de France, Manuscrit Français 88 and maintained that Lord Scales had died there, a curious error as he would have been aware that this was not the case. The Yorkists had lost many fewer prominent men, as we have seen: Lord Fitzwalter, John Stafford and Robert Horne were the only casualties named by contemporaries. Prospero Camulio and Master Antonio had heard Lord Scrope of Bolton was dead, but William Paston was better informed, writing that he was 'sore hurt'.[93] Rumours of Lord Scrope's demise at Towton persisted, however, and John Benet, writing after 1462, also listed him among the dead.[94]

There is no doubt that a significant proportion of the Lancastrian army and some of its most prominent leaders escaped. Somerset, Exeter, Lord Rivers, Lord Roos and Lord Richemount-Grey made it to York and the royal family. The Earl of Wiltshire escaped only to be eventually captured at Cockermouth and executed at Newcastle on 1 May.[95] What remained of the Lancastrian leadership had clearly fled the city by the time the first Yorkists arrived. The royal family fled first to Newcastle and eventually to Scotland, accompanied by a small band of adherents, many of whom would share their exile over the coming years. Edward's first act on arriving in York was to remove the severed heads of his father, brother and the Earl of Salisbury from Mickelgate Bar. His second was to execute the Earl of Devon. The two prominent Yorkist prisoners held in the city since their capture at St Albans, Lord Montagu and Lord Berners, were released and they interceded on behalf of the citizens of York for the new King's mercy.[96]

* * *

We can be reasonably certain that Towton was neither the biggest nor the bloodiest battle fought on English soil. Although we will never know for sure how many men fought there, nor how many were killed, we can safely discount the inflated numbers given by newsletter writers and chroniclers for this battle as we can for other, better documented battles and campaigns of the fifteenth century. Similarly, we can say with some confidence that the number of dead never approached even the lowest numbers provided by contemporaries and later writers. Yet it was a large and important battle, almost certainly the bloodiest, and without doubt the most politically significant, fought in this first stage of the Wars of the Roses. Its place in Yorkist mythology, however, has obscured many of the details and indeed the overall course of the fighting on Palm Sunday. The propaganda machine sprang into action within hours of Edward IV's victory. The scale of the victory was heralded in newsletters circulated in England and the Low Countries and featured in correspondence that was read in Paris, Milan, Venice and Rome. Within a decade there was a hotly

93 *Paston Letters and Papers*, ed. Davis, i., p.177; *Calendar of State Papers Milan*, pp.62, 65–66, 68, 73, 77; *Parliament Rolls of Medieval England*, Parliament of November 1461, item 28; *Mémoires de Jacques du Clercq*, iii., pp.118–19; BNF, MS Français 88, fo. 145v; Wavrin, v., p. 341. For Beaumont, see *Calendar of Patent Rolls, 1461–1467*, p.86.

94 *John Benet's Chronicle*, p.50.

95 *Paston Letters and Papers*, ed. Davis, ii., p.230.

96 *Three Fifteenth Century Chronicles*, pp.77, 174; *Paston Letters and Papers*, ed. Davis, i., p.165; *Calendar of State Papers, Milan*, pp.62, 78.

contested struggle over the Yorkist narrative of Towton between versions of the story favourable to the Earl of Warwick and those which championed the personal role of Edward IV as the victor of Towton.

Yet the Yorkist narratives, while they disagreed over Warwick's and the King's respective roles, presented a remarkably consistent account of the events of Palm Sunday 1461. They described how the Yorkist scouts discovered, probably late on Saturday, 28 March, that the crossing of the River Aire at Ferrybridge was held in force by the Lancastrians. The initial Yorkist assault on that day was rebuffed. They then told of a major battle at Ferrybridge, which began just before dawn the next day and resulted in a hard-fought and costly Yorkist victory. The outcome of Palm Sunday 1461 was probably decided at Ferrybridge, rather than at Towton Dale. The Yorkists then pursued the fleeing Lancastrians north, along the Great North Road, through Sherburn-in-Elmet. Between Sherburn-in-Elmet and Scarthingwell – perhaps around the area later known as 'Dintingdale' – the Lancastrians made a stand, and the second major engagement of the day was fought. Finally, on Towton Dale between Saxton and Towton, the Lancastrians made their final stand. Again, the Yorkist sources do not specify who these Lancastrians were. Presumably they included men who had survived the encounters earlier in the day, but the force on Towton Dale was probably comprised mainly of fresh contingents, led by Northumberland, who had made the 14-mile ride from York that day. A Lancastrian cavalry charge, possibly from the direction of Castle Hill Wood, threatened to overwhelm the Yorkists and many of their mounted men fled, until their commanders rallied their men and their superior numbers prevailed. Eventually, at some point in the late afternoon, the Lancastrian army broke and retreated towards Tadcaster and onto York. The pursuit seems to have turned into a bloody rout and by the next day, Edward was safely established in York, his foes – temporarily it would turn out – vanquished.

Within this broad outline of events, other events and details recorded by later commentators may have happened. The battle may have been fought entirely or partly in a snowstorm, but if it was, no contemporary afforded it the same importance as Edward Hall would do in the 1540s. The Yorkist archers must certainly have prevailed over their Lancastrian counterparts on Towton Dale, but that was as likely to have been down to their superior numbers as it was the wind direction and clever generalship of Lord Fauconberg. Lord Clifford may have played an important role in the fighting at Ferrybridge and died when he removed his helmet for a drink at Dintingdale, but if he did so, no contemporary thought it worthy of mention. The Duke of Norfolk may have arrived late to the fighting on Towton Dale, but if he did, no writer before the author of the Howard Chronicle thought to mention it. Equally, Cock Beck, swollen with the icy winter flood water, may have proved a choke point and witnessed the death of many fleeing Lancastrians. Yet if it did, no fifteenth-century writers differentiated what happened there from the rest of the Lancastrian flight to Tadcaster and on to York. Similarly, family legend, often set down in writing when heraldic visitations recorded the history of gentry families in the sixteenth and seventeenth centuries, embroidered the rich history of the Battle of Towton and added layers of myth and misunderstanding to the bare bones of the fifteenth-century narrative. By the time the nineteenth-century historians of the battle came to write their accounts, the battle's legacy as 'England's bloodiest battle' was firmly entrenched.

Further Reading

This chapter is heavily indebted to work of Tim Sutherland and conversations with Paul Dawson. A starting point for any serious study of the Battle of Towton must be Sutherland's 'Killing Time: Challenging the Common Perceptions of Three Medieval Conflicts – Ferrybridge, Dintingdale and Towton – "the Largest Battle on British Soil"', *Journal of Conflict Archaeology* 5 (2009), pp.1–26. The fullest 'traditional' account of the battle is Andrew Boardman's *Towton 1461: The Anatomy of a Battle*, first published in 1994 and now in its fourth edition (Cheltenham: The History Press, 2022). Most of the recent published accounts of Towton are derivative of Boardman's work and contain little original research or thinking, but Hugh Bicheno's is a well-written and thought-provoking interpretation (*Battle Royal*, pp.292–312).

Epilogue

The euphoria that Edward and his men must have felt as they entered the city of York on 30 March 1461 was short-lived. The fighting between Ferrybridge and Towton, it must soon have been apparent, was not the decisive victory the Yorkists had hoped for. The royal family, several prominent Lancastrian lords and a substantial portion of their army remained intact. Edward celebrated Easter in York, but soon the Yorkists were again assembling men and sending them against the Lancastrian rebels. Sir John Fogge, for example, raised 24 men from Beverley and they went north on 16 April resplendent in new livery jackets and carrying a new banner.[1] Edward himself remained in York until 17 April and then travelled north via Helperby, Northallerton, Durham and Newcastle-upon-Tyne before returning to York, via Middleham Castle, on 10 May. At Newcastle, the King executed the newly captured Earl of Wiltshire, sending his head to be impaled on London Bridge, and despatched Sir William Plumpton and the priests John Morton and Dr Ralph Mackerell to the Tower of London. From York, Edward made his way back to London via Preston, Chester, Stafford, Lichfield, Coventry, Warwick and Stoney Stratford before arriving in Lambeth on Sunday, 14 May.[2]

Rumours abounded: on 18 April John Paston heard that Henry VI was at large in Yorkshire and that Sir Robert Ogle had laid siege to a place called 'Corcumbre', killing half of the 6,000 or so men the Lancastrians had assembled there. A week later, according to the November Act of Attainder, Henry and Margaret, joined by Exeter, Somerset, Roos and Richemount-Grey, agreed to cede Berwick-upon-Tweed to the Scots in return for direct military assistance.[3] Even more worrying perhaps were the plans afoot on the continent. At the end of April, the Duke of Burgundy convened his council at Saint-Omer. The news from England was reassuring: the Dauphin Louis's support for the Yorkists and their victory could only help the Burgundians. As Bishop Coppini told the Duke of Milan on 8 May, 'this victory of King Edward is a great blow to the King of France'. Charles VII, however, was not idle. On 9 May Prospero de Camulio reported that the French had sent 1,500 men through the Duke of Burgundy's lands to lift the Yorkist siege of Hammes Castle. Although they had returned when told the castle had fallen, two days later they had returned with 12,000 men. By the beginning of June a French attack on England, with assistance from the Scots, was expected daily. Camulio reported that 20,000 men had left Normandy and were bound for the Bristol Channel with the intention of landing in Wales and raising the country for Queen

1 Poulson, *Beverlac*, i., pp.240–1.
2 TNA, C81/792, 793; *Paston Letters and Papers*, ed. Davis, ii., pp.229–30, 233.
3 *Paston Letters and Papers*, ed. Davis, ii., p.230; *Parliament Rolls of Medieval England*, Parliament of November 1461, item 21.

The much-damaged tomb of Ranulph, Lord Dacre, killed at the Battle of Towton, in Saxton churchyard. (Author's photo)

Margaret. The French did indeed attack the Channel Islands, and Castle Cornet was captured by men acting on the orders of Pierre de Brezé. Apparently, the Dauphin and the Duke of Burgundy had sent messengers to the Scottish regent, Mary of Guelders, to dissuade her from joining the French invasion.[4] The tense atmosphere in the weeks that followed the Yorkist victory at Towton is evident from documentary sources too. It is difficult to know what to make of the rumours of French invasion or the reference in Breton archives to the 'Army of England' assembled in Breton ports in early June 1461.[5] On 6 June Camulio told his master that he had heard that the French fleet had attacked Cornwall (although the Bretons had not joined in). It had 'done some damage by pillage and burning' but had since returned to Normandy. Further information followed on the 18th: the French fleet had attacked, been repulsed, and lost 4,000 or 2,000 depending on who you believed. 'The truth,' Camulio lamented, 'cannot be obtained from England, owing to the stupidity of the people there.'[6]

4 *Calendar of State Papers, Milan*, pp.84, 89, 90, 93–4.
5 BNF, MS Français 22318, p.57.
6 *Calendar of State Papers, Milan*, pp.95, 98.

Edward's government certainly took these rumours and threats seriously. The Earl of Warwick was compensated for £1,966 10*s*. for his costs in setting forth a navy.[7] Similarly, Lord Fauconberg was tasked with delivering victuals to Newcastle-upon-Tyne by sea and paid for taking men to subdue robbers and rioters in Norfolk.[8] Worse was to follow. On 12 June news was received that the Scots, accompanied by Queen Margaret, Exeter, Lord Richemount-Grey, Sir Humphrey Dacre and other Lancastrian rebels, had laid siege to Carlisle. Parliament, planned for early July, was postponed until November and the King made plans to return north. Just as the coronation, scheduled for 28 June, was about to be postponed, news was received that Lord Montagu had lifted the siege. Considerable damage was inflicted, however, and in December the citizens of Carlisle were compensated for the destruction of the King's mill and fisheries by the rebels.[9] In the south-west on 17 June, the mayors of Exeter and Plymouth and several local landowners were commissioned to arrest the inveterate Lancastrian Sir Baldwin Fulford and the surviving bastard brother of the Duke of Exeter, who were attempting to raise the people of the West Country for Henry VI and to aid and abet the French. Fulford set sail to Brittany to raise more men but was captured. He was kept prisoner in Bristol until September when, in front of the King, he was hanged, drawn and quartered. On 24 June, the inhabitants of Suffolk, Essex and Hertfordshire were ordered to raise funds to put ships to sea, after the example of the men of the northern counties who had provided for six ships furnished with 700 men-at-arms and archers.[10] Eventually, by the end of June, Yorkist fears began to subside. On 26 June Edward made his formal procession from Lambeth Bridge to the Tower in preparation for his coronation. The following Sunday, 28 June, he was crowned at Westminster Abbey. Some of those who had fought alongside him at Towton and Mortimer's Cross – Sir Humphrey Bourchier, Sir Walter Devereux, Sir William Hastings, Sir William Herbert, Sir Thomas Lumley, Sir Robert Ogle, Sir Humphrey Stafford and Sir John Wenlock – were elevated to the peerage, a new Yorkist aristocracy bound by ties of personal service to the new King.[11]

The battles of Ferrybridge and Towton did not mark the end of this stage of the Wars of the Roses, but they did mark a watershed moment. England may not quite have been the 'gay garden' celebrated by Yorkist poets in the spring of 1461, but a nationwide programme of commissions and arrests, made possible by the acquiescence of urban elites and landowners throughout the realm to the new regime, meant that Yorkist control was soon established.[12] Edward IV and the Earl of Warwick were no longer rebels. Instead, that mantle had passed to Henry VI, Queen Margaret and their followers. It was they who committed treason by conspiring with the King's enemies, imagining his death and raising war against him. Edward as king commanded the machinery of government and the institutions of state; formal royal authority lay in his hands. Warwick, on the other hand, held much of the real power: he remained popular among the Londoners and those portions of the population that had helped the Yorkist lords in their trials and tribulations between 1459 and 1461. Moreover, the Earl enjoyed formidable military and financial resources as captain of Calais, admiral and keeper of the seas, and steward of the duchy of Lancaster lands. His large

7 TNA, E404/72/1/11, 15, 32.
8 TNA, E404/72/1/35.
9 Scofield, *Edward IV*, i., p.180; *Calendar of Patent Rolls, 1461–1467*, p.82.
10 *Calendar of Patent Rolls, 1461–1467*, p.33; *The House of Commons 1422–1461*, iv., p.490.
11 Scofield, *Edward IV*, i., pp.181–4.
12 Hannes Kleineke, 'England, 1461: Predominantly Provincial Perspectives on the Early Months of the Reign of Edward VI', in *The Fifteenth Century XVIII*, ed Linda Clark and Peter Fleming (Woodbridge: Boydell and Bewer, 2020), pp.81–92.

affinity and network of servants, both military and political, was maintained not simply by his own estates at Middleham and elsewhere, but by the royal resources he could draw upon by virtue of his crown office.[13] In the second volume of this military history of the Wars of the Roses, we will see how Warwick put these to good use in crushing Lancastrian resistance in the north of England and how the embers of Lancastrian support in the north, in Wales and abroad were kept alive by the growing rivalry between Edward IV and the Earl.

13 Michael Hicks, 'Bastard Feudalism, Overmighty Subjects and Idols of the Multitude during the Wars of the Roses', *History*, 85 (2000), pp.386–403.

Colour Plate Commentaries

Plate A. Yeoman archer of the king's household, First Battle of St. Albans, May 1455.
The men of the royal household, as well as providing service to the king, were also a military force. Just prior to the First Battle of St. Albans, Henry VI ordered the purchase of 500 bows. In the following year, 82 bows were ordered for the yeomen of the king's household, suggesting the formation of a household band of archers, much like the Burgundian ducal *garde du corps*. As such, this archer wears a blue and white Lancastrian livery jacket over his padded jack and leg armour, consisting of cuisses, poleyns and greaves.

Plate B. Man-at-arms of the Earl of Salisbury's retinue, Battle of Blore Heath, September 1459.
This man is likely a member of Richard Neville's household or one of his indentured retainers. He has ridden to battle and is armed with a 'lancegay', an eight- and ten-feet long spear commonly carried by mounted men in the mid-fifteenth century. He wears a suit of West European harness, probably imported from Brabandt, suited for fighting on foot in the English manner, and carries a sword for dismounted combat.

Plate C. Edmund, Lord Grey de Ruthin, Battle of Northampton, July 1460.
Wavrin tells us that Lord Grey de Ruthin's actions in helping the Yorkists into the royal camp were decisive at Northampton. As a member of the nobility, he wears a heraldic tabard bearing the complex Grey de Ruthin arms over West European harness of a design typical for the late 1450s.

Plate D. Sir Ralph Percy, Wakefield, December 1460.
'The Battle of Wakefield' was not really a battle at all and, as one chronicle tells us, Richard, Duke of York was taken 'out of array' and murdered. Sir Ralph Percy, the younger brother of the third Earl of Northumberland was likely present at the duke's capture. He wears a brigandine, covered in red velvet, and leg armour, as well as gauntlets, vambraces, coulters and rerebraces on his arms. His sallet is based on the funeral effigy of Sir Hugh Cokesay in Kidderminster (c.1455-1460).

Plate E. Billman, Yorkist army, Battle of Mortimer's Cross, February 1461.
The bill was the standard polearm for English soldiers in the second half of the fifteenth century. The few contemporary musters and other documents that survive suggest that they may have outnumbered archers in most retinues. This individual is well equipped as befits a man of the retinue of Edward, the new Duke of York. He wears a Yorkist livery jacket over a mail byrnie. He also has armoured gauntlets and carries a sword and buckler. A woollen cloak protects him from the extreme cold.

Plate F. Lancastrian man-at-arms, Second Battle of St. Albans, February 1461.
The speed with which the Lancastrians overwhelmed the Yorkist position at the Second Battle of St. Albans suggests that a good proportion of their army was mounted. This well-equipped man-at-arms of the Duke of Somerset's retinue wears a mass-produced suit of Milanese harness and an armet-style helmet. Such suits reflected the Italian way of war which favoured mounted men-at-arms over the English fashion to ride to battle and dismount to fight.

Plate G. King Edward IV, London, March 1461.
Jean de Wavrin describes how Edward 'departed from London on a fine warhorse fully equipped with the arms of England, well accompanied by earls, lords, and barons' to head north in March 1461. He wears blackened Italian-style armour decorated with gilding, one of probably several suits of harness the King took with him for the Palm Sunday campaign. His armet-style helmet is topped with a golden crown and his heraldic caparison, bearing the arms of England, is a statement of royal magnificence.

Plate H. John Radcliffe, Lord Fitzwalter, The Battle of Ferrybridge, March 1461.
Fitzwalter was the prominent Yorkist casualty of the Ferrybridge/Sherburn-in-Elmet/Towton campaign. He is depicted here wearing a high-quality English harness with extensive gilding. He wears a heraldic tabard over his harness and carries a poleaxe, the weapon of choice for many English men-at-arms when fighting on foot.

Plate I. Banners and Standards

1. We know little about the banners and standards carried during the Wars of the Roses and most of the manuscript sources date from the sixteenth century. Banners carried the heraldic arms of lords and knights banneret. The banner of James Tuchet, Lord Audley bears his arms reflecting the family's various marriage alliances: Quarterly; land 4, Ermine a chevron Gules; 2 and 3, Gules a fret Or.
2. The banner of John, Lord Clifford: Quarterly: 1 and 4, Checky Or and Azure a fess Gules; 2 and 3, Gules 6 annulets Or; impaling, Sable a bend flory counter-flory Or.
3. Noblemen also carried a heraldic standard, comprising their heraldic badge, motto and their livery colours. Occasionally more than one standard was described and may have been carried, but the sources are less than clear. This is the standard attributed to Henry Beaufort, duke of Somerset: St George in the hoist. Field: Argent over azure a bordure company argent and azure. Badges: A yale argent spotted bezzante, horns, hooves and crowned and chained Or. Portcullis and chains Or. Motto: Souvent Me Souvient. The livery colours and badges could be worn by the lord's retainers and men under his command.
4. One of the few banners described by contemporary sources is that borne by Ralph Vestynden, one of the Edward IV's bearers on Palm Sunday 1461. He is said to have carried the standard of the 'Black Bull', a badge associated with the dukes of Clarence (from whom Edward claimed his descent and right to the throne): St. George in the hoist. Field: Azure over murrey a bordure company azure and murrey. Badges: A bull sable passant reguardant, crowned about the neck, horns and hooves Or. Roses en soleil Argent. Motto: Dieu Et Mon Droyt.

Plate J.

This diagram shows the scatter of archaeological finds on Towton battlefield. The arrow heads - in red - point to an archery duel north of North Acres and Bloody Meadow. The other finds are scattered across the Registered Battlefield area, with a further concentration to the south, around 'Dintingdale', and further finds north leading towards Tadcaster. The pattern of finds suggests a more fluid conflict, rather than the large set-piece battle suggested by Hall.

Appendix: The Nobility and the Wars of the Roses, 1459–61

Historians have long used the participation of members of the English nobility in the battles of the Wars of the Roses as a measure of the political commitment of the peerage to either side in the civil wars and of their involvement more generally in the political events of the time. Many historians, myself included, have argued that the apparently high rates of participation in the fighting, especially from 1459 to 1461, demonstrate how difficult it was for the King's greatest subjects to remain aloof from national events.[1] Colin Richmond, in an important article published in 1977, argued that 56 of the 70 members of the English nobility in this period actively participated in the fighting. Subsequent research on the subject has finessed the numbers but not radically changed the conclusion. Regardless of the measure of their support for each of the rival claimants, noblemen 'could not escape the responsibilities inherent in their political position'.[2] As the King's councillors, they were intimately involved in the affairs of the crown, and because of their networks of retainers, servants and friends in the areas where they held land they found themselves inexorably – and sometimes reluctantly – drawn into the conflict between Lancaster and York. The presence of large numbers of the peerage at the battles and sieges between 1459 and 1461 has important ramifications for how we view the Wars of the Roses more generally. It was, it is argued, the retainers and armed followers of the lords who provided the bulk of the armies, and certainly those men most experienced and capable in the art of war that typically decided a battle's outcome. The more nobles served, quite simply, the larger the armies and the resulting battles. The high percentage of participation in the battles fought between 1459 and 1461, and the higher proportion of noble casualties, compared to those of 1469 to 1471 and in 1485 suggests that the peerage as a group became increasingly demoralised and disengaged from the business of politics as the fifteenth century wore on.[3]

The conclusions of this study, however, suggest that we may have overestimated noble participation in the battles of these years and, as such, misunderstood their commitment to and involvement in the politics of the period. Richmond also counted Ludford Bridge among his battles, counting those lords who swore the oath of allegiance to Henry VI in the Coventry Parliament

1 Grummitt, *War and Martial Culture*, pp.12–15; Gerald Harriss, *Shaping the Nation: England 1360–1461* (Oxford: Oxford University Press, 2005), pp.639–49.

2 Colin Richmond, 'The Nobility and the Wars of the Roses, 1459–61', *Nottingham Medieval Studies*, 21 (1977), pp.71–85.

3 Grummitt, *Wars of the Roses*, pp.134–8; Colin Richmond, 'Identity and Morality: Power and Politics during the Wars of the Roses', in *Power and Identity in the Middle Ages: Essays in Memory of Rees Davies*, ed. H. Pryce and J. Watts (Oxford, 2007), pp.226–41.

among the Lancastrian ranks. I have not considered Ludford Bridge in this analysis, first because our sources for which lords were in the King's camp are so deficient and, second, because there was no fighting on the night of 12 and 13 October 1459. The nature of the sources generally is such that merely counting the references to nobles in each of the battles obscures the complexity of the situation. Our sources for recreating noble participation in the battles of 1459 can be divided into two broad categories. First, and most importantly, are the chronicles. We have already noted how these are almost exclusively pro-Yorkist in tone. They are also derivative of each other and of the newsletters, official acts and proclamations circulated in 1460 and 1461 by Warwick and later by Edward IV's government. The news contained in the Paston correspondence and that contained in the Milanese archives reflects the stories and rumours that fed Yorkist propaganda in the south of England and East Anglia. Equally, the chronicle accounts of Wakefield and St Albans mirror the newsletters circulated on the continent and in England. This explains the prominence of the Duke of Somerset as leader of the Lancastrian cause alongside Queen Margaret in 1460 and 1461. The list of Lancastrian lords present at Wakefield also largely maps onto those men attainted for York's murder in November 1461 (with Lord Clifford being an obvious and curious omission). Some London-based chroniclers, exemplified by the author of 'Gregory's Chronicle', tended to identify all northern lords as supporters of Henry VI, although the well-informed author of the *Annales* noted that as the Lancastrians prepared to march south early in 1461 two of those lords, Henry, Lord Fitzhugh, and John, Lord Greystoke, 'were under strong suspicion and therefore many hardships' for their kinship to Salisbury and Warwick. Eventually, and under duress, they swore loyalty to Queen Margaret and Prince Edward. They did not take up arms against Edward IV but equally they were not trusted members of the Neville inner circle in the early 1460s.[4] It is also difficult to judge how much weight to give to a single mention of an individual at the battle. The presence of Richard Fiennes, Lord Dacre of the South, at Towton is only recorded in one version of *The Brut* chronicle, although the prospect of him reclaiming the northern Dacre lands may have been incentive enough for him to march north in March 1461. Other times chroniclers were simply mistaken, confusing names and places. The author of the same version of *The Brut* chronicle was almost certainly in error when he named Lord Fauconberg among the Yorkist lords at St Albans in February 1461 as he was still in Calais, serving as his nephew Warwick's deputy.[5]

However well-informed the author of the *Annales* was over Fitzhugh's and Greystoke's allegiances, he may have been mistaken to suggest Henry, Lord Grey of Codnor, was with the Lancastrian army at the Second Battle of St Albans. Lord Richemount-Grey, later attainted for taking up arms against Edward IV at Towton, is probably a more likely candidate. He was not alone in mixing up the various lords Grey. In his second, shorter account of Northampton, Jean de Wavrin misidentified the man who had betrayed the Lancastrians as the Northumberland knight Sir Ralph Gray, another notorious turncoat, instead of Lord Grey de Ruthin.[6] John Benet listed Lord Grey of Codnor among the Lancastrian lords at Towton, again probably confusing him for Lord Richemount-Grey. The young Grey of Codnor, born in 1435 and first summoned to the Coventry Parliament in 1459, appears to have remained aloof from political affairs despite his age and being a ward of Viscount Beaumont. If he did fight for Lancaster – and his lands seem to have been seized by Edward IV in the summer of 1461 – he soon made an accommodation with the new

4 *Letters and Papers*, ii(2)., p.775; Pollard, *North-Eastern England During the Wars of the Roses*, pp.274–6.

5 *The Brut*, i., pp.602–3. For Dacre, see above, p.123.

6 Wavrin, v., p.323; *The House of Commons 1422–1461*, iv., pp.635–9.

regime, and he marched north with the King the following year. He took no part in the struggles of 1469 to 1471, but he crossed the Channel with Edward IV in 1475 and three years later he was appointed to a short-lived term as deputy of Ireland. He appears to have supported Richard III's accession, but not enough to fight for him at Bosworth, and he died peacefully in his bed in 1496.[7] Grey of Codnor may have fought at both St Albans and Towton, but we cannot be certain from the chronicle evidence and, if he did, he would seem to epitomise Colin Richmond's category of 'reluctant warriors'.

The second group of sources are royal or seigneurial administrative records. They are perhaps the most reliable in establishing an individual's presence at a battle. The duchy of Lancaster accounts for Wakefield, for example, confirm that the Earl of Northumberland and Lord Clifford visited the town in the aftermath of York's capture, but do not name any other of the Lancastrian lords mentioned in either the chronicle accounts or the 1461 Act of Attainder. Similarly, the record of the Lancastrian council meeting held at York on 20 January 1461 is a reliable list of the lords who had committed themselves to Queen Margaret.[8] Both the chronicle sources and the Act of Attainder attest to their subsequent defence of the Lancastrian cause. Such records are, however, very few and far between.

One important document is the hastily scribbled note of Yorkist and uncommitted lords probably written during the short final session of the 1460 Parliament. Composed between 28 January and 3 February 1461 and now in The National Archives, it has also been the subject of an article by Colin Richmond, allowing him to revisit and revise his analysis of noble participation in the events of those years.[9] Twenty-one lay and spiritual peers were identified as supporters of Edward, Duke of York: the Duke of Norfolk, the earls of Warwick and Arundel, Viscount Bourchier, and lords Berners, Bonville, Grey of Powis, Scrope of Bolton, Abergavenny, Clinton, Fitzwalter, de la Warre, Montagu, Cobham, Saye and Sele, Stanley and Grey de Ruthin. There are 'no surprises' among the list, Richmond concludes, save perhaps for Lord Stanley (whose inclusion would suggest we might need to accept the accusations made against him in the 1459 Parliament and Wavrin's account of the Battle of Northampton) and de la Warre. De la Warre's inclusion implies he accepted the Yorkists' good graces if he had been among those defending the Tower against Salisbury and Wenlock in July 1460 and that, significantly, John Benet was mistaken to include him among the Lancastrian lords who attacked the Duke of York at Wakefield. John, Lord Berners, a younger brother of Viscount Bourchier, *is* a surprising omission as he was clearly a committed Yorkist and was captured fighting alongside Lord Montagu at St Albans some two weeks later. Equally, the young Duke of Suffolk, York's brother-in-law, was not included simply because he had not been summoned to Parliament. The document then goes on to name 16 'newtri galis', presumably uncommitted lords. The lay peers in this category were the new Viscount Beaumont, the Earl of Oxford, lords Sudeley, Stourton, Rivers, Willoughby, Greystoke, Fitzwarin, Zouche, Beauchamp of Powick, Dudley, Latimer and Scales. Of these George Neville, Lord Latimer, was pronounced a lunatic in 1451 and his lands given to his half-brother, the Earl of Salisbury, while Dudley had been injured and captured at Blore Heath. John, Lord Beauchamp of Powick, a long-time Lancastrian servant and knight of the Garter with extensive military experience in France, appears to have retired from

7 *Complete Peerage*, vi., pp.130–2; *Three Fifteenth Century Chronicles*, p.152.

8 Hicks, 'A Minute of a Lancastrian Council', pp.214–21.

9 TNA, E163/28/5; Colin Richmond, 'The Nobility and the Wars of the Roses: The Parliamentary Session of January 1461', *Parliamentary History*, 18 (1999), pp.261–9.

public life by the late 1450s, as had the other veteran Lancastrian peers, Ralph, Lord Sudeley, and John, Lord Stourton. The elderly Northamptonshire peer William, Lord Zouche, was also probably in ill-health as he died in December 1462. William Bourchier, Lord Fitzwarin, another younger brother of Viscount Bourchier, appears to have avoided political entanglements altogether.[10] Was the compiler of the list being optimistic, however, when he included both the Woodvilles, Richard, Lord Rivers, and Anthony, Lord Scales? According to Wavrin, the two men would play a prominent role at Towton and Scales was rumoured to be among the Lancastrian casualties, yet both he and his father survived the battle and neither suffered the penalties of attainder and forfeiture, receiving a pardon for all offences in July 1461.[11] Equally, did Lord Willoughby really leave Westminster on 3 February when the Parliamentary session ended to join Queen Margaret in the north and then ride south again with her to St Albans just two weeks later as Robert Bale and the author of *Annales* claim? Perhaps he did, as both 'Gregory' and John Benet listed him among the Lancastrian lords at Towton, where he fought alongside his father, Lionel, Lord Welles. Professor Richmond probably impugned the reputation of Warwick's kinsmen Latimer and Greystoke when he doubted their neutral stance. Although they were named as being with the Lancastrian lords in the north of England before York's death, neither were at the January York council meeting. Perhaps bound by the oath the author of the *Annales* tells us he had made to Queen Margaret, Greystoke was unwilling to take the field against the Lancastrians, while Latimer was probably incapacitated. By May, however, Greystoke was with his Neville kinsmen suppressing Lancastrian rebels in the North Riding.[12]

By contrast, the Acts of Attainder of 1459 and 1461 leave little doubt as to the identities of the most committed partisans on either side. At Coventry, York, Salisbury, Warwick, Rutland, March and Clinton were attainted for taking up arms against Henry VI, but others, such as Grey of Powis and Stanley, were either pardoned or escaped punishment altogether. The granting of pardons for men who had committed treason by taking up arms against the King may have been even more widespread in 1461. In the November Parliament Exeter, Somerset, Wiltshire, Northumberland, Pembroke, Beaumont, Clifford, Dacre, Hungerford, Neville, Richemount-Grey, Roos and Welles were attainted, but others who had probably done likewise but submitted to Edward IV's grace, like the Woodvilles and Lord Willoughby, were pardoned. The general pardons granted did not specify the crimes and treasons committed, but it seems highly unlikely that a prominent lord who had taken up arms against the King would not have had to sue out a pardon. It is likely therefore that neither John de Vere, Earl of Oxford, nor Ralph Neville, Earl of Westmorland, were with the Lancastrians at St Albans in February 1461, as Robert Bale claimed, nor that Westmorland was at Towton the following month. Indeed, whatever the political allegiance of an individual during the Wars of the Roses, to actually take up arms and participate in a battle was a step which, it seems, only some were willing to take. Illness, accident and circumstance could also prevent participation, however willing an individual may have been to fight, and further reduce the number of men who fought.

At most, 37 of the 50 peers summoned to the Parliament of 1460 fought in at least one battle or siege during the years 1459 to 1461. Of the eight peers who were not summoned, either through age, illness, rebellion or because they were overseas, seven were probably actively engaged. The

10 *Complete Peerage*, ii., pp.47, 153; v., pp.507–8; vii., pp.479–81; xii., pp.301–2, 419–21, 944–5.
11 *Calendar of Patent Rolls, 1461–1467*, p.97.
12 *Calendar of Patents Rolls, 1461–1467*, p.30.

previous year, 30 of the 50 summoned had done likewise, while of the 13 not summoned, only John Tiptoft, Earl of Worcester (who was in Italy throughout), was not recorded to have seen battle.[13] In total, of the lords summoned to Parliament in 1459 and 1460, those peers not summoned, and Lord Audley who was killed at Blore Heath, 47 of 68 were said to have engaged in the fighting on at least one occasion. I have not counted two children (John Talbot, second Earl of Shrewsbury, and Edward, Prince of Wales) among this number.[14] Yet this simple headcount does not tell the whole story. Chroniclers, as we have seen, got it wrong, either through misidentification or, occasionally, by claiming lords were present when conclusive evidence proves otherwise. Moreover, the proportion that participated in more than one battle was probably much smaller still, although that conclusion comes with the caveat that the chroniclers' frequent addition of 'and many more' to their lists of lords may obscure the true number. The Yorkists won the throne in 1461 with the active support of a minority of lords: Norfolk, Warwick and his immediate Neville kinsmen, as well as the Bourchiers. To this group might be added the Earl of Arundel and lords Clinton, Fitzwalter, Scrope of Bolton and Stanley. They were assisted, of course, by a group of committed and capable gentry supporters, many of whom were themselves elevated to the peerage in Edward's first Parliament. The Yorkists defeated an equally narrow Lancastrian party – Somerset, Exeter, Devon, Northumberland, Pembroke, Wiltshire, Clifford, Neville and Roos – who never fought together on the same battlefield. Other northern lords – Dacre, Welles and Richemount-Grey – as well as Lord Hungerford and the new Viscount Beaumont may have fought and in some cases died at Towton, but they were not part of a large and committed opposition to the ambitions of the House of York. It is simply not true 'that almost all the nobility of England was assembled for Towton'.[15] It is tempting to suggest that Northampton in July 1460 marked an important watershed, and that the extraordinary violence visited on the lords in the royal party both removed prominent Lancastrian partisans and convinced others to shy away from confronting the Yorkist rebels. Contrary to the generally held view, by the beginning of 1461 most of the English nobility were probably no longer minded to fight to preserve the Lancastrian crown – if they had ever been so in the first place – but they appear equally unwilling to have risked their lives and wealth to place Edward of York on the throne.

---

13 For the lords summoned to each Parliament in this period see W.C. Wedgwood, *History of Parliament: Register of the Ministers and of the Members of Both Houses 1439–1509* (London: HMSO, 1938).

14 I have also not included William Bonville, Lord Harington in the right of his wife, Elizabeth, daughter and heir of William, 5th Lord Harington (d. 1458), who was not summoned to Parliament. Bonville was heir to William, Lord Bonville, who was killed at St Albans in 1461. Lord Harington was himself killed alongside his father-in-law, the Earl of Salisbury, at Wakefield: *The Complete Peerage*, vi., pp.318–20.

15 Boardman, *Towton 1461*, p.167.

Table 1 Blore Heath

	An English Chronicle	Jean de Wavrin	'Gregory'	Robert Bale	Short English Chronicle	John Benet	Abbot Whethamstede	Act of Attainder (1459)	The Brut	Jacques Du Clercq
Lancastrians										
Audley†	x	x	x				x	x	x	x
Dudley		x						x	x	
Exeter		x								
Beaumont		x								
Welles		x								
Yorkists										
Warwick		x								
Salisbury	x	x	x	x	x	x	x	x	x	x

Table 2 Northampton

	An English Chronicle	Jean de Wavrin	Brief Notes	Brief Latin Chronicle	Annales	'Gregory'	Robert Bale	Short English Chronicle	John Benet	Abbot Whethamstede	The Brut
Lancastrians											
Exeter		x									
Somerset		x									
Buckingham†	x	x	x	x	x	x	x	x	x		x
Shrewsbury†	x	x	x	x	x	x	x	x	x		x
Northumberland		x									
Beaumont†	x	x	x	x	x	x	x	x	x		x
Egremont†	x	x?	x	x	x	x	x	x	x		
Grey de Ruthin	x	x			x					x	
Yorkists											
Norfolk		x									x
Warwick	x	x	x	x	x	x		x	x	x	x
March	x	x	x	x	x			x	x	x	x
Arundel		x									
Fauconberg	x	x							x	x	
Abergavenny	x										
Audley	x										
Scrope of Bolton	x	x									
Saye and Sele	x										
Clinton	x										
Stanley		x									
Bourchier	x										

Table 3 Seige of the Tower of London

	An English Chronicle	Short English Chronicle	John Benet	'Gregory'
Lancastrians				
Scales	x	x	x	x
Hungerford/Moleyns	x		x	
De la Warre	x			
Vessy	x			
Lovell	x	x	x	
Yorkists				
Salisbury		x		
Cobham		x		

Table 4 Wakefield

	An English Chronicle	Jean de Wavrin	Brief Notes	Brief Latin Chronicle	Annales	'Gregory'	Robert Bale	Short English Chronicle	John Benet	Abbot Whethamstede	Act of Attainder (1461)	The Brut
Lancastrians												
Somerset	x	x	x	x	x	x	x	x	x		x	x
Exeter						x		x				
Northumberland	x					x	x		x		x	x
Wiltshire								x				
Devon						x			x		x	
Clifford	x			x	x	x	x		x			x
Neville	x			x	x	x	x		x		x	x
Roos						x	x	x	x		x	
Fitzhugh									x			
Greystoke									x			
De la Warre									x			
Yorkists												
York†	x	x	x	x	x	x	x	x	x	x	x	x
Salisbury†	x	x	x	x	x	x	x	x	x	x		x
Rutland†	x	x	x	x	x	x	x	x	x			x

Table 5 Mortimers Cross

	An English Chronicle	Jean de Wavrin	Worcester, Itineraries	Annales	'Gregory'	Tanner MS 2	Short English Chronicle	John Benet	Act of Attainder (1461)	The Brut	Milanese Letters
Lancastrian											
Wiltshire	x	x	x	x	x	x	x	x	x	x	
Pembroke	x		x	x	x	x	x	x	x	x	
Exeter										x	
Yorkists											
March	x	x	x	x	x	x	x	x	x	x	x
Lord Grey de Wilton			x								
Fitzwalter			x								
Audley			x								

Table 6 Second St Albans

	An English Chronicle	Jean de Wavrin	Brief Notes	Brief Latin Chronicle	Annales	'Gregory'	Robert Bale	Short English Chronicle	John Benet	Abbot Whetham-stede	Act of Attainder (1461)	The Brut	Milan Letters
Lancastrian													
Somerset		x	x	x	x	x	x		x		x		x
Exeter	x				x	x	x						
Northumberland					x		x		x	x	x		
Devon	x				x	x	x		x				
Oxford							x						
Shrewsbury					x								
Westmorland							x						
Clifford				x		x	x			x		x	
Neville						x							
Roos					x	x	x						
Grey of Codnor					x								
Fitzhugh					x								
Greystoke					x								
Willoughby					x		x						

	An English Chronicle	Jean de Wavrin	Brief Notes	Brief Latin Chronicle	Annales	'Gregory'	Robert Bale	Short English Chronicle	John Benet	Abbot Whetham-stede	Act of Attainder (1461)	The Brut	Milan Letters
Welles					x							x	
Yorkists													
Norfolk	x	x	x	x	x	x	x	x				x	x
Suffolk	x												x
Arundel	x			x	x	x	x						
Bourchier				x		x						x	x
Warwick	x	x	x	x	x	x	x	x				x	
Montagu					x								x
Berners													x
Bonville†	x		x	x	x	x	x	x			x	x	x
De la Warre				x									
Fitzwalter							x						
Abergavenny							x						
Fauconberg												x	

Table 7 Towton

	Jean de Wavrin	Brief Latin Chronicle	Annales	'Gregory'	Short English Chronicle	John Benet	Abbot Whethamstede	Act of Attainder (1461)	The Brut	Milanese Letters	'The Rose of Rouen'
Lancastrians											
Exeter	x			x		x		x		x	
Somerset	x			x		x		x	x	x	
Northumberland†	x		x	x		x		x	x		
Devon	x					x		x			
Westmorland										x	
Beaumont				x				x		x	
Dacre†								x		x	
Welles†				x				x		x	
Cifford†	x		x	x				x	x	x	
Neville†				x		x			x	x	
Rivers	x			x							

	Jean de Wavrin	Brief Latin Chronicle	Annales	'Gregory'	Short English Chronicle	John Benet	Abbot Whethamstede	Act of Attainder (1461)	The Brut	Milanese Letters	'The Rose of Rouen'
Richemount Grey								x			
Willoughby	x			x		x				x	
Roos	x			x		x		x		x	
Scales	x			x						x	
Grey of Codnor						x					
Grey of Groby				x							
Lovell				x							
Yorkists											
Norfolk		x	x	x	x	x	x		x	x	x
Suffolk	x										
Warwick		x	x	x	x	x	x		x	x	x
Bourchier											x
Fauconberg	x	x	x	x	x	x	x		x	x	x
Fitzwalter†	x		x	x		x				x	
Scrope of Bolton	x					x				x	x
Dacre of the South									x		
Grey de Ruthin											x
Clinton											x
Stanley										x	

Manuscript Sources

Paris: Bibliothéque Nationale de France
Manuscrit Français 84, 85, 88, 15491, 20354, 20356, 20428, 20683, 22318

Chippenham: Wiltshire and Swindon Archives
Salisbury Leger Book B 1452–1567, G 23/1/2

Dijon: Archives Départementales de la Côte-d'Or
Archives Municipales de Dijon, B 450

Kew: The National Archives
C1 Court of Chancery: Six Clerks Office: Early Pleadings and Proceedings
C49 Chancery and Exchequer: King's Remembrancer: Parliamentary and Council Proceedings
C76 Chancery: Treaty Rolls
C81 Chancery: Warrants for the Great Seal, Series I
C219 Chancery and Lord Chancellor's Office: Petty Bag Office and Crown Office: Parliamentary Writs and Returns
CP40 Court of Common Pleas: Plea Rolls
DL29 Duchy of Lancaster: Accounts of Auditors, Receivers, Feodaries and Ministers
DL37 Duchy of Lancaster: Chanceries, Enrolments
E13 Exchequer of Pleas: Plea Rolls
E28 Exchequer: Treasury of the Receipt: Council and Privy Seal Records
E101 Exchequer: King's Remembrancer: Various Accounts
E159 Exchequer: King's Remembrancer: Memoranda Rolls
E163 Exchequer: King's Remembrancer: Miscellanea of the Exchequer
E364 Exchequer: Pipe Office: Foreign Account Rolls
E403 Exchequer: Treasury of Receipt: Issue Rolls
E404 Exchequer: Treasury of Receipt: Warrants for Issue
E405 Exchequer: Treasury of Receipt: Tellers' Rolls
KB9 Court of King's Bench: Ancient Indictments
KB27 Court of King's Bench: Plea Rolls
SC8 Special Collections: Ancient Petitions

Kingston-upon-Hull: Hull History Centre
Bench Book 3A, 1449–1552, BRB1
Chamberlains' Accounts, BRF2
Letters, Petitions etc. 1412–1835, BRL

Lille: Archives Départementales du Nord
Archives Civiles, Serie B, Chambre des Comptes de Lille

London: British Library
Harley 4424, 7353

Stafford: Staffordshire History Centre
Stafford Great Cartulary, D.172/1/1

Index

Anson, Richard 84, 93, 95

Bay Fleet 57–58
Battles Blore Heath (1459) 6, 33-46, 73, 101, 156, 158-9; Ferrybridge (1460) 3, 6, 62, 122-47; Ludford Bridge (1459) 6, 46-51, 53, 58, 64-5 90, 127, 154-5; Mortimer's Cross (1461) 3, 62, 98–107, 109, 120, 150, 152, 161; Newnham Bridge (1460), 62-3; Northampton (1460) 3, 6, 9, 44, 46, 62-3, 67, 69-82, 84, 86, 90, 100, 106, 108, 156-7, 158-9; St. Albans (1455) 22-32; St. Albans (1461) 108-21, 125, 145, 155-7, 161; Towton (1461) 1, 3-4, 6, 44, 62, 76-7, 107, 110, 115, 117, 122-50, 155-8, 162-3
Brezé, Pierre de 73, 109, 126, 149
Bristol, city of 16, 126, 148, 150

Cade, Jack 13-15, 69
Clifton, Sir Gervase 60, 70, 78, 87, 95
Clinton, John, 5th Lord Clinton 24, 48, 73, 156-9, 163
Coventry, city of 23–24, 34–42, 48, 52, 65, 70, 72, 74, 79, 82–83, 106, 108, 126, 133, 148, 154–155, 157

Dartford (Kent) 16–17, 31, 37, 72, 92
De la Pole, John, 2nd Duke of Suffolk 111, 137, 156, 162-3
De la Pole, William, 1st Duke of Suffolk 13, 18, 34
De Vere, John, 12th Earl of Oxford 24, 157, 161
Denbigh Castle (Clwyd) 82, 106
Devereux, Sir Walter, 1st Lord Ferrers of Chartley 11, 37, 49, 52, 79, 82, 98-100, 106, 150
Dynham, Sir John, 1st Lord Dynham 52, 59–60, 62–63

Edward IV, King of England 62–65, 75, 80, 84, 92–96, 105, 109–110, 115, 117, 121, 123–124, 127, 130–131, 133, 137, 141–142, 144–146, 150–151, 153, 155–157
Edward of Lancaster, Prince of Wales 18, 34-6, 41, 53, 71, 83, 108, 110-11, 116, 118, 123, 155, 1587

Fiennes, Sir William, 2nd Lord Saye and Sele 72-3, 156, 159
Fitzalan, William, 9th Earl of Arundel 40, 73, 111, 117, 156, 158-9, 162
Fitzgerald, Gerald, 8th Earl of Kildare 65
Fitzgerald, Thomas, 7th Earl of Desmond 65
Fitzhugh, Henry, 6th Lord Fitzhugh 84, 87, 108, 111, 155, 160, 161
Fogge, Sir John 70, 148

Gray, Sir Ralph 123-4, 144, 155
Grey, Sir Thomas, 1st Lord Richemont–Gray 144-5, 148, 150, 155, 157-8, 162
Grey, Sir Edmund, 4th Lord Grey of Ruthin 74, 76, 81, 152, 156, 159
Grey, Sir Edward Grey, 1st Lord Grey of Groby 163
Grey, Sir Henry, 7th Lord Grey of Codnor 111, 155-6, 161, 163
Grey, Sir John Grey 117
Grey, Sir Richard, 1st Lord Grey of Powis 48-9, 156-7
Grey, Sir Reynold, 7th Lord Grey de Wilton 99, 161
Grimsby, William 35, 87, 94, 123

Harrington, Sir James 43, 85
Hastings, Sir William 52, 99, 150
Henry VI, King of England 9, 12–14, 16–18, 20–23, 26, 31, 34–39, 42, 48, 54, 57, 67, 70, 72, 74, 78, 80, 84, 90, 94–95, 97–98, 100, 106, 109, 111, 116–117, 121–123, 126–127, 129, 140–141, 148, 150, 152, 154–155, 157

Herbert, Sir William, 1st Lord Herbert 11, 52, 79, 82, 98-100, 106, 150
Holland, Henry, 2nd Duke of Exeter 13, 18-20, 31, 38-40, 44, 48, 58, 62, 71, 74-5, 79, 82-4, 87, 90, 92, 94, 108, 118, 123, 133, 144-5, 148, 150, 157-62
Horne, Robert 70, 129, 138, 145
Humphrey of Lancaster, Duke of Gloucester 12, 14, 20, 31, 54

James II, King of Scotland 34, 38, 65, 82
James III, King of Scotland 82
John of Lancaster, 1st Duke of Bedford 9, 12, 54
Joseph, William 25

Kemp, John, Archbishop of Canterbury 18-19
Kenilworth Castle 35, 72
Kingston–upon–Hull, town of 83-4, 90, 93, 95, 108, 126
Kyriell, Sir Thomas 111, 118–119

Louis XI, King of France and Dauphin 7, 115, 123-4
Loveday, The (1458) 36, 92
Lumley, Sir Thomas, 1st Lord Lumley 150

Margaret of Anjou, Queen of England 13–14, 18, 34, 36–37, 39, 42, 51, 53, 70, 82–83, 87, 91–92, 99, 101, 107–110, 112, 116, 118–121, 123, 125, 133, 150, 155–157
Mary of Guelders, Queen of Scotland 83, 108, 149
Moleyns, Robert, 2nd Lord Hungerford 13, 71, 78, 157–158, 160
Mowbray, John, 3rd duke of Norfolk 8, 13, 18, 24, 30, 71, 73, 111–112, 117–118, 122, 124–125, 127, 133, 139, 141–142, 146, 150, 156, 158–159, 162–163

Neville, Cecily, Duchess of York 50, 127,
Neville, George, Bishop of Exeter 70, 79, 122, 134,
Neville, George, 1st Lord Abergavenny 71, 73, 156, 159, 162
Neville, George, 1st Lord Latimer 156
Neville, John, 1st Lord Montagu 111, 117-19, 145, 162
Neville, Sir John of Raby, 1st Lord Neville 6, 84, 87, 89, 108, 138, 157-8, 160-3
Neville, Ralph, 2nd Earl of Westmorland 157, 161
Neville, Richard, 1st Earl of Salisbury 6, 14, 17, 19-20, 22-31, 36-51, 52, 59, 63-4, 69-70, 73, 77-9, 82-97, 145, 155-60
Neville, Richard, 16th Earl of Warwick and 2nd Earl of Salisbury, 'The Kingmaker' 7-8, 17, 19, 22-31, 33, 35, 37-40, 44-52, 56-82, 84-5. 90, 94, 97, 107, 109-125, 131, 133-42, 146, 150-1, 155-9, 162-3
Neville Sir Thomas 18, 39, 85, 95
Neville, Sir William, 1st Lord Fauconberg 24, 39, 56, 58-9, 62-3, 71-3, 77, 81, 124-5, 129, 133, 137-9, 142, 146, 150, 155, 159, 162-3
Normandy 13–15, 17–18, 21, 73, 78, 109, 126, 148–149
Norwich, city of 61

Ogle, Sir Robert, 1st Lord Ogle 28, 124, 148, 150
Oldhall, Sir William 16–17, 40
Ormond, James, 1st Earl of Wiltshire 30, 35, 39, 48, 61, 65, 67, 69, 71, 74, 77, 84, 87, 98-107, 123, 145, 148, 157-8, 160-1

Parliament (1455) 22-6, 31, 33-4 ; (1459) 38-40, 41, 43, 45-6, 48-9, 52-3, 56, 76, 83, 89, 106, 154-5, 159; (1460) 79-80, 85, 90, 110, 156-8; (1461) 118, 138, 144, 150, 156-8, 160–163
Parr, Sir Thomas 40, 85
Percy, Henry, 2nd Earl of Northumberland 19, 24, 30-1
Percy, Henry, 3rd Earl of Northumberland 39, 48, 51, 71, 74, 79, 83-4, 87-8, 92-3, 96-8, 108, 118, 123, 138, 140, 144, 159-63
Percy, Sir Ralph 87, 95, 108, 123, 144–145, 152, 155
Percy, Sir Richard 19, 87, 99, 123, 131, 144–145
Percy, Sir Thomas, 1st Lord Egremont 19, 39, 74-6, 81, 84, 90, 92, 159
Plantagenet, Edmund, 1st Earl of Rutland 24, 48, 52, 84, 92-4, 97, 157, 160
Plantagenet, Richard, 3rd Duke of York 13-21, 24-31, 33-44, 46-51, 52, 54-6, 64-8, 77-97, 155-6

Radcliffe, Sir John, 8th Lord Fitzwalter 99, 136-7, 145, 153, 156, 158, 162-3
Roos, Thomas, 9th Lord Roos 24, 59, 63, 74, 83-4, 87, 96, 98, 108, 123, 144-5, 148, 157-8. 160-1, 163
Rouen, Normandy 126

Sandwich, (Kent), town of 36, 59-63, 69, 71-2, 84, 124
Scrope, Thomas, 6th Lord Scrope of Masham 84
Scrope, John, 5th Lord Scrope of Bolton 72-3, 75, 145, 156, 158-9, 163
Somnium Vigilantis (1459) 53, 69
Stafford, Sir Henry 144

Stafford, Humphrey, 1st Duke of Buckingham 13, 17, 24, 26-7, 30, 35, 38, 48, 55, 71, 74-7, 81, 159
Stafford, Humphrey, of Grafton 150
Stafford, Sir Humphrey 35, 150
Stafford, John 75, 77, 129, 145
Stanley, Thomas, 1st Lord Stanley 24, 35, 42
Stanley, Thomas, 2nd Lord Stanley 41-2, 48, 52, 73-4, 156-9, 163
Stanley, Sir William 41, 73
Sutton, John, Lord Dudley 19, 24, 31, 35, 42-3, 45, 101, 156, 159,

Talbot, John, 1st Earl of Shrewsbury 14, 17, 72,
Talbot, John, 2nd Earl of Shrewsbury 24, 35, 38, 48, 69, 71, 74, 76, 79, 86, 159
Talbot, John, 3rd Earl of Shrewsbury 111, 118, 161
Thorpe, Thomas 25, 30, 76, 93
Tiptoft, John, 1st Earl of Worcester 20, 23, 158
Tuchet, James, 5th Lord Audley 41-3, 45, 158-9
Tuchet, John, 6th Lord Audley 59, 62, 72-3, 99, 159, 161
Tudor, Edmund, 1st Earl of Richmond 37, 39
Tudor, Jasper, 1st Earl of Pembroke 24, 39, 48, 82, 85, 87, 98-107, 123, 157-8, 161
Tudor, Owen 99–100, 106,

Vaughan, Roger 79, 82, 98-100
Vaughan, Thomas 40, 79, 82

Waynflete, William, Bishop of Winchester 35-6, 38, 70
Welles, Lionel, 6th Lord Welles 56, 83, 111, 123, 144, 157-9, 161-2
Wenlock, Sir John 30, 33, 60, 62, 78, 99, 119, 124, 150, 156
Woodville, Anthony, 8th Lord Scales 60-1, 141, 157
Woodville, Richard, 1st Lord Rivers 13, 56, 60-1, 137, 140-1, 144, 157

About the author

David Grummitt

David Grummitt is a Staff Tutor at the Open University, having previously worked at the universities of Oxford and Kent, as well as the History of Parliament Trust. He is author of several books on the period, including *The Wars of the Roses: War and Martial Culture in England, 1455-1487* (OUP, 2025), *A Short History of the Wars of the Roses* (2nd edn. Bloomsbury, 2025) and *Henry VI* (Routledge, 2015).

About the artist

Bruno Mugnai

Bruno Mugnai was born in Florence in 1962 and still lives there with his partner Silvia. Active for years as a historical researcher and illustrator, he is the author of several titles published by, among others, the Historical Office of the Italian Army and Helion & Co. His books focus on the historical periods and geographical areas of his interest – the ancient Italian states, Central and Eastern Europe in the sixteenth, seventeenth, and eighteenth centuries, and South America after the conquest. He is a member of `La Sabretache', the French Society for Military History Studies, and of the Italian Society of Military History. As an illustrator, he collaborates with Italian and foreign specialists, and with the Stibbert Museum of Florence. Bruno is a Rugby Football Union enthusiast, who still believes in an Italian Grand Slam in the Six Nations Tournament.

Other titles in the From Retinue to Regiment series:

1. *Richard III and the Battle of Bosworth* Mike Ingram
2. *Tanaka 1587: Japan's Greatest Unknown Samurai Battle* Stephen Turnbull
3. *The Army of the Swabian League 1525* Doug Miller
4. *The Italian Wars Volume 1: The Expedition of Charles VIII into Italy and the Battle of Fornovo* Massimo Predonzani & Alberici Vincenzo, translated by Irene Maccolini
5. *The Commotion Time: Tudor Rebellion in the West, 1549* E.T. Fox
6. *The Italian Wars Volume 2: Agnadello 1509, Ravenna 1512, Marigna1515* Massimo Predonzani & Alberici Vincenzo, translated by Rachele Tiso
7. *The Tudor Arte of Warre Volume 1: The Conduct of War from Henry VII to Mary I, 1485-1558* Jonathan Davies
8. *The Ethiopian-Adal War 1529-1543: The Conquest of Abyssinia* Jeffrey M. Shaw
9. *The Ōnin War: A Turning Point in Samurai History* Stephen Turnbull
10. *One Faith, One Law, One King: French Armies of the Wars of Religion 1562–1598* T J O'Brien de Clare
11. *The Italian Wars Volume 3: Francis I and the Battle of Pavia 1525* Massimo Predonzani & Alberici Vincenzo
12. *On the Borderlands of Great Empires: Transylvanian Armies 1541-1613* Florin Nicolae Ardelean
14. *The Art of Shooting Great Ordnance: A History of the Development, Manufacture and Use of Artillery, 1494–1628* Jonathan Davies
15. *The Italian Wars Volume 4: The Battle of Ceresole 1544 – The Crushing Defeat of the Imperial Army* Massimo Predonzani & Simon Miller
16. *The Men of Warre: The Clothes, Weapons and Accoutrements of the Scots at War 1460–1600* Jenn Scott
17. *The German Peasants' War 1524–26* Douglas Miller
18. *The Tudor Arte of Warre Volume 2: The conduct of war in the reign of Elizabeth I, 1558–1603: Diplomacy, Strategy, Campaigns and Battles* Jonathan Davies
19. *The Kalmar War 1611–1613: Gustavus Adolphus's First War* Michael Fredholm von Essen
20. *Hojo: Samurai Warlords 1487–1590* Stephen Turnbull
21. *The Battle of Castillon 1453: The Death Knell for English France* Peter Hoskins
22. *The Tudor Arte of Warre Volume 3: The Conduct of War in the Reign of Elizabeth I 1558-1603: The Elizabethan Army* Jonathan Davies
23. *Sweden's War in Muscovy 1609-1617: The Relief of Moscow and Conquest of Novgorod* Michael Fredholm von Essen
24. *'Of Kerns and Gallowglasses': Irish Armies of the Sixteenth Century, 1487-1587* Robert Gresh
25. *'The Italian Wars Volume 5: The Franco-Spanish War in Southern Italy 1502-1504* Massimo Predonzani
26. *The Sieges of Rhodes 1480 and 1522* Jonathan Davies
27. *The Swabian War of 1499: The first confrontation between Landsknechts and the Swiss* Albert Winkler
28. *'A Mighty Fortress of God': The Siege of Münster 1534-35* Doug Miller
29. *The Nine Years War 1593-1603 Part 1: The ascendancy of Irish arms and the road to Yellow Ford, 1593-1598* James O'Neil
30. *Elephants and Gunpowder. Southeast Asian Warfare 1380-1700* Stephen Turnbull
31. *The English Longbow – Investigating a Myth Volume 1: Performance and employment 1298-1485* Jonathan Davies
32. *The War of the Roses Volume 1: The Triumph of York 1455-1461* David Grummitt